Islamic
Fundamentalism

Islamic Fundamentalism

edited by

Abdel Salam Sidahmed
Anoushiravan Ehteshami

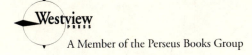

Westview PRESS

A Member of the Perseus Books Group

Copyright © 1996 by Westview Press, Inc., A Member of the Perseus Books Group

Published in 1996 in the United States of America by Westview Press, Inc., 5500 Central Avenue, Boulder, Colorado 80301-2877, and in the United Kingdom by Westview Press, 12 Hid's Copse Road, Cumnor Hill, Oxford OX2 9JJ

Library of Congress Cataloging-in-Publication Data
Islamic fundamentalism / edited by Abdel Salam Sidahmed and
Anoushiravan Ehteshami.
    p. cm.
  Includes bibliographical references and index.
  ISBN 0-8133-2429-7. — ISBN 0-8133-2430-0 (pbk.)
  1. Islam and politics. 2. Islamic countries—Politics and
government. I. Sidahmed, Abdel Salam. II. Ehteshami,
Anoushiravan.
BP60.I82 1996
322'.1'0917671—dc20   96-16463
                                                         CIP

PERSEUS
POD
ON DEMAND   10   9   8   7   6   5   4   3

Contents

Part Three: Parallels

Preface

Political Islam has emerged as a potent force in the Middle East and North Africa, dominating the political and social map of the region. Engaged in an increasingly open struggle for power with the ruling elites in the Arab world, the Islamists have become the main source of political instability in many Arab states. Political developments in the Middle East and North Africa since the late 1970s show that the "fundamentalist phenomenon" is neither a single movement nor the same force in all corners of the region.

This book offers an in-depth, timely analysis of the rise of Islamic fundamentalism and other Islamic movements in the contemporary Middle East and North Africa. In original and specially commissioned essays, the contributors examine important differences between the movements and discuss the dissimilar circumstances in which they have emerged, offering new perspectives on their role in the region and prospects for the future. Through detailed case studies, our international team of authors traces the various manifestations of the "fundamentalist phenomenon" and its implications for the divergent nations of the Muslim world and beyond. They map out the power, influence, and presence of the movements in the emerging post–Cold War order and initiate a new dialogue with due appreciation for the current realities and the coming winds of change.

We hope that the interdisciplinary nature of this study will provide specialists, observers of the region, and policymakers with unique insights into the state of Islamist movements and states of the Middle East and North Africa. The book is divided into three parts. The first part, comprising four chapters, tackles issues of a thematic nature, such as Islamic state theories, the paradigm of Islamist movements, and Islamist attitudes about international relations. Youssef Choueiri's discussion of the political discourse of the Islamist movements is complemented by Suha Taji-Farouki's examination of the intellectual and practical problems the

Islamists have faced when "formulating" for government. Charles Tripp's panoramic survey of Islamist movements in action provides evidence for the view that the secular aspects of the structures of power in Middle Eastern states tend to shape Islamic political activity, a conclusion that forms the heart of David George's contribution to this book. George develops the view that the Islamists' main predicament is how to counter the existing international order and replace it with "pax Islamica."

The second and third parts of the book are based on empirical observations of the Islamists in their domestic, natural habitats. The reader is taken on a journey of discovery, from Algeria (Claire Spencer), Tunisia (Muhammad Mahmoud), Sudan (Abdel Salam Sidahmed), and Egypt (Maha Azzam) in North Africa to Syria (Raymond A. Hinnebusch), Jordan (Beverley Milton-Edwards), and Palestine and Israel (Iyad Barghouti) in the Mashreq. One of the highlights is Mahmoud's focus on one of the most controversial themes in contemporary Islamist discourse—women's issues—through a detailed analysis of Rashid al-Ghannushi's writings on the subject.

In addition, in his chapter on Yemen, Eric Watkins traces the rise of Islamism in united Yemen and its place in the country's post–civil war political order. The successes and failures of non-Arab Iran, the region's first revolutionary Islamic state, are closely scrutinized by Anoushiravan Ehteshami. Mehdi Mozaffari's research provides insights into the differences between the 1979 revolution in Iran and the explosive situation in Algeria, complementing the findings of Ehteshami in the case of Iran and Spencer's observations on Algeria.

Finally, we hope that the reader's lasting impression of this book will be that "Islamic fundamentalism" is not a single monolith but is still a dynamic political force. These movements are, by definition, political and as such are subject to the secular rules of playing for power. It should become clear that, where in power, the Islamists no longer uphold the ideological purities that they appeared to be fighting for. Many contributors to this book illustrate that Islamist leaders have increasingly realized that power, though sweet, demands responsibility if it is not to turn sour. With responsibility comes cost-benefit analysis and the need to temper and balance utopian expectations of the zealous with the requirements of the state.

Abdel Salam Sidahmed
Anoushiravan Ehteshami

Note on Terminology and Transliteration

This book does not follow particular transliteration systems for Arabic and Persian words. Diacritical marks have been kept to a minimum, except for the Arabic 'ayn ('). Most transliterated words are italicized at every appearance. Proper nouns, however, including names of sects and organizations, are capitalized but not italicized. Where "Jama'a" and "Jihad" are capitalized, they indicate names of organizations.

Throughout the text we have used the terms "Islamist(s)" and "Islamism," rather than "Islamic" or "Islamicist," to denote the movements of political Islam and its activists.

The list that follows includes only the most common Arabic and Persian words used in the book, that is, those that appear in more than one chapter or are used as key terms in one chapter. "Pers." indicates Persian words; all others are Arabic.

Terms and Phrases

adawat	tools, procedures (synonymous with *asalib;* see *uslub*)
ahadith	sayings and tradition of Prophet Muhammad; sing. *hadith*
ahd	covenant
ahdath	events
ahl	people
ahl al-hall wal-'aqd	those who resolve public matters
akhondism (Pers.)	ecclesiastical

alim	scholar
Allah	God; *l'Allah* means "to God"
Allahu akbar	God is great
amir	leader; adj. *imara*
amr	order, preach
amr bi al-ma'ruf	preaching good deeds
amwal	wealth, finances
asr	age, epoch
ata'	charity, allotment
awqaf	endowments
'awra	vice
azadi (Pers.)	movement
bay'at	allegiance
bay'at in'iqad	investiture
bayn	between
bazaar (Pers.)	market
bonyad (Pers.)	foundation
bozorg (Pers.)	great
chehellum (Pers.)	fortieth day
dar al-harb	abode of war (non-Muslim land)
dar al-Islam	abode of Islam (Muslim land)
dastur	constitution
da'wa	call, propagation, mission
dawla	state
din	religion
dunya	world
faqih	jurisconsult
faridah	duty
fasad	corruption
fasl	separation
fatwa	authoritative religious decree
fikr	thought
Filistine, Filistiniyya	Palestine, Palestinian
fiqh	jurisprudence
fitna	political upheaval
fuqaha	jurisconsults
ghaybat	occlusion (of the hidden Imam)
Haftum (Pers.)	seventh day
al-hajj	pilgrim
hajj	pilgrimage
hakimiyya	sovereignty
haq	truth

harim	womenfolk; also the separate section of women in the household, the women of a rich person or a sultan (English: harem)
hijab	veil
hisba	procedure of accountability of public officials
hishma	decency
hizb	party
hurriya	freedom; pl. *hurriyat*
'ibada	worship; *'badat* means acts of worship (prayer, fasting, reciting)
'iffa	chastity
ijmma'	consensus
ijtihad	independent interpretation of Qur'an and Sunna (Islam's primary sources) and formulation of rules and regulations (see also *mujtahid*)
Ikhwan	Muslim Brotherhood
'ila	to, toward
imam	leader
imami	shi'i rite (of the twelve Imamites)
iman	faith
infitah	economic liberalization
inhitat	decadence
Islami	Islamic
istedh'af	subjugation, oppression
istikbar	hegemony, oppression
jabhat	front
Ja'fari	related to Ja'far al-Sadiq, the fourth Imam of the Shi'a and their most renowned scholar
jahil	ignorant
jahili	from *jahiliyya* (pre-Islamic, or non-Islamic, epoch)
jama'a	group
jama'at	groups
jidd	seriousness
jihad	effort, struggle, holy war
jins	sex
kafir	infidel, nonbeliever
kayd	guile
khitab	address, discourse
kitab	book; when capitalized, denotes the Qur'an
kubra	largest
kufr	infidelity, unfaithfulness

lahw	lasciviousness, lechery
mahkamat al-mazalim	court of iniquities
majlis	council, assembly
mar'a, mar'atu	woman
mashrutah (Pers.)	constitutional
mashura	council (derivative of *shura*)
maskh	distortion, alienation
mazalim	grievances (see also *zalama*)
millah	sect
mirath	inheritance
mu'amalat	(legal) matters pertaining to human dealings, mostly used in contrast to *'badat,* which deals with a person's relationship with God
Muharram	first month in the Islamic calendar
mujahideen	fighters (driven by jihad)
mujtahid	One who interprets the Qur'an and Sunna (Islam's primary sources) and formulates rules and regulations (see also *ijtihad*)
munhal	permissive
muqaddimah	introduction
Muslimah	feminine of "Muslim"
Muslimin, Muslimun	plural ("Muslims")
mustadh'afun	oppressed
mustakbirun	oppressors
mutlaqah	absolute
nahda	renaissance
nahy 'an al-munkr	preaching abstention from sin
nayib	deputy, caretaker
qabaliyya	tribalism
qanun	law
qaumiyya	nationalism
qiyamah, qiyamatu, qiyamati	Doomsday
Qur'an	the Holy Book of Islam
Qurban	sacrifice; also an annual festival that takes place during Pilgrimage
Rashidun	the first four righteous Caliphs of Islam's early history
rastakhiz (Pers.)	party
salafiyya (from *salaf*)	"the previous," mainly denoting an orthodox Islamic creed
sana'at	industries

Saqifat bani Sa'ida	the place where the selection of the first Caliph to Prophet Muhammad took place
sawm	fasting
sawt	voice
Sewwum (Pers.)	third day
shabab	youth
sha'bb	people
shahada	martyrdom; testimony pronouncing that there is no other God but Allah and that Muhammad is his messenger
shahid	personality, identity
shari'a	Islamic law
sharikat	companies; sing. *sharikah*
shaykh	religious or tribal leader
al-shaytan	Satan; the devil
Shi'a	Islamic sect; followers of the Prophet's cousin, son-in-law, and fourth righteous Caliph; Shi'ism, Shi'ite
shura	council (see also *mashura*)
sirat	the Prophet's biography
Sufism	mysticism; Sufi, Sufist
Sunna	mainstream and largely legalistic school in Islam; Sunnism, Sunnite
suq	market
ta'awun	cooperation
tafsir	exegesis
taghut	extreme oppression (same as *istikbar, mustakbirun*)
tahaluf	alliance
tahrir	liberation
tajdid	renovation, renewal
talaq	divorce
talfiq	piecing together (mainly of ideas)
taqlid	imitation, traditionalism
taqwa	piety
tarbiyya	education
tawhid	unification, oneness of God
tawzif	employment, investment
ta'ziah	condolence
ulama	scholars
umad	mayors; sing. *umdah*
umma	community of Muslims

umum	general, universal
umum al-khitab	universal address
uslub	style, procedure, technique; pl. *asalib*
usrat	family; cell (basic unit of an organisation)
usul	fundamentals; *usuliyya, usulyyun*
vilayat (Pers.)	vice regency; Arabic *wilayat*
wa'i	consciousness
waqi'i	realistic
watani	patriotic
wilaya khassa	provincial/local authority
wilaya mutlaqah 'amma	central authority
wizarat al-tanfidh	executive authority
yaum	day
zakat	alms in tax
zalama	oppressors, usurpers

Introduction

ABDEL SALAM SIDAHMED
ANOUSHIRAVAN EHTESHAMI

The phenomenon of "political Islam" continues to dominate the political and social map of the Middle East and North Africa. The region's political scene since the Kuwait crisis of 1990–1991; events in Algeria since the aborted elections of 1991–1992; the resurgence of Islamist groups in Egypt, the Palestinian occupied territories, and Jordan in the 1990s; the ascendancy of an Islamist force to power in Sudan in 1989; and other events show that "Islamic fundamentalism" is marked by great diversity. This book highlights the differences in these movements and the varying circumstances in which they have emerged and still flourish.

The contributors map out the power, influence, and presence of Islamist movements in the post–Cold War order of the Middle East and North Africa.

The case studies included in Parts 2 and 3 provide a basis for a comparative study and link theoretical considerations to current realities. In looking at these cultures and trends, the authors investigate the causes of Islamic fundamentalism and consider how and why it became the most conspicuous phenomenon in the Middle East during the 1980s and 1990s. They address other important questions as well: For example, do the movements essentially share a common ideology while operating in divergent conditions and circumstances, or do they adopt various ideological discourses and postures in response to divergent sociopolitical circumstances? What are their attitudes toward power, democracy, secularism, international relations, and so on?

In this introduction we neither provide conclusive answers to these questions nor attempt an exhaustive treatment of them. Rather, we preview some of the common themes and answers that emerge from the individual contributions. Before we go on to address these problems, however, a word on the term "Islamic fundamentalism" and its adequacy as a concept is in order.

Fundamentalism: A Label or a Concept?

The use of the label "Islamic fundamentalism" has become widespread, especially in the media, and is increasingly penetrating academic circles. Yet, if tolerated or even employed as a *label*, the term is still far from being established as a *concept*. Scholars still find it difficult to accept and use it because of its indiscriminate deployment by the media and similar circles and because of its popular association with extremism and fanaticism. Other critics argue that the term gives the mistaken impression of the existence of a monolithic movement throughout the Muslim world, that the term is offensive to those who are regarded as fundamentalists, and, most significantly, that the term was taken from a particular Christian context and deployed into the Islamic field without due appreciation for the appropriate differences and peculiarities of the respective religious contexts.

This assessment is concerned less with apologies for adopting or discarding the term than with identifying the potential or actual problems to be encountered if the term is to be employed as a *concept* in an Islamic context. To this end it is helpful to go back to the Christian genesis of the term. It originated in America early in this century, "when it was applied to ultraconservative Protestant Christian biblical literalists and inerrantists who propounded a list of 'fundamentals' that all true Christians should follow."[1] This definition involves: (1) a tendency to take the Holy Scripture literally and a belief in its inerrancy and (2) adherence to a number of elaborated *fundamentals* as the line of demarcation between true believers and the rest.

How applicable are these features to the Islamic "fundamentalists"? Let us first examine the scripture metaphor. In the case of Islam, the Holy Scripture is the Qur'an. Unlike the scriptures of other Abrahamic religions, the Qur'an has a central place in Islam. According to one scholar of Islam, "Just as Christianity is the religion of and about Jesus, Islam is the religion of the Qur'an."[2] It is therefore imperative that all Muslims, regardless of rite, sect, or piety, essentially believe in the inerrancy of the Qur'an as the revealed word of Allah. Hence, if one is to judge by their attitude toward scripture, all Muslims may be classified as "fundamentalists."[3]

If Muslims agree on the authenticity and primacy of the Qur'an, however, they occasionally differ with regard to its meaning. By its very nature the text of the Qur'an is formulated in a way that is far from self-explanatory. Accordingly, there is no way of taking the entire text of the

Qur'an literally. It has to be interpreted, a task reserved only for the learned jurists and ulama. The most common form of interpretation is called *tafsir,* or "exegesis." Over the course of time, the exegesis literature has grown in size and diversity to become almost as important as the text itself. Some exegetes emphasized legislation and others labored on theology.[4] The most important differences, however, occurred between the orthodox and mystical traditions, with the latter more concerned with the hidden meanings of the text. A similar dichotomy may be found between the Shi'i and Sunni schools.

Within this framework there is indeed room for a literalist interpretation as contrasted against a more liberal or rationalist tendency. An important dimension of the problem, however, is that Muslim interpretations of scripture have changed over time with changing conditions and the growth of human knowledge. Consequently, despite the abundance of classical exegesis literature, Islamic revivalists and reformers of the nineteenth and twentieth centuries found it important to reinterpret the Qur'an in the light of new circumstances and in respect to the new message they sought to emphasize for Muslims of their own time. In its turn this exercise triggered the growth of modern and contemporary exegesis, which vowed to produce neointerpretations of the Qur'an in a form and content more accessible to contemporary Muslims and more suited to their needs.

Within this framework it is possible to reflect on the attitude of the contemporary Islamist movements toward the Holy Scripture. Curiously enough, there are very few works of exegesis by leaders of the contemporary Islamist movements. In fact, apart from al-Maududi (d. 1979) and Sayyid Qutb (d. 1966), there is hardly any significant work by Islamists in this regard. Here, one can only agree with Martin E. Marty and R. Scott Appleby, who argued: "As lay scholars of Islam, leaders of . . . fundamentalist movements are not theologians but social thinkers and political activists."[5]

Because of their preoccupation with political activism, leaders of contemporary Islamism have been more concerned with emphasizing segments of the Qur'an that serve their purposes (sometimes the exercise is reduced to extensive quoting of verses) than with interpreting the text itself. Consequently, the line of demarcation that sets the Islamist leaders and followers apart from their coreligionists is their political activism rather than a dogmatic or literalist attitude toward Holy Scripture.

If their attitude toward scripture is not a distinguishing factor of the Islamists, what about the second feature of emphasizing a set of *fundamentals*? Again, all Muslims share a common belief in basic fundamentals known as the pillars of Islam: pronouncement of *shahada* (i.e., to testify explicitly that there is no other God but Allah and that Muhammad is his messenger); prayer; fasting; almsgiving; and Hajj (pilgrimage to Mecca). There are also six articles of the faith (*iman*): belief in Allah, His messengers, Holy books, angels, the Day of Judgment, and Destiny. Together, the pillars of Islam and the *iman* constitute the fundamentals of the Islamic religion and give it much of its particular character.

Since adherence to these fundamentals is an integral part of the faith, then, no distinction between Islamic groups would be possible on these grounds either. Furthermore, these are not the points of emphasis in the discourse of the contemporary Islamist movements, which instead focus on the necessity of establishing an Islamic government or authority to enforce the *shari'a* law. As we shall see, an integrated and common blueprint of what constitutes an authentic Islamic state is still wanting. As for the *shari'a*, there is abundant tradition in this field, but the Islamists rather narrowly focus on the *hudud*—the canonical penalties of the *shari'a*. Since these cover only certain aspects of criminal law, they may not be regarded as *the* fundamentals of Islam.

There is, however, another aspect to the problem of fundamentals. The Arabic equivalent of the term is the word *usuli*, which is one of the key concepts of Islamic jurisprudence. In fact, there is an entire discipline called *'ilm usul al-fiqh* (science of the fundamentals of jurisprudence) that is concerned mainly with the genesis and sources of the general jurisprudential rules. These are to be searched first in the Qur'an, then in the Sunna (Prophet Muhammad's authentic tradition), and finally in the consensus of the jurists (*al-ijmma'*). Scholars who specialize in this field are known as *'ulama al-usul*, or just *al-usulyyun*, which may be literally translated as "fundamentalists."

Interestingly, when translated into Arabic the terms "fundamentalism" and "fundamentalist" become *'usuliyya* and *usuli*, respectively. Equating the English and Arabic terms, however, can be both misleading and confusing given the inherent juristic connotations of the original Arabic concept *usul* and its derivatives. Similarly, when the Arabic terms are applied to contemporary Islamist movements, they may imply either an association with Islamic jurisprudence or an association with a certain set of Islamic fundamentals. On both accounts the usage can only be misleading.

Thus, the word "fundamentalism," with its original Christian implications, should not be brought into an Islamic context for reasons associated both with the particularity of Islam itself and with the discourse of the contemporary Islamist movements.

In recognition of this problem several scholars have attempted a redefinition of the term after stripping it of its Christian connotations.[6] The most profound examples in this class are Marty and Appleby, who argued that "fundamentalism is here to stay" and that scholars must define or redefine the term rather than "seek idiosyncratic and finally precious alternatives."[7] Furthermore, they maintained that fundamentalism is useful as "a comparative construct encompassing movements within [various] religious traditions." Accordingly, Marty and Appleby advanced the following definition:

> Religious fundamentalism has appeared as a tendency, a habit of mind, found within religious communities and paradigmatically embodied in certain representative individuals and movements, which manifests itself, as a strategy or set of strategies, by which beleaguered believers attempt to preserve their distinctive identity as a people or group. Feeling this identity to be at risk in the contemporary era, they fortify by a selective retrieval of doctrines, beliefs and practices from a sacred past. These retrieved "fundamentals" are refined, modified, and sanctioned in a spirit of shrewd pragmatism: they are to serve as a bulwark against the encroachment of outsiders who threaten to draw the believers into a syncretistic, areligious, or irreligious cultural milieu. Moreover, these fundamentals are accompanied in the new religious portfolio by unprecedented claims and doctrinal innovations. By the strength of these innovations and the new supporting doctrines, the retrieved and updated fundamentals are meant to regain the same charismatic intensity today by which they originally forged communal identity from the formative revelatory religious experiences long ago.[8]

Indeed this is a rigorous, comprehensive, and inclusive definition. By being both general and comprehensive, it contains many features of the "fundamentalist" movements and hence is useful as a comparative category across the religious board. Yet, when one attempts to apply it to one religious tradition, it becomes less adequate. First of all, the definition is too broad for one religious context. Second, though lengthy beyond practicality, any attempt to narrow it down would most likely be at the expense of its comparative utility. Finally, our assessment has already pointed to the problematic nature of what might constitute Islamic "fundamentals" in general and what is emphasized in the discourse of contemporary Islamists in particular.

Thus, although "fundamentalism" is here to stay as a label, it is yet to be established as a generic concept or comparative category in the field of Islam and Islamist movements. As a label the term is sometimes explicitly rejected or silently avoided by scholars. In other cases it is tolerated and/or redefined narrowly or comprehensively. This is more or less the case with the contributors and editors of this volume.

Genesis and Context

Returning to the questions raised in the beginning of this introduction, let us have a brief look into the genesis of the phenomenon. That is, why has

Islamism become the most conspicuous force in the current political scene of the Middle East? Only general patterns will be identified here, as most of the chapters address the question through individual case studies.[9]

Contemporary Islamism is the product of a sociopolitical process of two decades or more. The roots go back to 1967 when, instead of recapturing Palestine, the Arab states, led by Nasserite Egypt, lost further territories to Israel. The disaster, which shook the credibility of Arab nationalist/populist regimes and forces, sowed the seeds of discontent that later sprouted as Islamist extremist forces. The death of Nasser a few years later seemed to have closed a chapter in the history of the region characterized by slogans of liberation, development, and socialism. Thereafter, although other populist regimes thrived in the region (in Iraq, Syria, Libya, and Algeria), with similar structures and discourses, the tide was permanently reversed. A new force was maturing rapidly—namely, Islamism.

Arab Nationalism had dominated the postcolonial political scene and its failure left the region with few alternatives. Two ideologies might have counted: Marxism and liberalism. The latter, however, was a spent force since it was effectively supplanted by the populist Nationalist regimes and was already discredited because of its association with the constitutional experiments pursued under the shadow of colonialism. These experiments were mostly dominated by often corrupt parties of traditionalists, landowners, and other propertied classes. In turn, the social base of these groups was significantly eroded by measures of "land reform" and nationalization adopted by the populist regimes. The Marxist Left, whether organized in Communist parties or not, suffered from two fatal problems: structural disintegration due to oppression by Nationalist regimes, on the one hand, and those regimes' appropriation of Marxist ideological credentials, on the other. Thus, the Marxist Left was no more ideologically attractive than the Nationalist regimes themselves, which had even contracted "strategic alliances" with the Soviet bloc. It was indeed hard for the Marxist forces to appeal to the public on the grounds of who was the "authentic" socialist.

It was against this background of uncertainty and "ideological vacuum" that the slogan "Islam is *the* solution" was raised and gradually came to gain grounds. The process was aided, however, by other important developments. The oil boom of the 1970s had significantly disrupted the balance in the Middle East by raising the political and economic stakes of Saudi Arabia and other oil-rich states in the Arabian Peninsula. Through its wealth and "religious" prestige, Saudi Arabia was able to ascend to the top of the region's politics. By implication and design this Saudi dominance had unfolded gradually, causing a consolidation of Islamist ideology throughout the region.

This state of affairs coincided with a systematic policy of rapprochement and even encouragement of Islamist forces in individual countries. As always, Egypt was a pioneer in the process. Sadat, who succeeded Nasser, was eager to undo the legacy of the latter for personal and political reasons. After emerging victorious from a struggle for power with the Nasserite establishment (May 1971), Sadat sought to shore up his legitimacy by relying more and more on Islamist overtones and to consolidate his power by encouraging the Islamists to counter the Nasserite and Marxist Left. A similar process was noted in the Sudan under Nimeiri, who changed course after a collision with the Sudan Communist Party in July 1971. This pattern was to be repeated about a decade later by Chadli Benjedid in Algeria, who, in seeking to undo the legacy of the populist Bommediane regime, also courted embryonic Islamist groups.

At the societal level conditions were conducive to the growth of Islamist forces. Social dislocation resulting from or accompanying economic "development," rapid urbanization, destruction of traditional institutions, expansion of education, and social mobility had resulted in the growth of deep social tensions and discontent. This environment was compounded by the growing inability of the states to provide necessary services for their subjects as a result of mounting economic crises.

The combination of these factors created fertile ground for the growth of the Islamist forces and movements either in the form of a revival and consolidation of the "multinational" Muslim Brotherhood movement, as occurred in Egypt, Sudan, and Jordan, or in the form of the emergence of a new movement with similar credentials, as in Algeria and Tunisia. The process was facilitated further by many forms of assistance and funding from Saudi Arabia and its allies. Moreover, in the spirit of Cold War politics, the United States and its Western allies also sought to aid the Islamist groups in the Middle East as a bulwark against infiltration of Communist influences in that strategic region. Then came the Iranian revolution.

Despite its particularity and Shi'ite ideology, the Iranian revolution was a grand moment for the Islamist forces at large. It provided them with a strong sense of inspiration and encouragement and demonstrated that an Islamic revolution was indeed a realistic objective. From being a center of westernization and secularism, Iran had overnight become a center of Islamist politics and agitation. Saudi Arabia, hitherto the champion of Islamism, did not take kindly to that dramatic development. At best it meant the creation of another center, and a Shi'ite one for that matter, competing for the leadership of the Islamic world. However, the worst was to be expected from Iran, which soon engaged in actual or suspected attempts to export its revolution across the Gulf. The primary concern of Saudi Arabia and its regional and international allies became how to contain revolutionary Iran. The outbreak of the war between Iran and Iraq in

1980 provided Saudi Arabia et al. with their best chance. The *secular* Iraq was unreservedly supported against an overtly *Islamist* regime.

The rising Islamist forces, however, were not less pragmatic. Despite their declared sympathy with Iran they were careful not to cross the line and fall out of favor with the Saudi Party. If anything, they even benefited from the overt and covert competition between Riyadh and Tehran over the patronage of the Islamist movements.

Down to the end of the 1980s the Islamist forces held a delicate balance between Riyadh and Washington on the one hand and Tehran on the other, while enjoying the support of all. A case in point in this regard was the Afghan mujahideen, who were supported by a combination of all these forces.

As a result of this complex process of support and relationships, the mainstream Islamist forces were able to build a formidable international network extending through a broad range of religious, political, economic, and welfare institutions. In its turn this network enhanced their power and eventually enabled them to assume independent postures.

At the end of the 1980s and in the beginning of the 1990s, three important developments disrupted the balance: the rise to power of an Islamist force in Sudan in 1989, the collapse of the Soviet bloc in 1989 and 1990, which effectively ended the Cold War, and the second Gulf war, which occurred in 1990 and 1991.

The end of the Cold War meant that an alliance between the West and the Islamist groups was no longer a necessity for both sides. Moreover, the collapse of the Soviet bloc had effectively removed even the remotest possibility of a "socialist" alternative in the region. During the second Gulf war the majority of the Islamist forces, to the surprise of many observers, sided with Iraq against Kuwait and its allies.[10] Regardless of the calculations involved and the outcome of the war, that position achieved something for the Islamists. It was during the Gulf crisis and war that these movements definitely parted company with Saudi Arabia and its U.S. allies—that is, they made the vital transition from a pro-Western to an anti-Western force. The significance of this step is that it enhanced their ideological and political independence to challenge the legitimacy of entire regimes in the region, including that of Saudi Arabia, as non-Islamic. By the same token, the anti-American rhetoric was needed to enhance their legitimacy as proponents of the most authentic and original *Islamic* alternative. The government in Sudan, which underwent "conversion" to Islamist control in 1989, sets an example for these movements, provides them with a "haven," and could serve as a springboard for further bids of power.

It is against this background that current Islamist movements arose in individual countries. As subsequent chapters show, these patterns did not produce uniform results throughout the region. Thus, whereas some movements achieved substantial influence and growth, others struggled for survival. Some movements were co-opted in the political process and allowed a degree of legal or semi-legal operation, and others were banned and actively suppressed. Essentially, these manifestations and experiences differed owing to differences in history, social conditions, political structures, and processes, on the one hand, and to differences in interpretations of the message of Islam and its meaning for our times, on the other. Taken together, these two aspects might explain the divergent discourses and postures of Islamist movements and their multiplicity even in the same country.

Ideology and Pragmatism

The common underlying feature of contemporary Islamist movements is that they all believe in the "cause" of establishing an Islamic state or order. The central theme in this process is that within the framework of this order the Islamic *shari'a* law would be thoroughly enforced. Apart from this insistence on the *shari'a* there is no monolithic approach toward what should constitute an authentic Islamic order. This issue may be investigated at three levels: theory, practical approaches, and political adjustment.

On theoretical grounds there are some models and blueprints for an Islamic order. Famous among these is Khomeini's blueprint of *vilayat-e faqih*, which now constitutes the official ideology of the Islamic Republic of Iran. Another was the project of the Islamic Liberation Party (Hizb al-Tahrir al-Islami), which called for reestablishing the Islamic Caliphate in the contemporary world since it is regarded as the most "authentic form of Islamic government" (see Chapter 2). Despite important concessions made by Taqi al-Din al-Nabhani in recognition of contemporary realities, the idea of resurrecting the Caliphate reflects nostalgia more than it sets an objective for practical implementation. It did not gain any significant ground among the Islamist forces and remained confined to the minority Islamic Liberation Party, which could not achieve multinational expansion similar to that of the Muslim Brothers.

Khomeini's vision, though representing an important innovation in the traditional Shi'i political thought, remained mostly confined to that tradition. His main achievement was to successfully advocate the necessity and possibility of establishing an "Islamic government" under the guardianship of the jurists rather than waiting for the return of the "hidden Imam." The concept of *vilayat-e faqih* is rooted in and substantiated by the existence of an institutionalized and hierarchical Shi'a "clergy" unmatched in the Islamic Sunni world. Hence, despite the immense influence of the Iranian revolution on the Islamist movements, the concept of *vilayat-e faqih* remained peculiar to Iran.

Nonetheless, other aspects of "Khomeinism" came to have a greater impact and influence on contemporary Islamism. Khomeini's rhetoric of the "disinherited of the earth," his dire hostility to the West and its "arrogance" and materialism, and more significantly, his populism penetrated with varying degrees the discourse of contemporary Islamist movements.

Alongside Khomeini two other theoreticians figured prominently in the ideological foundation of contemporary Islamism: al-Maududi and Sayyid Qutb. To al-Maududi is attributed the foundation of an "Islamic" political theory, the central theme of which is the concept of God's sovereignty (*hakimiyya*). Among other things, this concept entails that human beings can exercise power only in the name of Allah and in pursuit of His teachings and regulations. Sayyid Qutb elaborated the peculiar thesis that today's world is essentially living through an epoch of *jahiliyya* (godlessness and perplexity) and that true Muslims have a duty to withdraw from this society, establish their own righteous one, and reconquer the *jahili* order.

Emphasizing common ground between the three ideologues—Khomeini, Maududi, and Qutb—Youssef Choueiri's assessment in Chapter 1 reveals that in the projection of those Islamist theoreticians Islam is essentially incompatible with the modern "secular" reality and that an Islamist blueprint can only grow and flourish at the expense of this reality and as a negation of it.

Another vision adopts a vaguer attitude toward state and society while emphasizing political activism in the name of Islam and an emphatic call for enactment of an Islamic constitution and/or *shari'a* law. This view may be traced to the founder of the Muslim Brothers organization, Hasan al-Banna, and today is perhaps best represented by Hasan al-Turabi of Sudan and Rashid al-Ghannushi of Tunisia. Of course, the three do not hold identical views on all matters, but in general they are more concerned with establishing and expanding their movements and achieving power through whatever means. In the process, they are willing to make necessary ideological concessions either in recognition of the requirements of contemporary realities or in order to attract new recruits who could be put off by strict adherence to dogmatism. Consequently, an Islamist movement may coexist with or operate within a non-Islamist sociopolitical framework until the moment is ripe to replace it.

It could be argued that whereas the first discourse, which emphasized a withdrawal from and a break with the "godless" world of today, gradually produced and nurtured the extremist movements, the second discourse produced mainstream movements. Whereas the former operate on the edge of society and on the periphery of its political structures, the latter, whether legalized or not, work through sociopolitical means for mobilization of the populace to their cause. Although essentially correct, this distinction is not as categorical as it appears.

Indeed it was Qutb's, Maududi's, and Khomeini's ideas that inspire the proliferating extremist groups (commonly known as al-Jama'at) who are currently engaged in violent struggles with the regimes in Egypt, Algeria, and elsewhere (see Chapters 5 and 6). Those ideologues, however, were no founders of extremist minority groups. Khomeini led a massive revolution that overthrew a powerful regime and replaced it with an Islamist one, al-Maududi founded a mainstream organization—Jamati Islami of Pakistan—and Sayyid Qutb was a prominent figure of the mainstream Egyptian Muslim Brotherhood. Rather, it was the unique interpretation of the ideas of these leaders that gave rise to the current extremist movements.

Two conclusions may be drawn from this assessment. First, the extremist groups are essentially the children, legitimate or not, of the mainstream movements. Second, and consequently, the difference between the two is less a question of ideology or ultimate objectives than a matter of practical approach. In other words, both aspire to the realization of an "Islamic" order and state; the problem is how to achieve that goal.

Elaborating further, one might suggest that there are no clear, definitive lines of demarcation between the mainstream and extreme groups, only points of engagement and disengagement. Take, for example, the attitude toward violence. It was Hasan al-Banna, the founder of the mainstream movement(s), who first legitimized violence and established a secret organization for that purpose, which soon became associated with assassinations and killings during the 1940s and early 1950s. The revolutionary Iran became widely associated with acts of violence and terrorism on a world scale and served as a source of inspiration and assistance to extremist groups throughout the region. Today, the Sudanese regime, led and backed by the National Islamic Front, a mainstream movement, is reportedly harboring extremist groups, particularly from neighboring countries. In a word, the mainstream movements are not necessarily immune to the violent tactics associated with extremist groups. Much depends on the strategy of the movement in question and the reality under which it operates. Accordingly, the movements that operate in an atmosphere of legality or semi-legality need not use violence against the state or other adversaries. However, they can watch the latter engage in almost daily skirmishes with their kin, the Jama'at. They may count on the expectation that this deadly dispute between the regimes in question and the Jama'at would weaken the former and eventually erode its ability to rule, therefore strengthening their chances of attaining power. Another facet of the problem is the ruthless violence and oppression inflicted by the Islamist regimes in Tehran and Khartoum against their opponents. Consequently, violence could be a point of both engagement and disengagement between the mainstream and extreme.

A clear point of disengagement, however, arises from their divergent tendencies toward dogmatism and pragmatism. In the case of the extremist Jama'at, there is a strong reductionist and exclusivist tendency in identifying what is Islamic and what is not. Sometimes, the boundaries are reduced to the number of the group, which implies condemning the rest of the society to infidelity or *jahiliyya*. The mainstream movements, in contrast, have a strong sense of pragmatism, either adjusting to particular political realities, as in the cases of Jordan, the Palestinian occupied territories, and Israel, or adjusting to realities of power, as in the cases of Iran and Sudan. Each of these two categories has its own logic and implications. In the case of the Islamist movements in Jordan and Israel, the process mainly involves adopting a more flexible and concessionary program for the purpose of attracting a wider spectrum of the population and electorate. It also involves postponing some of the important, albeit controversial, themes, such as the nature of their project of creating an Islamic state, for fear of antagonizing the respective regimes. As for the Islamist regimes, however, the process involves a more fundamental concession: It means succumbing to reality, be it local or international, rather than engaging in a process of transforming it. Ironically, this kind of pragmatism might eventually involve "secularizing" the avowed Islamist project rather than Islamicizing the respective structures of state and society.

Islamists and Democracy

It is essential to conclude this introduction with a word on Islamism and democracy. The universality of democracy is the predominant feature of the current post–Cold War order. Yet, although various democratic experiments are being pursued from Latin America to southern Africa, the Middle East has lagged behind. Has this anything to do with Islam as the religion of the majority of the Middle Eastern peoples? In other words, is Islam inherently incompatible with democracy?

These are indeed abstract questions—to answer them is similar to considering whether Islam is a religion only, or a religion and a state! History shows that when it comes to public and societal matters religions and religious teachings are what people make of them, not what they inherently entail. Thus, the Islamic institution of the Caliphate came into existence, evolved, and was even legitimized after the death of the Prophet Muhammad and the termination of revelation. Likewise, some of today's Muslims are at pains to legitimize democracy on the grounds of the Islamic tradition of *shura* (council), and others condemn it as an encroachment on God's supremacy.

More appropriate, perhaps, is to inquire about the attitude of the Islamists toward democracy as a system and a concept. This question is increasingly becoming a center of controversy and heated debate, particularly since the cancellation of parliamentary elections in Algeria (January 1992). One dimension of the question is whether the Islamists *believe* in democracy.

To deal with this question in an appropriate manner, it is important to remember that democracy is both a procedure and a system of government. With regard to democracy as a procedure of transition to power, the positions of the Islamist movements fall primarily into two categories: One endorses democracy as a way of attaining power, and the other disapproves of this option (see Chapter 1). In other words, most of these movements are happy with democracy as long as it provides them with freedom of organization and action and even the prospect of power.

Nevertheless, if while enjoying freedom of organization and expression the Islamists were presented with a chance of reaching their goals through means other than the ballot box, they would utilize it without remorse. This attitude appears cynical but there is contemporary evidence that it is prevalent—as in the case of the Sudanese National Islamic Front (NIF, al-Jabha al-Qawmiyya al-Islamiyya), which overthrew a democracy in which it enjoyed representation in parliament and even government in order to rule the country alone. The leader of NIF, Hasan al-Turabi himself, once endorsed all means of attaining power—whether revolutionary, democratic, or a coup d'état—as legitimate.[11]

The problem of democracy as a system of government is complex because it is associated with the essence of the Islamist project—that is, the establishment of an Islamic state or order. Here it does not help much to search in the conflicting literature and statements of Islamists concerning the "democratic" nature of the projected Islamic state. Neither does it serve any purpose to resort to speculative questions, such as whether the Islamists would uphold democratic principles if they came to power through elections. An alternative approach is to look in the essential tenets of the Islamist ideology itself.

In the first place, there seems to be an inherent contradiction between the *absolutist* nature of Islamist ideology and the *relativist* character of democracy. It is a contradiction between a force that sees itself as a custodian of the divine message, hence as having a monopoly on truth, and a system built on relative truths and opinions.[12] Second, even when an Islamist party endorses democracy, not just as a procedure but also as a concept and principle, it will not have the same value for them as it has for a liberal secularist. This attitude is intimately associated with the Islamic Utopia. As put by Lahouari Addi, the Islamic Utopia means "a City not regulated by politics but by morality."[13]

Finally, Islamists adhere with varying degrees of emphasis to the supremacy of the *shari'a*, to which both rulers and society must be subjected. The essential problem with this scheme lies less in the qualifying feature it imposes on the full adoption of democratic principles than in the additional and largely unaccountable power given to those entrusted with interpretation of the *shari'a*. Here, unlike the classical Islamic Ages, interpretation of the *shari'a* is no longer the prerogative of specialized ulama but the jurisdiction of Islamist leaders and movements. By appropriating for themselves the right of solely deciding what is Islamic and what is not for the rest of the community, Islamist leaders have assumed the roles of both governors and adjudicators while denying everyone else a similar share in public affairs.

It follows, therefore, that the Islamist ideology and the ideology of democracy are inherently incompatible. This is, however, not a conclusive judgment. The authoritarian nature of the Islamist discourse is more a question of political agenda and choice than a matter of cultural authenticity, as is often claimed. In reality, the Islamist leaders have borrowed liberally from Western culture and ideologies, including fascism and communism.[14] Theoretically, there is no reason why this borrowing should not be extended to democracy and modernity. In other words, a synthesis between Islamism and democracy may be possible.

Such a synthesis is possible, however, only if democracy becomes the dominant tradition to which the Islamist movements are forced to adapt themselves and their ideology. The present political scene in the Middle East and North Africa does not point in this direction. Democracy is not likely to blossom out of the current conflict between the authoritarian regimes, populist or oligarchies, and the equally authoritarian Islamist opposition.

Yet, put in its wider context, the present conflict between the regimes and the Islamist opposition is an important manifestation of the accelerated disintegration of the ailing social order that came to dominate the region after World War II in association with the rise of postcolonial states.

If, judging by the experience of other regions, the key word in the establishment of a new order is "democracy," then the future invariably involves complex questions of structures, forces, ideologies, and frameworks, and above all a consensus that this is indeed the most appropriate alternative. The basic prerequisite in such a process would be the rise of a force or coalition of forces that would come out in favor of democracy and fight it out. Then and only then would a discussion of a synthesis between Islamism and democracy become meaningful.

Notes

1. Frederick M. Denny, *An Introduction to Islam* (London: Macmillan, 1994), p. 345.

2. Ibid.

3. John L. Esposito, *The Islamic Threat: Myth or Reality?* (Oxford: Oxford University Press, 1992), pp. 7–8.

4. Cf. Kenneth Cragg, *The Mind of the Qur'an* (London: George Allen & Unwin Ltd., 1973).

5. Martin E. Marty and R. Scott Appleby, *Fundamentalism Observed* (The Fundamentalism Project) (Chicago: The University of Chicago Press, 1990).

6. Ibid.

7. Ibid.

8. Ibid.

9. For further accounts of these processes, see Gilles Kepel, *The Revenge of God: The Resurgence of Islam, Christianity and Judaism in the Modern World* (translated by Alan Braley) (Oxford: Polity Press, 1994), pp. 21–46, and Nazih Ayubi, *Political Islam: Religion and Politics in the Arab World* (London: Routledge, 1991).

10. See James Piscatori (ed.), *Islamic Fundamentalisms and the Gulf Crisis* (The Fundamentalism Project) (Chicago: American Academy of Arts and Sciences, 1991).

11. Abdel Salam Sidahmed, "Iran, Sudan and Algeria: A Setback in the Grand Plan?" *Middle East International,* February 1992.

12. For an inspiring discussion on the issue of Islamism and democracy, see Lahauari Addi, "Islamicist Utopia and Democracy," and William Zartman, "Democracy and Islam," in *The Annals of the American Academy of Political and Social Sciences,* special issue on *Political Islam,* edited by C. E. Butterworth and W. Zartman, November 1992, pp. 120–130 and 181–191, respectively.

13. Addi, "Islamicist Utopia and Democracy."

14. Aziz Al-Azmeh, *Islams and Modernities* (London: Verso, 1993).

Part One

General Framework and Themes

1 ❧

The Political Discourse of Contemporary Islamist Movements

YOUSSEF CHOUEIRI

The second Gulf war afforded various Islamist movements a rare opportunity to put some of their ideas into practice. After all, it was Saddam Hussein who throughout the crisis espoused and expounded various fundamentalist themes and ideas. The slogan *Allahu Akbar* ("God is Great") was decreed to be inscribed on the Iraqi flag. The confrontation itself was invariably depicted as being between belief and unbelief, faith and atheism, good and evil. The slogan of jihad, the hallmark of contemporary fundamentalism, pervaded all the statements, speeches, and announcements put out by the Iraqi president or broadcast on his behalf. Arab nationalism, the official ideology of the regime, figured as a subtext needing constant decoding, or, at best, an anomalous survival in the context of a new terminology. Allusions to the early career of the Prophet were made, analogies drawn, and lessons to be learned reiterated in the best traditions of fundamentalist discourse. The world was thus divided into two diametrically opposed camps: the believers and unbelievers (or infidels). As a matter of fact, anyone familiar with the vocabulary and terminology of Islamic fundamentalism would have detected an unmistakable transformation in the theoretical and political analysis of the Iraqi regime.

The rhetoric of fundamentalist notions made it possible for a whole host of Islamic movements to rally to Baghdad's cause. Some Islamist movements, such as the Islamic Liberation Party (Hizb al-Tahrir al-Islami), called on Saddam to declare himself the new Caliph of all Muslims. Various Islamic activists visited Baghdad to declare their allegiance and full-hearted support.

Although it is not my intention to analyze the political background of such a transformation, it remains of direct relevance to the long-term prospects of Islamic fundamentalism in the Arab world as a whole. To simplify matters, one could put forward the following proposition: During the past decade Saddam Hussein's policies and strategy have dealt Islamic fundamentalism a double blow. During the Iran-Iraq War (1980–1988) he succeeded to a large extent in discrediting the viability of Khomeinism as a revolutionary or alternative force. His adoption of an openly Islamic rhetoric throughout the Gulf crisis served, as it turned out, to weaken the credibility of all other Sunni groups. Whereas his relatively efficient military performance against Iran deprived Shi'ite fundamentalism of its potential influence and appeal, Saddam's defeat in his reincarnation as an Islamic fundamentalist robbed the Arab Islamic parties of their opportunity to assert themselves or gain direct power. Both in his victory and defeat Islamic fundamentalism suffered moral and political losses.

It is perhaps appropriate at this juncture to highlight the complex and varied nature of the political forces that proclaimed their support of Iraq. Nevertheless, one cannot escape the conclusion that the ideological battle assumed Islamic dimensions, forcing secular, nationalist, and other trends to adjust their pronouncements in the same direction.

The hard core of the pro-Iraq alliance, the Islamist movements and parties in the Arab world, may be divided into three groups or categories: The first includes radical groups that consider themselves in a permanent state of war. These groups condemn democracy both as a means of attaining power and a process of government. Relying on the theoretical analysis of Sayyid Qutb, the Egyptian Muslim Brother, their perception of democracy makes its application a direct violation of God's sovereignty. The desires and opinions of secular majorities, it is contended, represent an outright usurpation of divine laws. Democracy implies human agents devising their own legislation. The legislative exclusiveness of God (*hakimiyya*) is inseparable from the question of doctrine. To these groups, Islam has ceased to exist outside their immediate circles. Humanity as a whole has therefore reverted to the age of ignorance (*jahiliyya*). Consequently, multiparty politics and all practices that derive their legitimacy directly from a sovereign electorate are rejected. The nation is not entitled to legislate at will. Or, as Sayyid Qutb explains, "Muslim scholars confuse the act of exercising power with that of its source." In other words, people do not possess, nor do they delegate, the right of sovereignty. Rather, they implement what God has legislated in accordance with His exclusive authority. In this sense, Islam must first be restituted, then discussions of technical procedure, such as elections, can proceed. Political power has to be gained before all other considerations. The Egyptian Jihad (al-Jihad al-

Islami) organization is the most prominent representative of this trend (see Chapter 6).

Democracy is seen in the same light as Arab nationalism, secularism, and socialism and considered a manifestation of Western decadence and corruption. The immediate enemy, however, remains the local political elite rather than external forces such as Zionism or imperialism.

The second category includes movements and parties such as the Muslim Brethren of Jordan and the Islamic Front in Algeria. These parties represent a political trend that accepts the means and practices of multiparty politics and democratic institutions without an equal acceptance of democracy as a permanent process or the ultimate form of government. Their acceptance of multiparty politics does not, therefore, constitute an integral part of their ideological aim. This aim remains an Islamic state, which by its very nature excludes non-Islamic platforms and ideas. It seems that the willingness of some Arab governments to tolerate, implicitly or explicitly, the presence of an Islamic trend, be it a party or a movement, which is the case in Egypt, grants this trend the opportunity to take advantage of a situation in which certain Arab regimes are pursuing open-door policies in both the economic and political fields. These Islamist parties are then the strange bedfellows of democracy: Their sympathies embrace its immediate advantages, while they remain skeptical of its ultimate aims.

The third category has been officially deprived of the implicit or explicit legality of our second category. This is the case of the Renaissance Party (al-Nahda) led by Rashid al-Ghannushi in Tunisia, and the Syrian Muslim Brethren (al-Ikhwan al-Muslimun Suriyya). These two organizations have been banned in both Syria and Tunisia and judged by the officials of these two countries to be terrorist bands bent on violence and destruction. The public pronouncements of the Tunisian and Syrian Islamic fundamentalists are sometimes designed to highlight the peaceful and democratic credentials of their struggle; their resort to violence is often attributed to the harsh treatment meted out to their members at the hands of the security forces. However, ideologically and politically, Tunisian and Syrian fundamentalism is virtually indistinguishable from the first category. There is, moreover, factional strife within these movements and a tendency to rely on outside forces in order to change the political structure in their respective countries.

By and large, these three trends share a number of common ideological features that lend their discourse a coherence of tactics and strategy. This discourse is fundamentally opposed to Islamic reformism and its main representatives, particularly Muhammad 'Abduh, Rashid Rida, and Ibn Badis. Thus, democracy is either excluded at the outset or tolerated as one of the available means to attain exclusive political control. The Islamic fundamentalist belief in God's sovereignty goes hand in hand with the doctrine of *jihad* as the sixth pillar of Islam. This entails a method of armed struggle, coupled with an assertion of Islam as a religion that has to be ultimately embodied in a totalitarian state.

Islamic radicalism postulated the restoration of Islam as an eminently political endeavor. Consequently, other activities, such as elections, demonstrations, and propaganda campaigns, were subordinated to this overriding idea. Its other hallmark is the belief that the method of struggle must be commensurate with the goal and of direct relevance to its realization.

In this sense, an Islamic state can only be brought about by waging jihad, or armed struggle in its widest connotations, and under the leadership of a dedicated, well-organized elite. This triad—the state, armed struggle, and a revolutionary organization—is reminiscent of Leninist forms and arguments perfected at the turn of the twentieth century. These forms, however, do not necessarily imply a convergence of content or ultimate aims.

The discourse of contemporary Islamic radicalism derives its possibilities and rules of formation from the writings of three Muslim thinkers and activists: Abu al-A'la al-Maududi (d. 1979), Sayyid Qutb (d. 1966), and Ayatollah Khomeini (d. 1989). This chapter is devoted to an initial exposition of the main themes of their texts as the unique founders of this particular "discursivity."[1]

God's Sovereignty

This concept seeks to go beyond the mere affirmation of the existence of God in order to assert His authority in the daily life of His creatures and servants. Hence, the universe is judged to be one single organic unity, both in its formation and movement.[2] The unity of the universe mirrors the absolute oneness of God. The Qur'an is the word of God. It is seen by Sayyid Qutb as a divine symphony with its rhythmical tones, reverberations, and movements of climax.

Islam is then a manifestation of a harmonious cosmic order that conveys its fixed order in the similar messages handed down to a chain of prophets extending from Adam to Muhammad. Without God's guidance, the human intellect swims in the sea of the unknown.[3] Consequently, *jahiliyya*, or pagan ignorance, becomes "a psychological state which rejects God's guidance, and a system that refuses to conduct its affairs according to God's commands." Moreover, such a rejection leads "to inevitable deviations, entailing misery, destruction and suffering."[4]

Jahiliyya is bound to rear its head whenever people's hearts are devoid of a divine doctrine and their lives cease to be governed by legal injunctions derived from this doctrine. It also has the same characteristics, irrespective of time and place. Humanity today is living a second *jahiliyya*, more sinister in its implications than the *jahiliyya* of pre-Islamic days.[5]

Human life is therefore a battle of moral and religious values. Those who forsake God and become atheists turn into "brutish animals." In other words, without spiritual beliefs human beings cannot be differentiated from beasts and savage creatures.[6] Seen in this light, European history consists of a connected series of *jahiliyyas*: Hellenism, the Roman Empire, the Middle Ages, the Renaissance, the Enlightenment, and the French Revolution. It is no wonder that modern European colonialism is pronounced to be "a perverse appetite of a pagan society."[7]

Thus, Islam is "knowledge"; all other ideologies and theories are mere "opinions," in the Aristotelian understanding of these two terms. This is all the more so since Islam accords with nature and represents an authentic reproduction or representation of a harmonious universe. The universe is the visible book of God, and the Qur'an is His recited word. Moreover, just as Islam is a method that remains permanent in its fundamentals and constituent parts, so is man's essence. All alterations and developments associated with man's life do not change his nature. Such a premise becomes self-evident when faith is shown to be instinctive, whereas atheism is a transient and false phase.[8]

Whereas human reason is limited by space and time, divine revelation is universal and absolute. Islam, as a result, has an independent existence outside the actual conditions of any generation of Muslims.[9] Nevertheless, the cosmic order, regulated by God, places man on this earth to be His functionary and lieutenant.

Rituals (*'ibadat*), such as praying and fasting, form an integral part of the wider domain of human transactions and politics (*mu'amalat*). As a matter of fact, all human activities have to be performed as acts of worship.[10] This view is adopted not only to preserve Islam but also to make it more amenable to change. Hence, institutions or practices that could no longer be revived, such as slavery, were explained away as having been temporary devices created to deal with a transient and transitional situation.[11]

In Qutb's exegesis, the Qur'an is treated like another cosmos, possessing its structures, harmonious components, and complementary functions. Both teem with their stars and planets, seas and rivers, plants and animals, human beings, angels, and jinns. Furthermore, the Qur'an resonates with that mysterious and hidden silence that emerges out of a vast firmament. At that moment, grains of sand and bright stars merge into each other in an embrace of cosmic love.[12]

Nevertheless, God's attributes—divinity, lordship, omnipotence, omnipresence, and omniscience—reiterated by Qutb, al-Maududi, and Khomeini—are directly dependent for their elaboration on Islamic theology and Greek philosophy. This is a paradoxical state of affairs since these two disciplines were not integrated into the main doctrinal corpus of Islam until almost two centuries after its emergence. It is also ironic that Qutb often stigmatized these two disciplines and called upon the members of his well-disciplined vanguard to reject them as intellectual distortions developed under the influence of pagan currents of thought.

Aristotle asserts that man is a political animal by nature. Contemporary Islamic thought appropriates this notion and amalgamates it in its contention that holds the sound instinct of man to be essentially religious. The apparent contradiction is then obliterated or sublated by redefining religion to encompass all aspects of life, particularly its focal political organization.

Politics and Democracy

In contemporary Islamic thought, democracy is denuded of its neutral connotations and descriptive attributes. Like socialism, it is considered to rest on a comprehensive worldview. Being an expression of a philosophical substructure, it cannot be confined to administrative procedures. Its adoption is automatically accompanied by its wider domain and conclusions.

To Qutb, the general characteristics of a political system are governed by one predominant feature. It is this particular feature that authorizes the relative position and function of all the other elements. In addition, the dominant feature is itself conditioned by a deeper and more comprehensive theory. Institutions and their attendant theoretical justifications are therefore mere manifestations of an interrelated organic entity.

The dominant feature of liberal democracy is the concept of majority rule and the sovereignty of the people, whereas that of communism is the dictatorship of the proletariat, which is basically the absolute authority of a single party. In an Islamic polity, *shura* (mutual consultation) is the essential quality that defines the criteria of selecting the leader of the community (the Imam), members of a consultative assembly, and the executive officials of the state.[13]

In a democratic system, it is a small minority that controls the levers of power and wealth. This minority conceals its real aims behind a number of political and cultural façades. These façades serve to divert attention away from the actual wielders of power, on the one hand, and subject the entire society to a consistent operation of indoctrination and brainwashing, on the other. All social classes are thus in the grip of a few thousand usurers who own and run the principal financial companies and credit banks.[14]

Under communism, the party bosses, acting in the name of the proletariat, use the state apparatus to unleash a reign of terror, placing all society under a system of constant surveillance. Common ownership becomes synonymous with the supremacy of the state, which is in turn under the absolute control of the party machine. Although usury is prohibited, the exaltation of production and the satisfaction of materialistic needs lead to depravities and emotional vacuity. Similarly, capitalism's sole aim is to lend money at exorbitant rates of interest. Capital, labor, land, and the market are thus dominated and manipulated by Jewish usurers, according to this view. This is the epitome of a parasitic system that is alien to the insistence of Islam on productive work and useful goods. Hence, Islam singles out licit and illicit activities. It acknowledges private ownership of property but restricts its scope. All members of society are de jure shareholders of wealth, since it is originally bestowed by God on man. God has created all things and is consequently the owner of His own creation, including wealth and property. Man is a trustee of God and engages in certain economic activities, exerting his productive labor according to divine injunctions.[15]

Whereas capitalism is built on usury, and Marxist socialism on the abolition of private property, Islam has its system of social solidarity, mutual obligations, and security. It restricts private property without abolishing it. This is accomplished by the collection of the religious tax known as *zakat*. Levied on incomes, property, and fixed capital, its rate varies between 3 and 20 percent. Its main purpose is to eliminate poverty and economic misery.[16] Except for its insistence on the prohibition of direct interest-earning, an Islamic economic system is an "enlightened" form of capitalism. According to al-Maududi, its hallmark is the way it eradicates extravagance in spending, hoarding, and accumulation. The prevention of accumulation consists in handing over the surplus income to the needy and less fortunate. Should moralistic promptings and Islamic ethics fail to curb individual tendencies of greed and reinvestment of capital, legal limitations would become operative. Lending for the sake of earning interest on accumulated savings is thus strictly prohibited. However, joint ventures and investment in industry are considered lawful, provided no usurious transactions are involved. If accumulation of wealth does occur, the state would have the right to levy an annual percentage rate on the accumulated sum and spend it on welfare benefits. This is the *zakat* system prescribed by the Qur'an. A public treasury or exchequer has therefore to be set up in order to cater to the needs of the poor and the unemployed. These procedures eliminate the necessity of taking out insurance policies or keeping deposit accounts in banks—the two evil features of capitalism. Moreover, the social agency of *zakat* produces an additional bonus: It restores "a proper balance between production and consumption" by improving the purchasing power of the less fortunate sections of society, as well as obviating the need to export surplus production to other countries.[17]

The diffusion of wealth, designed to prevent its concentration in a few hands, is also the aim of the Islamic law of inheritance. According to this legal rule, all near and distant relatives of a deceased person are entitled to well-defined shares in his legacy. By excluding primogeniture, the circulation of wealth is thus assured in a process of full equity and as part of God's wisdom.[18]

Nationalism

The idea of the oneness of God and of His exclusive sovereignty is meant to reinstate Islam as a political system. Whereas secular nation-states implement their own laws and consider religion a spiritual affair or a national heritage, Islamic fundamentalism, particularly in its Sunni branch, condemns the pagan connotations of nationalism. According to al-Maududi, Qutb, and Khomeini, the underlying strength of Islam is its universal doctrine. Its basis, ever since its inception, denotes a sublime endeavor that dissociates itself from nationalist notions of race, color, and language.

Qutb, for example, points out that the Arabs did not succeed in "conquering Kingdoms and destroying thrones" until they had become oblivious, for the first time in their history, of their Arab identity. They suppressed their national and racial chauvinism, thinking of themselves as being nothing else but Muslims. Today as in the early days of Islam, the only valid and legal division in all societies is that between "the Party of God" (Hizb Allah) and "the Party of Satan" (Hizb al-Shaytan).[19]

Hence, individuals do not become human and proper members of society except as believers and Muslims. This concept was of particular relevance to the identity of the Arabs, given the fact that they occupy a distinctive position in Islam as its founders and propagators.

To al-Maududi the concept of both the nation and nationalism is as old as human civilization. However, the Qur'an does not justify or commend the bond of nationalism, be it linguistic, racial, economic, or territorial. Moreover, the Prophet Muhammad combated the nationalist fanaticism of the Arabs in order to pave the way for the universalist mission of Islam. The only differentiation that was then allowed revolved around belief and unbelief, polytheism and monotheism, atheism and Islam. All other differences were relegated to the background or obliterated altogether.[20] Qutb often spoke disparagingly of "inferior and brutish" human beings who adopt secular or nationalist ideologies. He rejected Arab nationalism out of hand, ridiculing its narrow and sterile theoretical basis. God's choice of Arabia as the cradle of His final message had nothing to do with the nationalist qualities of its inhabitants. He did so for reasons connected with the absence of "state structures and political coercion in the Arabian Peninsula." In other words, Arabia was simply a more convenient conduit to receive and nurture the prophetic message.[21]

Qutb goes on to point out that the Arabs today have nothing to offer the world except their religion. In all other fields—literature, arts, sciences, industrial production, and social philosophy—they have been overtaken by others. Without Islam, the Arabs would be worthless and useless. Thus, each nation has a special mission in life and particular skills: The Greeks and the Germans are noted for their philosophical investigations; the British excel in scientific discoveries and empire-building; and the Japanese are known for their mass-production and technological products.[22]

As for Khomeini, Islamic history is reduced at his hands, apart from the brief period of the Prophet's career, A.D. 610–632, to a span of five years, which is the duration of the reign of the fourth caliph, 'Ali b. Abi Talib (656–661). Consequently, apostasy took place in Islam at an early stage and persisted down to the twentieth century. To him, "the age of ignorance" (*jahiliyya*) set in with the advent of the Umayyad dynasty in 661. The most prominent factor in the degeneration of Islam was the adoption of Arab nationalism:

> Unfortunately, true Islam lasted for only a brief period after its inception. First the Umayyads and then the Abbasids inflicted all kinds of damage on Islam. . . . The process was begun by the Umayyads, who changed the nature of government from divine and spiritual to worldly. Their rule was based on Arabism, the principle of promoting the Arabs over all other peoples, which was an aim fundamentally opposed to Islam and its desire to abolish nationality and unite all mankind in a single community, under the aegis of a state indifferent to the matter of race and color.[23]

Leadership and Jihad

Contemporary Islamic thought, particularly in its radicalist variety, accords political struggle and power the most pivotal function in its strategy as a whole. It is essentially an elitist conception of politics. It projects life as a vital force imbued with an instinctive drive. Hence, direct action becomes the substitute for detailed programs and compensates for lack of material power. Although Qutb called for the emergence of "a Muslim vanguard," composed of resolute individuals and turning itself into "a living organism," Khomeini directed all his efforts toward recruiting a new corps of young clerics and students of religion who would dedicate their lives to political action. He also affirmed the permanent role of the men of religion in his state as well as the absolute rulership of the jurist.

To al-Maududi the question of leadership takes priority over all other political issues, for the leaders of society decide its general development and value system. Thus states dominated by corrupt and immoral politicians mold all institutions and the citizenry in their own image. By contrast, a pious and God-fearing political elite is bound to impart its virtues to various sectors of the population. The quintessence of human life is undoubtedly manifested in political leadership. The central task of an Islamic revolutionary party is to topple idolatrous governments and wrest power from their representatives. It is, in al-Maududi's analysis, a religious obligation incumbent on the community as a whole. The establishment of a virtuous Imamate is required by divine law in order to embody moral values in society at large.[24] Moreover, the distinguishing marks of a human being are nobility of character and high moral standards. Morality has always been the decisive factor in winning or losing a battle. A compact group, armed with the moral ideals of Islam, must therefore be formed, regardless of the material resources it has at its disposal. A well-organized, self-disciplined, hardened group, relying on faith and material power, is bound to overcome its enemies. Islam is simply "the manifestation of belief in action."[25]

Qutb adopted al-Maududi's idea of political struggle, singling out the latter's lecture on "Jihad in Islam" as one of the most valuable theoretical contributions to contemporary Islamic thought. In that lecture al-Maududi called for the establishment of an "International Revolutionary Party" in order to wage jihad against tyrannical governments. Its members were called "the functionaries of God" and their duty would consist in wiping out "oppression, mischief, strife, immorality, high-handedness and unlawful exploitation from the world by force of arms."[26]

Perhaps Qutb's most important legacy to Islamic activists was his system of classifying societies according to well-defined criteria. This system provided Islamic movements a tool of analysis with which they could clearly identify their task. Since he thought that the task of these movements was no less than the reenactment of the two phases of the Prophet's career, it would be useful at this stage to give a brief account of the Meccan and Medinan phases so as to be able to gauge Qutb's contemporary contribution.

The first Islamic state in history, and irrespective of its rudimentary organization, came into being through a process of peaceful means. The

Meccan phase (c. 610–622) was confined to a series of warnings and admonitions directed at the pagan Arabs, particularly the wealthy members of al-Quraysh, Muhammad's tribe. This led to a series of provocative reactions on the part of the Prophet's opponents. Despairing of his tribe's support, and following the death first of his uncle who was his protector, and then of his first wife, Khadija, in 618, he traveled to the neighboring town of al-Ta'if, seeking support from another tribal group. Disappointed and downcast, he returned to Mecca only to face further hostility.

It was not until a delegation from the city of Yathrib (later renamed Medina) met Muhammad during the pilgrimage season in Mecca that new horizons opened up. The delegates affirmed their belief in his message and confirmed that he was indeed God's messenger. A second and larger delegation arrived in the following year. Its members invited him to travel to Medina and act as a trusted arbitrator between its warring factions. This request gave rise to the idea of *Hijra,* or migration, whereby Muhammad, in A.D. 622, secretly left Mecca under the cover of darkness and traveled with a select group of his companions to a different environment.

Once in Medina, he built a mosque and living quarters and initiated the application of the legal injunctions of Islam. By the mere implementation of those rules, which were revealed in a gradual process, an Islamic state is said to have come into being. This decade is known as the Medinan period (622–632).[27]

It was after the emergence of what may be called "political structure" that jihad against polytheists, Meccans, and recalcitrant Jewish tribes of Medina was proclaimed to mean fighting the way of God. After Muhammad's victory over the polytheists and the Jews, whereby Mecca itself was conquered, he began to prepare for military campaigns outside the Arabian Peninsula.

Qutb, al-Maududi, and Khomeini, unlike the Prophet Muhammad, confronted a totally different situation. Their immediate aim was not to build a nonexistent state but to overthrow well-established and highly developed state structures. Perhaps the seizure of power by the Bolsheviks in 1917, or the march on Rome organized by Mussolini in 1922, would serve as better models in inspiring twentieth-century radicalists.

To Qutb and al-Maududi jihad was a total state of war, designed to disarm one's enemy in order to reinstate the *shari'a.* Both thought that the backwardness of Muslims in the contemporary world resided in the absence of a reliable and organized Islamic movement. An Islamic revolution could not, therefore, be brought about without the existence of a well-disciplined group with its own leadership and agents and a proper moral environment. The history of the French, Russian, and Nazi revolutions, according to al-Maududi, furnished the best evidence of this theory.

Thus "German Nazism" could not have succeeded in establishing itself except as a result of the theoretical contributions of Fichte, Goethe, and Nietzsche, coupled with "the ingenious and mighty leadership of Hitler and his comrades."[28]

Qutb contends that Islam does not have to justify itself or present its precepts in a defensive manner. An Islamist has to be bold, strident, and radical in stating his case. His tone and conduct should never be apologetic, hesitant, or conciliatory. Unflinching and infused with pride, he stares death in the face. A believer stands his ground, never runs away, and meets the enemy in open combat. If killed, he is promised martyrdom by God, the highest honor to be gained by a Muslim. A martyr is not washed but buried in his clothes, as he has already been purified. He enters paradise bearing his unmistakable labels and eternal identity. There he enjoys the everlasting pleasures promised by God. Triumphant and towering above his enemies, he paves the way for the advent of "the Kingdom of God" on earth and acts as a magnet that attracts the onlookers, who form the greatest majority of every society.[29]

In order to ensure the world domination and the unquestionable hegemony of Islam, the validity of jihad must become perpetual and timeless. Under such circumstances, terms such as "offensive" or "defensive" struggle lose their meaning and become redundant. The necessity of the daily assertion of God's absolute sovereignty demands the existence of a constant state of war. Hence, a clear distinction must be drawn between "the Party of God" and "the Party of Satan," or righteousness and falsehood. Today, as opposed to former times, the danger of mixing with idolatrous individuals, without the prior purpose of admonition, surpasses in its repercussions all other innovations. Consequently, the nature of the task to be undertaken by the vanguard is itself imposed by the universality of religious ignorance.[30]

An Islamic vanguard, Qutb reiterates, has to arm itself with a clear-cut and permanent criterion. This criterion would ensure its doctrine against dilution and render its complete detachment from a corrupt environment a positive achievement. Accordingly, Qutb divides the world into two spheres: the Abode of Islam and the Land of War. The first includes every country in which the legal judgments of Islam are applied. This condition obtains even in countries that happen to be composed of a Christian or Jewish majority. As long as the wielders of political power are Muslim and adhere to the injunctions of their religion, conversion is not required. The second sphere comprises every territory in which Islamic rules are not applied, irrespective of claims made by their rulers or inhabitants.[31]

In the Abode of Islam, property, life, and public order are sacrosanct. Those who violate its laws would be punished in accordance with Islamic justice. The inviolability of an Islamic society is the result of its virtuous and sublime character. It is a society that guarantees full employment and affords financial sufficiency to its disadvantaged members. It also creates incentives to encourage righteous deeds and discourage vice or evil. Abounding with all these amenities, bestowing plentiful benefits on all its citizens, and governed by just instincts, an Islamic state is entitled to consider anyone who violates public order to be a transgressor and to treat him as a criminal deserving the severest punishment.[32]

As for the Land of War, its inhabitants are not worthy of such guarantees and rewards. As long as Islamic law is not applied there and the sovereignty of Islam is not recognized, it becomes for the Muslims an open territory to be conquered. Its inviolability or sanctity, as far as the Muslims are concerned, is null and void, unless a treaty is concluded between it and the Abode of Islam for a brief and prescribed period. In the contemporary world, Qutb continues, this division has become obsolete. Since no Islamic system of government exists anywhere in the world, no treaties are to be concluded or abided by. Consequently, the entire world has become for a true Muslim a Land of War.[33]

Thus, jihad is the only option available to the new Islamic vanguard. It is a spiritual, financial, and military endeavor undertaken to assert God's sovereignty. These multifarious aspects form an organic whole and constitute the process of political struggle. However, the highest and most honorable aspect is the military engagement—the violent act in which a believer either triumphs over the enemy or dies and becomes a martyr.[34]

Khomeini was less precise than either al-Maududi or Qutb in defining the characteristics of jihad or the validity of armed struggle. He simply contended that political authority in Islam rightfully belonged to the custodians of Qur'anic legal rules, the jurists. All other forms of government, be they democratic or monarchical, were illegitimate. This tenet applied in particular to the kingship of the Shah, an institution that was abhorrent in Islam. He thus called upon the religious leaders to denounce all tyrannical authority (*taghut*).

Such a straightforward message, Khomeini thought, would create its own momentum and mobilize millions upon millions. At that stage, and spurred on by their religious leaders, these millions would rush onto the streets, defying, with their faith, bare chests, and clenched fists, the bayonets and guns of the Shah's army. One martyr would follow another. Each would be given a mass funeral—a procession of remembrance—and each would be celebrated for his courage and envied for his success in winning a prominent place in paradise. As martyrs multiplied and funerals proliferated, the Shah, along with the two Satanic powers (the United States and the Soviet Union), would weaken and falter. With the cries of *Allahu Akbar* ("God is Great") resounding through the streets, alleys, and lanes of the land, the enemy would be steadily intimidated. The hour of his surrender would draw closer and closer. The masses' faith in God and revolution would steel them against all attempts to sow dissension in their ranks or force them to compromise. The downtrodden, the oppressed, and the deprived were for Khomeini the invincible army of Islam. To cleanse society of decadence and corruption, as defined by Khomeini, represented the urgent task of a new theocracy organized to exercise power under a self-appointed and absolute jurisconsult.[35]

Qutb, al-Maududi, and Khomeini articulated a new Islamic theory and established the contemporary discourse of a variety of Islamic political organizations. To them, change had to be total, comprehensive, and revolutionary. They saw no possibility of coexistence between Islam and other political or social systems. Gradual improvements and partial amendments of the status quo were considered inimical to the nature of a true Islamic approach. Society as a whole had to be remolded in the image and spirit of Islam.

They all opposed and argued against Western concepts of democracy, socialism, and nationalism. Their line of argumentation excluded even the remotest resemblance between Islam and other systems. To them, apparent similarities in the growth of human institutions were accidental and did not warrant a comparative and fruitful study.

Notes

A shortened version of this chapter was published under the title "Theoretical Paradigms of Islamic Movements," *Political Studies* 41, No. 1, March 1993, pp. 108–116.

1. See Paul Rabinow, ed., *The Foucault Reader* (Middlesex: Penguin Books, 1984), p. 114. It is interesting to note that despite postmodernist pronouncements on "the death of the author," Foucault had to admit that "founders of discursivity" were "unique in that they are not just the authors of their own works. They have produced something else: the possibilities and the rules for the formation of other texts." Foucault singled out Freud and Marx as such founders.
2. S. Qutb, *Fi zilal al-Qur'an* (Under the Aegis of the Qur'an) (Beirut: Dar al-Shuruq, 1981), p. 280.
3. Ibid., p. 1115.
4. M. Qutb, *Jahiliyyat al-qarn al-'ishrin* (The Pagan Ignorance of the Twentieth Century) (Cairo: Matba'at Wahbah, 1964), pp. 9–11.
5. S. Qutb, *Fi zilal al-Qur'an*, pp. 510, 3616.
6. S. Qutb, *Milestones* (Beirut: The Holy Koran Publishing House, 1978), pp. 181–186.
7. S. Qutb, *Fi zilal al-Qur'an*, p. 146.
8. Ibid., pp. 2665, 349, 556, 3451.
9. Ibid., p. 584.
10. Ibid., pp. 1937, 932–933.

11. Ibid., pp. 230, 500, 1743.

12. Ibid., pp. 3563, 2373.

13. Ibid., pp. 112, 3165, 3343, 1754, 3165.

14. S. Qutb, *Al-Islam wa mushkilat al-hadara* (Islam and the Problems of Civilization) (Beirut: Dar al-Shuruq, 1980), pp. 179–180.

15. A. al-Maududi, *The Economic Problem of Man and Its Islamic Solution* (Lahore: Islamic Publications Ltd., 1978), pp. 23–29; S. Qutb, *Fi zilal al-Qur'an,* pp. 331, 1087, 3524. Qutb often quotes the fictitious *Protocols of the Wise Men of Zion* to substantiate his claim regarding Jewish domination in high or international finance. Zionism is seldom mentioned by al-Maududi or Khomeini in the same context.

16. I. Khomeini, *Islam and Revolution,* translated and annotated by Hamid Algar (Berkeley, Calif.: Mizan Press, 1981), pp. 45, 77; S. Qutb, *Fi zilal al-Qur'an,* pp. 331, 3187, 3524.

17. Al-Maududi, *The Economic Problem of Man and Its Islamic Solution,* pp. 33–37.

18. Ibid., p. 38.

19. S. Qutb, *Fi zilal al-Qur'an,* pp. 1866, 3514–3515.

20. A. al-Maududi, *Bayna al-da'wa al-qawmiyya wa al-rabita al-islamiyya* (The Nationalist Creed and the Islamic Bond) (Cairo: Dar al-Ansar, 1967), pp. 9–38.

21. S. Qutb, *Fi zilal al-Qur'an,* pp. 1441, 1888–1889.

22. Ibid., pp. 511–512.

23. Khomeini, *Islam and Revolution,* p. 332.

24. A. al-Maududi, *Al-usus al-akhlaqiyya li al-haraka al-islamiyya* (The Moral Foundation of the Islamic Movement) (Cairo: Dar al-Ansar, 1952), pp. 6–18.

25. Ibid., pp. 19–52.

26. A. al-Maududi, *Jihad in Islam* (Lahore: Islamic Publications, Ltd., 1978), pp. 17–18.

27. This account draws on traditional Islamic historiography. It is thus not intended to be a critical account having as its premises more recent scholarly studies.

28. A. al-Maududi, *Minhaj al-inqilab al-islami* (The Method of Islamic Revolution) (Cairo: Dar al-Ansar, 1977), p. 19.

29. S. Qutb, *Fi zilal al-Qur'an,* p. 143.

30. Ibid., pp. 1013–1015, 1129–1130, 1946. For further elaboration, see Y. M. Choueiri, *Islamic Fundamentalism* (London: Pinter Publishers, 1992), pp. 125–140.

31. S. Qutb, *Fi zilal al-Qur'an,* pp. 873–874.

32. Ibid., pp. 294, 873–874.

33. Ibid., pp. 873–874.

34. Al-Maududi, *Jihad in Islam,* pp. 16–26; S. Qutb, *Fi zilal al-Qur'an,* pp. 1429–1469, 1634, 1735.

35. Khomeini, *Islam and Revolution,* passim.

2

Islamic State Theories and Contemporary Realities

SUHA TAJI-FAROUKI

The establishment of an Islamic state is the ultimate goal of most Islamist programs today. Islamists have devoted considerable attention to theorizing about the notion and nature of such a state, producing a substantial literature on the subject offering numerous and varied Islamic state-theories. This chapter explores the general relationship between these theories and contemporary realities, looking in particular at the state-model articulated by Taqi al-Din al-Nabhani (1909–1977), and calls into question the claims that the proposed paradigms are "exclusively and authentically Islamic." A survey of recent Islamist activism reveals that there is frequently a significant dichotomy between the ideology of Islamic movements and their actions. This dichotomy is paralleled in the theoretical realm of political thought. Here a dichotomy arises between the rhetoric of Islamic exclusivism and authenticity, with its rejection of Western forms and norms, and the implicit assumption of these very forms and norms in these "authentic and exclusively Islamic" state-theories. In fact, the rhetorical insistence on a distinctively and exclusively Islamic state-model represents the articulation of a pressing demand to reinstate forms rooted in the indigenous culture and consonant with its fundamental values, in the face of an increasingly global, Western-dominated culture that appears to deny the validity of all cultural and civilizational alternatives. The implicit assumption of aspects of the political discourse of this global culture by Muslim theorists casts a fresh light on the fears of many Westerners concerning the necessary implications of an Islamic state, especially were such a state to emerge on Europe's doorstep.

There is little agreement among modern Sunni theorists concerning what constitutes an Islamic state and government: This reality is reflected in the extensive variations in governmental systems existing among

states in the Muslim region that claim to be specifically Islamic. According to one group of theorists, there is an implicit diversity in the very general (and somewhat meager) guidelines addressing the Islamic community's political organization contained in the textual sources of Islam. This
is upheld as evidence of a generous and merciful scope for adaptability to
changing historical and social contexts.[1] For these theorists, a state-model
is Islamic as long as it achieves the supreme Islamic values and adheres to
certain general Islamic principles, regardless of its specific character and
the details of its systems, institutions, and offices. These values derive
from the Qur'an and Sunna and have allegedly been respected throughout Islamic history: They also represent the ultimate purposes (*maqasid*) of
the *shari'a*. In relation to the political context, they are generally identified
as justice, liberty for all, and equality. The principles of mutual consultation and governmental accountability complete the list.[2] As Mahmud A.
Faksh puts it: "Since *Shari'a* is silent on matters of form to which a state
must conform to deserve the appellation 'Islamic,' then there can be diverse forms of an Islamic state depending on the contextual social and
temporal conditions of each Muslim country. The only requirement is that
the state in its different forms must adhere to the general principles and
spirit of Islam."[3]

As evidenced by recent attempts to emphasize the democratic character of Islamic government against the background of moves toward liberalization and democracy in the Arab world, those who adopt this position
have little problem accommodating their Islamic paradigms to the dominant political discourse and the state-model it upholds. Without compro-
mising the theoretical underpinnings of their position, they are able to incorporate some of the central features of this model.[4] Such theorists hold
that the hallmark of an authentically Islamic state-system is the application of the *shari'a*, and not any particular political order. They construe
flexibility as one of the *shari'a*'s central characteristics. Separating out the
immutable core of the *'ibadat* (which regulate a Muslim's relation with the
divine), they hold that the remainder (the *mu'amalat*, which relate to all
other aspects of life, be these social, economic, or political) is changeable,
in that it constitutes a set of general guidelines that achieve the welfare of
the community in this life and the hereafter, leaving ample room for
human interpretation (*ijtihad*). There are, then, no explicit rules concerning the precise form of the state, and it is up to human reason to decide
this on the basis of relevant general guidelines. Effectively, this means
that the state itself is not a substantive part of the *shari'a*, but only a technique by which the *shari'a* can be implemented and its ultimate purposes
actualized. Techniques can be adopted from non-Islamic sources, provided that they do not incorporate any un-Islamic values. A precedent for
this notion arises in the early Islamic state's absorption of the administra-

tive infrastructure of the conquered territories. The form of government is hence a matter for people to decide and can legitimately be adopted from non-Islamic sources.

In contrast with this first position, certain other theorists advocate a more rigid definition of *shari'a* as "a comprehensive set of norms and values regulating human life down to the smallest detail." According to this view, the *mu'amalat* have been definitively regulated by the *shari'a* for all times, although the process of *ijtihad* makes allowance for differing positions on minor details.[5] This trend posits a more or less definitively defined archetypal Islamic state-form that any modern state claiming the appellation "Islamic" must replicate. According to these rigidly legalistic theorists, the Islamic state must not only achieve the supreme values of the *shari'a* and adhere to relevant general Islamic principles, it must also adhere in its systems and institutions to forms precisely defined by the *shari'a* itself. In other words, the state in Islam is held by these theorists to be a substantive part of the *shari'a*; it is not merely a technique.[6]

This position is much less accommodating to contemporary realities. For such theorists, the Islamic state-system has been comprehensively and finally defined by the revelation, later elaborated through the *shari'a*: Existing Western models are hence irrelevant. Muhammad Salim El-'Awa characterizes the approach of this trend, which is "satisfied with expounding rules previously extracted by the Muslim jurists," in the following terms:

> The followers of this course offer no solution to the difficulties of the problems which face the people nor do they try to distinguish among the pronouncements of the Muslim jurists in regard to what they determined as rules which were suitable during their time and that which constituted a statement of rules of Islamic law binding on Muslims throughout the ages. Their works on the political system ... still abound in discussions of such old topics as the executive ministry, the ministry of authorisations, the succession to the throne, the oath of allegiance, the qualifications of the people who should decide matters, the conditions of the Caliph and other topics which, except historically, are of no value now.[7]

The more blinkered posture of this trend, which is summarily dismissed by theorists from the other camp, generally articulates an ultra-conservative ethos. By upholding the *shari'a* as a comprehensive set of rules fixed for all times (and thereby marginalizing the potential for human interpretation), the ultra-conservative ulama resisted the modernist project of the late nineteenth and early twentieth centuries. Over the past three decades, the resort to such a notion of *shari'a* has provided a medium through which to articulate the rejection of the theoretical underpinnings of Islamic reform and a reassertion of Islamic authenticity (the twin concerns of Islamic radicalism). Although similarly expressed through a retreat to tradition, this position stems not from a desire to *ignore* the West, but to *separate* from it. It insists that because of the qualitative contradiction between Islam and Western civilization, a complete epistemological break with the West must occur. It also upholds Islam as a self-sufficient principle, perfect and complete unto itself.

The articulation of an incipient radicalism through the resort to neo-traditional beliefs, including the notion of *shari'a* outlined above, is represented with particular clarity in the writings of Taqi al-Din al-Nabhani (1909–1977). During the early 1950s, al-Nabhani elaborated a comprehensive and detailed state-model on the basis of a strictly neo-traditional legal theory. Consistent with his incipient radicalism, he explicitly rejected Western governmental forms and norms; further analysis, however, exposes his incorporation of the very forms and norms that he consciously repudiated. His model thus provides an excellent case study to explore the dialectics between modern Islamic state-theories and contemporary realities. These theories generally represent an attempt to reconcile the demands of Islamic authenticity with the requirements of modernity (with its undeniably Western cultural imprint): Al-Nabhani's state-theory presents a particularly rich case study in this respect, reflecting and magnifying the internal inconsistencies that can result from this endeavor.

Al-Nabhani, a judge from Ijzim in northern Palestine, was the ideologue and founder of Hizb al-Tahrir (Islamic Liberation Party), established in Jerusalem in 1953.[8] Its aim was, and still is, to revive Muslim societies by eradicating the legacy of colonialism and restoring an Islamic way of life: This would be achieved by establishing an Islamic state on the ruins of existing regimes in Arab countries. After outlining al-Nabhani's legal theory and its implications for the notion of Islamic state and government that he upholds, I shall examine his paradigm for Islamic government, especially his rejection of alien forms and norms. In so doing, I shall demonstrate that although he developed this paradigm as a denial of contemporary realities, some of its features implicitly rest on assumptions drawn from those realities. Al-Nabhani explicitly rejected the new political order in the post–World War I Middle East, shaped and dominated by the recently established territorial or nation-states. However, dimensions of his own allegedly authentic Islamic state-model are nevertheless premised on the forms and norms of the modern nation-state and its associated political concepts and practices.[9]

Owing perhaps to its evident unreality and anachronistic character, al-Nabhani's state-model has had little impact on modern Islamic political discourse. It undoubtedly contributes, however, to the current appeal of Hizb al-Tahrir for its young recruits. In contrast with the perceived vagueness of theorists from the first camp, who appear to marginalize the legacy of Islamic history in favor of stepping in line with existing realities, al-Nabhani's detailed and exhaustive blueprint for an Islamic state is rooted in Islamic history and assumes an assertively Islamic character. This attraction is reinforced by his denunciation of *all* alien governmental models as manmade systems of unbelief.

Shari'a, State, Constitution, and Government

According to al-Nabhani, all aspects of life have as their fountain and foundation the Islamic doctrine. This doctrine contains within it a life-system, represented in the *shari'a*, that must exclusively regulate all of life's affairs: Other sources of life-regulations constitute false gods. Anyone who fails to believe in even part of the *shari'a*, which is comprehensive and supremely suitable for all times and places, is denounced as an unbeliever. The scope of the *shari'a* does not imply flexibility or adaptability to evolving circumstances: It merely signifies that an unlimited number of rules can be deduced from the legislative texts and that each rule can apply to several issues.[10]

Reinforced by the conviction that Islam is self-sufficient, this notion of *shari'a* underpins al-Nabhani's claim that there exists a distinctively Islamic state and government, the form of which is prescribed precisely in the Qur'an and *hadith*. To counter the effect of the colonialist campaign to disseminate the notion that Islam does *not* stipulate a particular form of government,[11] he maintained that the Prophet Muhammad *himself* perfected the entire governmental apparatus, bequeathing an unequivocal paradigm later encapsulated in the *shari'a*.[12] The state is a permanent servant and vehicle of the *shari'a*,[13] making it possible for the latter to assume its rightful position at the apex of society's political, economic, and social organization. As long as the Islamic state existed (up to the abolition of the Caliphate in 1924), the *shari'a* was implemented "exclusively and comprehensively,"[14] although there were episodes of deficient or incorrect application. The debate over whether the state is an intrinsic part of Islam was dismissed by al-Nabhani because this is self-evident. Confusion among Muslims concerning this matter is attributed to a colonialist campaign to convince them that "they never had a state, or had a purely spiritual state . . . and that they must detach religion from the state in order to succeed in life, because these are two separate things."[15]

If the future state is to implement the *shari'a*, legislation must be prepared in advance, al-Nabhani reasoned. To this end he published a detailed constitution (182 articles) outlining political, economic, and social systems and educational and foreign policies for an ideal Islamic state.[16]

A detailed corpus of other state laws followed. With regard to terminology, although al-Nabhani endorsed the use of Western terms such as constitution (*dustur*) and law (*qanun*), he highlighted the fundamental difference between their sources in a Western (democratic) context and an Islamic one.[17] Laws pertaining directly to the Islamic doctrine or life-system must comprise Islamic legal rules exclusively, he said: Examples are laws detailing the penal system and those defining legal evidences admissible in court cases.[18] However, certain types of law, such as those defining purely administrative measures, can be adopted from alien sources.[19] Such laws determine techniques or procedures (*uslub*) for which no textual prohibitions exist. Al-Nabhani defined *uslub* as "a particular way of carrying something out."[20] In contrast with the first group of theorists, in his state-model it applies, at least in theory, only to very specific procedural points in the running of state and government: It cannot be cited in relation to the *forms* of these entities.

According to al-Nabhani, the state must adopt comprehensive legislation to prevent potential chaos as people arrive, through the practice of *taqlid* (adopting the opinions of past jurists), at contradictory attempts to apply the *shari'a*. With some exceptions, the historical Islamic state adopted legislation pertaining to its political and administrative unity only, so as to encourage *ijtihad* among state officials. The scarcity of *mujtahidun* and general ignorance of Islam today make this approach impracticable.[21]

All articles in the constitution detail comprehensive legal rules or general legal principles either adopted from recognized *mujtahidun* or deduced directly through *ijtihad* from the sources of jurisprudence upheld in al-Nabhani's legal theory. As such, the constitution is a purely abstract model informed by a denial of existing realities, a refusal to accommodate these realities, and an attempt to offer an exclusively and authentically Islamic alternative. Indeed, al-Nabhani declared that he drafted the document "without paying any attention whatsoever to the sorry circumstances of Muslim societies, the conditions of other nations, or non-Islamic systems."[22]

The second chapter of the constitution details the governmental system of the Islamic state. In reconstructing the blueprint encapsulated in the *shari'a* for a contemporary state, al-Nabhani's overwhelming concern was to recover its authentic form free from alien influences. He was perturbed that Muslims were now accustomed to "the political systems of unbelief" and might unwittingly conceive of Islamic government in terms of these: "It is imperative that we overcome our habituation to these forms of government. We must transcend our current situation together with systems of government the world over. Our choice must be Islamic government as a distinctive political system. We must attempt neither to compare it with other systems of government nor to interpret it as we like to bring it into conformity with another system or to make it resemble anything else."[23]

To this end, he insisted on rejecting Western terms that denote realities in conflict with the "distinctive Islamic political system": "president," "minister," "republic," and the like.[24] The only authentic form of Islamic government is the Caliphate, which has become Hizb al-Tahrir's self-professed hallmark.[25] For al-Nabhani, "Caliphate" designates a divinely prescribed, complete, and definitively detailed system, which can be broadly identified with the medieval Caliphate.[26] His concept of "state" rests on four principles (article 22): The *shari'a* (and not the people) is sovereign; authority to govern itself is vested in the *umma*; it is a religious obligation for Muslims to appoint a single Caliph; and finally, the Caliph has the exclusive right to adopt legal rules and to enact the constitution and all other laws. The state apparatus rests on eight pillars (article 23): the Caliph; his authorized aide; his executive aide; the jihad commander; the judiciary; provincial governors; state departments; and the Umma Council. Al-Nabhani, hence, effectively called for a resurrection of the medieval Caliphate, complete with its traditional accompanying institutions and functionaries. Reinforced by a preoccupation with authenticity, his passion for defending the self-sufficiency and exclusiveness of the perceived Islamic paradigm constrained him to slavishly adopt anachronistic forms in a forceful if naive rejection of contemporary political realities. Thus, he targeted in particular the concepts of democracy and the nation-state.

Rejecting the Concepts of Democracy and the Nation-State

Al-Nabhani condemned democracy as a man-made system of unbelief that is incompatible with Islam, which considers the *shari'a*, and not the people, to be sovereign.[27] He denounced notions that Islam is "the religion of democracy" or that democracy is "part of Islam," calling these notions lies planted during the cultural assault of colonialism on Muslim lands, especially following the destruction of the Caliphate. Repudiating the apologetics of Islamic reform, he highlighted the distinction between democratic notions and the Islamic notion of mutual consultation (*shura*) and restored the latter to its original Islamic context.[28] He insisted that *shura* is not a principle of Islamic government and has nothing to do with governing per se, but only with taking opinions. On the basis of Qur'an 3:159, he furthermore argued that it is only recommended (not obligatory) for the Caliph to implement *shura*; if he does not, although he will have been remiss, his government continues to be Islamic.[29] Nevertheless, al-Nabhani's Caliph is obliged to consult his subjects in relation to affairs concerning *mashura*. *Mashura* is a particular case in the application of *shura* that applies to certain matters that require majority opinion, but not to technical or intellectual matters. In relation to the latter category (which includes legal opinions), the purpose of consultation is merely for the person in authority to gain insight into the matter in question: He is hence not bound by the majority opinion. As far as policymaking in the Islamic state is concerned, the affairs regulated by mashura obligations are subject to a stipulation requiring possession of adequate knowledge on the part of those consulted (article 107 [i]).[30]

An emphasis on the gulf between Islam and democracy informs several aspects of al-Nabhani's state-model. He made reference to it, for example, in his first principle of the Islamic state (see above). The emphasis is also discernible in his virtual exclusion of the Muslim populace from the legislative process, which is the Caliph's prerogative: The opinions of the elected Umma Council concerning legal rules adopted by the Caliph are hence not binding on him (article 107 [iii]).[31] This rejection of democracy can be explained by al-Nabhani's conviction that the democratic experiments erected in the region's new states following World War I were part of a neocolonialist strategy for continuing control over it.[32] Equally, it mirrors the disillusionment with parliamentary democracy characteristic of the interwar generation: In 1953, indeed, al-Nabhani wrote that the bankruptcy of democracy as a system of government had become clear worldwide.[33] His specific historical context thus partly explains his stance toward democracy, expounded during the years immediately after World War II.

Rejection of the nation-state as a concept (it was of course accepted as an elemental political fact) likewise informs aspects of al-Nabhani's state-model. According to the proposed constitution (article 185 [i]), a nuclear Islamic state established in an Arab country must not consider relations with other Muslim states to fall within its foreign relations: It must not exchange diplomats or establish treaties with them, for example.[34] This attitude is a denial of these separate states (which are frequently condemned as "cardboard constructions"), together with their boundaries. The party's own sphere of operation, and the proposed Islamic state, are divided into administrative units based around major cities (*wilayat* Baghdad; *wilayat* Mosul, for example) as a further denial of the existing nation-states.[35] The promotion of a single, universal Caliphate itself constitutes an implicit denial of the legitimacy of the modern nation-state.

Consistent with his rejection of the concepts of democracy and the nation-state, in 1979 the successor to al-Nabhani, as leader of Hizb al-Tahrir, pronounced the constitution of the Islamic Republic of Iran un-

Islamic because it was informed by notions of democracy and Iranian nationalism.[36]

A Critical Assessment of Al-Nabhani's State-Model

In exhuming the perceived paradigm of authentic Islamic government, al-Nabhani drew heavily on medieval Sunni juristic theories of the Caliphate (Abu-l-Hassan al-Mawardi's *al-Ahkam al-Sultaniyya* [The Ordinances of Government] and Taqi al-Din Ibn Taymiyya's *al-Siyasa al-Shar'iyya* [Political Jurisprudence], for example), undeterred by the fact that these were typically formulated as an apologia for the historical status quo and constituted an endeavor to harmonize *existing* political realities with the *shari'a*.[37] On very few occasions he approached the political history of Islam with a critical eye and contextualized the views of the classical jurists in deference to the lessons of history and in the service of pragmatism.

Two examples illustrate this point. The first concerns the role of the Court of Iniquities (*mahkamat al-mazalim*) in dismissing the Caliph. Departing from early Islamic practice, al-Nabhani recommended that the Caliph permanently delegate the sensitive sphere of *mazalim* jurisdiction to a distinct, autonomous body of judges authorized to dismiss him if needed by the requirements of the *shari'a* (article 40).[38] To safeguard this function, he insisted that the Caliph himself should not be authorized to dismiss *mazalim* court judges; thus, he cannot dismiss them when he discovers they are about to dismiss him. Al-Nabhani noted that the classical jurists failed to address this aspect of the Court of Iniquities:[39] His own proposals represent an attempt to redress this weakness in the classical theory, providing a check on the Caliph's powers and potential despotism.

The second example concerns the extent of powers enjoyed by the provincial governor. Although there is no awareness of dangers inherent in the virtually all-powerful office of authorized aide (articles 41–47), al-Nabhani did recommend that the state restrict the authority of provincial governors to matters of provincial government exclusively (*wilaya khassa*) in order to stave off pretensions to provincial independence or sovereignty. Deferring further to the lessons of history, he advised the central authorities to keep a close watch on provincial governors and to prevent them from continuing in office for unreasonably long periods.[40]

Such rare examples aside, however, on the whole al-Nabhani wrenched out of context the institutions and practice of the historical Caliphate, construing these as timeless models of universal relevance. The office of authorized aide is a case in point: Ann Lambton notes that the classical jurists introduced the distinction between authorized and executive ministries (*wizarat al-tafwid* or *wizara mutlaqa 'amma*, and *wizarat al-tanfidh*) in an endeavor to keep within a theoretical framework of Islamic government those officials who had usurped power or neglected the Caliph in their exercise of it.[41] More generally, al-Nabhani overlooked the fact that specific institutions were created to meet particular socio-historical situations. He rigidly attempted to resurrect models reflecting the socioeconomic life of societies much less complex than today's, making no allowance for the new needs and circumstances of the contemporary age. Having said that, however, it can be demonstrated that aspects of al-Nabhani's state-model assume political forms and norms indisputably associated with the modern nation-state and the political fields that developed in relation to it. Three examples illustrate this fact.

First is the institution of direct elections to appoint the Caliph. According to al-Nabhani's second principle of state, authority to govern is vested in the Islamic *umma* as a whole. The third principle requires that it delegate this authority to a single Caliph to exercise power on its behalf. This principle derives from al-Nabhani's understanding of the Islamic conception of leadership (*imara*) as obligatory and individual, a notion based on the following *hadith*: "It is not permitted for three people to be in an open stretch of land without appointing one of their number as their *amir* (leader)."[42] The Caliph hence derives his legitimacy as ruler through his installation by the *umma*. Al-Nabhani insisted on the historical contractual pledge (*bay'at in'iqad*) as the divinely prescribed method for appointing a Caliph. Although the pledge itself is a collective religious duty, for it to be legally binding *all* Muslims concerned must be able to exercise their right to participate in the appointment. As a mechanism for achieving this ideal, al-Nabhani advocates a one-Muslim/one-vote direct election, that is, universal suffrage and the modern paraphernalia of the secret ballot. He justified these methods as merely procedures and devices (*asalib; adawat*), concerning which the *shari'a* is silent.[43] The pledge is, hence, a method for *investing with office* a candidate who has been *selected* by election: It is a manifestation of the Muslim populace's "unquestioning recognition of the fact of the Caliph's election."[44]

Seeking precedents for this approach in historical Islam, al-Nabhani argued that the influential circles referred to by the classical jurists as *ahl al-hall wa-l-'aqd* were the *umma*'s de facto representatives.[45] The legally binding character of their contractual pledge hence derives from the fact that their selection of the Caliph, which necessarily preceded this pledge, constituted an indirect election by the populace at large. In contrast, in al-Nabhani's constitution the role of the *umma*'s representatives (in the Umma Council) is not to select the Caliph, but to list candidates for the office: The Muslim populace must elect the Caliph directly (article 33).

Through a proleptic treatment of the earliest decades of Islam, al-Nabhani furthermore insisted that each of the rightly guided Caliphs was appointed by election and then invested with office through the contractual pledge.[46]

The second aspect of al-Nabhani's state-model that deserves attention is the provision for a representative institution in the form of an elected state council (*majlis al-umma*). Its function is to represent the *umma*'s opinions in calling the state to account for its actions, expressing dissatisfaction with state officials, discussing proposed legislation, exercising a limited right to *shura,* and determining the list of Caliphal candidates. It has no right to govern or legislate, as the *umma* itself possesses neither of these rights within the context of the Caliphal contract. Al-Nabhani upheld the membership of non-Muslim representatives, elected by non-Muslim subjects, on the basis that all subjects have the right to express their opinions regardless of religion, sect, or gender. They are excluded from certain of the council's activities, however.[47]

Finally, al-Nabhani's proposed state-model contains a provision for political parties. The modern political party is upheld as the only means for achieving an effective implementation of the process of *hisba.* This is a classical concept that denotes the Caliph's accountability before his subjects, and conversely, his subjects' right and duty to scrutinize his actions and call him to account. Al-Nabhani construed it as the fundamental principle governing the relationship between Caliph and subjects. As an expression of the Qur'anic injunction to "bid to honor and forbid dishonor," it is obligatory. Although the Umma Council serves to institutionalize the pursuit of *hisba,* al-Nabhani argued that neither the *umma* as a whole nor individual subjects within it can fulfill *hisba* effectively. What this duty requires is the creation of centers of leadership within the *umma* that can engage it in debate with the state, scrutinize the latter's conduct, and call it to account. On the basis that the modern political party is the only practical instrument for achieving this end, al-Nabhani advocated party plurality in the Islamic state, the only proviso being that all parties be based on Islamic doctrine (article 21).[48] Political parties, animating an active and orderly opposition, are the ultimate guarantee for the implementation of the faith. They must assume responsibility for Islam, for refreshing the *umma's* understanding of it, for purifying its ideas, and so on.[49] Imposing modern categories on the early decades of Islam, al-Nabhani construed the Companions and the first generation of Muslims ("sixty thousand out of over ten million Muslims") as the Islamic party (*al-hizb al-islami*) left by Prophet Muhammad on his death. He attributed the increasing misapplication of Islam to the disappearance of this party by the time of the successors to the Companions' successors.[50]

According to the constitution (article 21), al-Nabhani envisaged political parties as vehicles for assuming power and promoting potential Caliphal candidates. He insisted that it is not reprehensible to compete for the office of Caliph, citing the dispute between the Companions at Saqifat Bani Sa'ida in Medina following the death of the Prophet and concerning his succession. The platforms of these parties will also reflect different juridic positions: Whereas implementing rules enacted by a Caliph is obligatory, *embracing* these is not.[51] Although parties can mobilize support for a particular candidate and stance, they are compelled by the principle of obedience embodied in the *bay'a* to operate within the parameters stipulated by the state. Although many Islamic political theoreticians who advocate the multiparty system have yielded to the prevalent "democratization of culture,"[52] al-Nabhani's views in this respect are incongruous, given his vigilance against the influence of Western liberal and democratic notions.[53]

Conclusions

Al-Nabhani's attempt to return to the status quo ante by rehabilitating the Ottoman Empire in its Islamic dimensions was an affirmation of the continuity of history and a denial of European intervention, which was seen to have caused a rupture in the political and religious development of the Islamic world. The abolition of the Caliphate in 1924 symbolized the institution of the modern nation-state in the old territories of the empire. In his endeavor to reverse this development, al-Nabhani offered a state-model that explicitly rejected the new realities. Deconstruction of this model exposes the dichotomy between the rejectionism of his rhetoric and the implicit assumption of forms and norms associated with the new political context.

There is evident tension in al-Nabhani's state-model between the attractions of modernity, on the one hand, and the demands of perceived Islamic authenticity, on the other. This tension can be attributed to his peculiar location, with regard to his theoretical assumptions, between two distinct camps within modern Islamic thought. These are the culminating phase of Islamic reform (represented in Hassan al-Banna and the "old" Muslim Brotherhood), on the one hand, and mature Islamic radicalism (as articulated by Sayyid Qutb), on the other. Al-Banna embraced modernity, reworking modern political concepts such as the nation-state so that they became an integral part of his Islamic political discourse. In contrast, Qutb rejected modernity as an expression of the negation of God's sovereignty, refusing to adopt the political idiom of the modern nation-state in the service of a rediscovery of Islamic authenticity.[54] As al-Nabhani had a foot in each camp, his state-theory draws together the major concerns of both, issuing in a curiously hybrid model.

More generally, it is paradoxical that an ideologue who so vehemently rejected democracy (then much discredited as a system of government) should incorporate so many of its basic elements, including the rule of law, political participation, and governmental accountability, for example. The need to reappropriate a culturally authentic model in the face of Western encroachments issued in the elaboration of a Caliphal state-form that in some respects is utterly remote from existing realities. This model must be understood not at face value but as an articulation of the demand for cultural authenticity. Al-Nabhani's state-model resembles in broad outline that proposed by 'Abd al-Qadir 'Awda (the Muslim Brotherhood's most significant political theoretician), as expounded in his *al-Islam wa Awda'una al-Siyasiya* (Islam and Our Political Reality), published in 1951.[55] Unlike the Brotherhood, however, al-Nabhani insisted on the establishment of the state as the only means to inaugurate the Islamic order. As the vehicle for restoring a life-system rooted in the region's indigenous culture, it was hence crucial that the state conform to the most rigorous criteria of Islamicity or Islamic authenticity. The appropriation of alien forms and norms, albeit justified in terms of Islamic discourse, reflects both the influence of the culturally dominant West (if only unconsciously) *and* the extent of the author's pragmatism in accommodating existing realities and maintaining a certain openness to these. The development of an Islamic state-theory that confidently accommodates contemporary realities must assume a West that will respect both the culturally specific framework within which these realities are incorporated and the values to which they are subordinated. The "democratic" theory of Islamic government, developed especially against the backdrop of very recent Western-backed democratization programs in the Arab countries, provides a significant opportunity for testing Western attitudes in this respect.

Notes

1. See, for example, M. S. El-'Awa, *On the Political System of the Islamic State*, 6th edn. (Indianapolis, Ind.: American Trust Publications, 1980), p. 119; Q. Khan, *Al-Mawardi's Theory of the State* (Lahore: Islamic Book Foundation, 1983), pp. 4–6.

2. See El-'Awa, *On the Political System*, pp. 83–86, for an example.

3. M. A. Faksh, "The Islamic State System: A Paradigm for Diversity," *Islamic Quarterly* 28, no. 1 (1989), p. 20.

4. This tendency is well illustrated by progressive Islamist writers such as F. Huwaydi and M. S. El-'Awa. See G. Kramer, "Islamist Notions of Democracy," *Middle East Report*, July-August 1993, pp. 4–5.

5. Ibid. The author poses the question of how the *shari'a* is to be defined as the focus of debate among Islamists who uphold the functional theory of government, which sees government merely as the executive of the *shari'a*.

6. For examples, see Z. al-Qasimi, *Nizam al-Hukm fi al-shari'ah wa-al-tarikh al-Islami* (The System of Government in Islamic Law and History) (Beirut: Dar al-Nafais, 1974); M. Hilmi, *Nizam al-Hukm al-Islami muqaranan bi-al-nuzum al-muasirah* (The Islamic System of Government: A Comparison with Contemporary Systems) (Cairo: Dar al-Fikr al-Arabi, 1970); F. Abdul Karim, *al-Dawla wa-l-Siyada fi-l-Fiqh al-Islami* (State and Sovereignty in Islamic Jurisprudence) (Cairo: Maktabat Wahbah, 1977); S. Dabbous, *Al-Khilafa: Tawliyatuhu wa 'Azluhu* (The Caliph: His Appointment and Dismissal) (Alexandria: Universal Culture Establishment, 1972).

7. El-'Awa, *On the Political System,* pp. 117–118.

8. The party is presently active in most Muslim countries and parts of Europe. It has participated in parliamentary elections (Jordan 1954, 1956), attempted coups (Jordan 1968, 1969), and sustained its effort to win support in the face of universal proscription. For an introduction, see D. Commins, "Taqi al-Din al-Nabhani and the Islamic Liberation Party," *The Muslim World Journal* 81 (1991), pp. 194–211; S. Taji-Farouki, *A Fundamental Quest: Hizb al-Tahrir and the Search for the Islamic Caliphate* (London: Grey Seal, 1996).

9. Compare with S. Zubaida, *Islam, the People and the State: Essays on Political Ideas and Movements in the Middle East* (London and New York: Routledge, 1989), pp. 38–55; 121–181.

10. Al-Nabhani assumes an independent position in his views concerning *usul al-fiqh* (the principles of jurisprudence), elaborating a system that minimizes and strictly controls the role of reason in the process of juridic elaboration and displays a concern to strip away additions made by jurists after the age of Muhammad and his Companions. *Ijma'* (consensus) is confined to the consensus of the Companions; the rational legal occasion is rejected as a basis for *qiyas* (analogical deduction), and *al-maslaha al-mursala* (public interest) is not admitted as a legal evidence. This rigorous legal theory is consonant with his theological position, which upholds revelation, rather than reason, as the final arbiter in all matters defining, for example, the categories of good and evil. For his legal theory, see Taqi al-Din al-Nabhani, *al-Shakhsiya al-Islamiya* (3 vols), 2nd edn. (Jerusalem: n.p., 1953), Vol. 3.

11. Leaflet, "Al-dimuqratiyya nizam kufr," June 25, 1965.

12. Taqi al-Din al-Nabhani, *al-Dawla al-Islamiyya,* 2nd edn. (Jerusalem: n.p., 1953), pp. 93–95.

13. Taqi al-Din al-Nabhani, *Nizam al-Hukm fi-l-Islam,* 2nd edn. (Beirut: Dar al-Kashshaf, 1953), p. 10.

14. M. M. Isma'il, *Al-Fikr al-Islami* (Beirut: Maktabat al-Wa'i, 1985), pp. 39, 78–82; leaflet, "Qur'an 5:52," April 17, 1984; Taqi al-Din al-Nabhani, *Nizam al-Islam,* 5th edn. (Jerusalem: n.p., 1953), pp. 40–44; 47–50.

15. Al-Nabhani, *Nizam al-Hukm,* p. 2.

16. Al-Nabhani, *Nizam al-Islam,* pp. 80–113. An amended version (187 articles) appears in *Mudhakkara min Hizb al-Tahrir hawl al-dustur al-Irani* (hereafter cited as

Mudhakkara) (addressed to Ayatollah Khomeini), August 30, 1979, pp. 55–109. References to the constitution here are to the amended version.

17. Al-Nabhani, *Nizam al-Islam*, pp. 75–77.

18. A. al-Maliki, *Nizam al-'Uqubat* (n.p., 1965); A. al-Da'ur, *Ahkam al-Bayyinat* (Beirut: Matabi' al-Ghandur, 1965).

19. Al-Nabhani, *al-Tafkir* (n.p., March 1973), pp. 90, 92–93.

20. Taqi al-Din al-Nabhani, *Mafahim Hizb al-Tahrir,* 2nd edn. (Beirut: Matabi' al-Istiqlal, 1953), p. 45.

21. Al-Nabhani, *Nizam al-Islam,* pp. 75–77; see also al-Maliki, *Nizam al-'Uqubat,* pp. 194–196.

22. Al-Nabhani, *Mafahim Hizb al-Tahrir,* p. 45.

23. Al-Nabhani, *Nizam al-Hukm,* p. 9.

24. Ibid., pp. 30, 105–108; al-Nabhani, *Mafahim Hizb al-Tahrir,* pp. 68–71. Compare with Qutb: See Y. M. Choueiri, *Islamic Fundamentalism* (London: Pinter, 1990), p. 113.

25. Leaflet, "Nass al-ijaba 'ala risalat ahad al-shabab," March 31, 1983; London-based journal *al-Fajr,* no. 16 (April 1990), p. 8.

26. Theorists from the first camp maintain, in contrast, that the term does not indicate a specific system of government; rather, the Caliphate merely became the *symbol* for government in the historical Islamic state. See El-'Awa, *On the Political System,* p. 64, for example.

27. *Mudhakkara,* pp. 12, 21–22, 30–31, 37, 42, 44–47. This notion highlights the incompatibility of republican democracy (as represented in the constitution of the Islamic Republic of Iran) with the Islamic system of government.

28. The modernists were first to reformulate *shura* as parliamentary democracy. For comments on the distinction between the two, see B. Tibi, "Islam and Modern European Ideologies," *International Journal of Middle East Studies* 18 (1986), p. 16.

29. Leaflets "Al-dimuqratiyya nizam kufr," June 25, 1965, and "Al-shura fi-l-Islam," March 14, 1961; *Hadith al-Siyam* (al-Ram: Matba'at al-Risala, n.d.), p. 80. In contrast, the dominant tendency in contemporary Islamic political discourse is to construe *shura* as the first pillar of Islamic government. See I. R. al-Faruqi, "The Islamic Critique of the Status Quo of Muslim Society," in B. Freyer Stowasser (ed.), *The Islamic Impulse* (London: Croom Helm, 1987), p. 229, for example.

30. Al-Nabhani, *Nizam al-Hukm,* pp. 16, 26, 28. For the distinction between *shura* and *mashura,* see leaflet, "Al-shura fi-l-Islam"; al-Nabhani, *Al-Shakhsiyya al-Islamiyya,* Vol. 1, pp. 207–221.

31. *Mudhakkara,* pp. 29–32. Compare with the insistence among theorists from the first trend that legislation evolves through consensus achieved via consultation, necessitating a sharing of legislative power between the head of state and an elected body representing the people. In line with this view, theorists frequently use the terms "consultative council" and "legislative assembly" interchangeably. See, for example, F. Hassan, *The Concept of State and Law in Islam* (Lanham, Md.: University of America Press, 1981), p. 82; Richard P. Mitchell, *The Society of the Muslim Brothers* (New York: Oxford University Press, 1969), p. 248; J. Esposito, *Islam and Politics,* 3rd edn. (New York: Syracuse University Press, 1991), p. 147.

32. Leaflets, "Khutut 'arida," May 18, 1976; "Al-dimuqratiyya kufr wa la narda 'an al-Islam badila," May 1960; "Al-dimuqratiyya nizam kufr," July 25, 1965.

33. Al-Nabhani, *Nizam al-Hukm*, p. 9.

34. *Mudhakkara*, p. 4.

35. *Al-Qanun al-Idari li-Hizb al-Tahrir* (Jerusalem: n.p., 1953); leaflet, "Qanun al-intikhabat li-lijan al-wilayat," April 23, 1960, p. 1.

36. *Mudhakkara*, pp. 8–11. Compare with Zubaida, *Islam, the People and the State*, pp. 172–179.

37. A.K.S. Lambton, "Khalifa," *The Encyclopaedia of Islam*, 2nd edn. (Leiden: Brill, 1979), p. 948; H.A.R. Gibb, *Studies on the Civilization of Islam* (Princeton: Princeton University Press, 1962), pp. 162ff.

38. Compare with E. Tyan, "Judicial Organization," in M. Khadduri and H. J. Leibesny (eds.), *Law in the Middle East*, Vol. 1, *Origin and Development of Islamic Law* (Washington, D.C.: The Middle East Institute, 1958), p. 266.

39. Al-Nabhani, *Nizam al-Hukm*, pp. 90, 94–96.

40. Ibid., pp. 66–79.

41. A.K.S. Lambton, *State and Government in Medieval Islam (An Introduction to the Study of Islamic Political Theory: The Jurists)* (Oxford: Oxford University Press, 1981), pp. 95–96.

42. *Muqaddimat al-Dustur: Al-Asbab al-Mujiba lahu* (n.p., 1963), p. 87; al-Nabhani, *al-Shakhsiyya al-Islamiyya*, Vol. 2, pp. 110–114. The corollary is that there can be only one universal Caliphate: Al-Nabhani, *Nizam al-Hukm*, pp. 30–31.

43. Al-Nabhani, *al-Tafkir*, pp. 94–97.

44. Al-Nabhani, *Nizam al-Hukm*, pp. 29, 33–34, 38.

45. Al-Nabhani, *Al-Khilafa* (Kuwait: al-Matba'a al-'Asriyya, 1967), pp. 17, 32–34; al-Nabhani, *al-Shakhsiyya al-Islamiyya*, Vol. 2, p. 39. Compare with modernist arguments: See Y. M. Choueiri, *Islamic Fundamentalism*, pp. 33–34.

46. Al-Nabhani, *Nizam al-Hukm*, pp. 34, 42–52; al-Nabhani, *Al-Shakhsiyya al-Islamiyya*, Vol. 2, p. 35.

47. Al-Nabhani, *Nizam al-Hukm*, pp. 16–19, 24.

48. Ibid., pp. 36–40.

49. Al-Nabhani, *Al-Shakhsiyya al-Islamiyya*, Vol. 2, p. 123.

50. Al-Nabhani, *Nizam al-Hukm*, pp. 119–123; al-Nabhani, *al-Takattul al-Hizbi*, 3rd edn. (Jerusalem: n.p., 1953), p. 56.

51. Al-Nabhani, *Al-Dawla al-Islamiyya*, p. 181; al-Nabhani, *al-Shakhsiyya al-Islamiyya*, Vol. 2, p. 121.

52. N. A. al-Khatib, "Islamic Thought and Political Parties," *Islam Today*, no. 4 (April 1986), pp. 13–14; K. M. Ishaque, "Political Parties and Leadership in the Islamic State," *Islamic and Comparative Law Quarterly* 6, nos. 2–3 (1986), pp. 136, 155–156.

53. See al-Nabhani, *Nizam al-Hukm*, p. 9, for example.

54. Choueiri, *Islamic Fundamentalism*, p. 48; E. Sivan, *Radical Islam: Medieval Theology and Modern Politics* (New Haven, Conn.: Yale University Press, 1990), pp. 28, 67; Zubaida, *Islam, the People and the State*, pp. 52–53.

55. See F. Jaddane, "Notions of the State in Contemporary Arab-Islamic Writings," in G. Salame (ed.), *The Foundations of the Arab State* (Kent: Croom Helm, 1987), pp. 132–133; the author argues that al-Nabhani's model is "better defined, more concise, clear, complete, and radical" than 'Awda's.

3

Islam and the Secular Logic of the State in the Middle East

CHARLES TRIPP

There are a number of ways of approaching the subject of the renewed salience of Islamic themes and movements in Middle Eastern politics. One approach would be to take the essentialist road and suggest that the basic values of an undifferentiated Islam are permanent features of Middle Eastern societies and therefore irrepressible. This approach is associated with the idea of cultural determinism and produces the thesis that fundamental or essential values will always find expression, particularly at moments of social and political crisis. A contrasting view is to suggest that distinctively Islamic forms of political expression and organization are better explained with reference to the material conditions of the people concerned than to anything specifically "Islamic." In this reading, "Islam" simply becomes a label used to convey mundane social grievances. The thesis here is that people have the capacity to choose their symbolic vocabulary according to their perception of their interests at the time. Clearly, each of these views is connected to and underpinned by rather different understandings of the relationship of ideas, beliefs, and identities to social action.

However, in the context of contemporary manifestations of self-consciously Islamic political activity, it seems more fruitful to seek to understand the ways in which Islamist movements in Middle Eastern politics have been shaped, if not necessarily created, by the same political forces as those which have been associated with the emergence of Middle Eastern states. I shall argue that manifestations of self-consciously Islamic political activity are best understood as responses to encounters with particular forms of power, of which the state may be the most public symbolic and actual repository. The goals and methods of the organizations associated with the reassertion of Islamic values in political life are to a large degree shaped by the structures of imagination and power appropriate to the state. Precisely because of the particular features of the organization of power found in different Middle Eastern states, as well as of the variety of legacies and value-systems they incorporate, the Islamic responses have varied. So, too, have the reactions of governments seeking to control and deploy the resources of the state for their own purposes.

One particular feature that merits attention is the secular "logic," or, perhaps more accurately, the different forms of secular logic, associated with the state in the late twentieth century. The proponents of a distinctively "Islamic politics" have sought to differentiate it from the secular impulse and the forces of secularism, while at the same time seeking to reclaim the terrain of political activity in the name of Islam by declaring that there is no distinction between religion and politics. It will be instructive, therefore, to understand the degree to which politics, insofar as it must perforce be played out in a world of states and human societies, may in fact be subject to a secular logic or to secularizing impulses. The consequences of this analysis for those who would assert Islamic obligations as the foundation for all political life may be troubling, since they may find that their activities are resting, in turn, on a set of distinctly secular preoccupations.

The nature of these preoccupations will depend upon the understanding of the term "secular." One sense attached to the term is that associated with secularism as a distinctive ideology that seeks to privatize religious belief. In this respect, it is a program advocating the elimination of all religious symbols, authorities, and organizations from public life and the foundation of political authority on worldly ethical principles. Such an understanding is directly related to the emergence of Western forms of political thought, informed by a humanist sensibility and associated with liberal distinctions between the private and the public. In this sense, therefore, secularism represents a determined effort to relegate religion to the private domain. From this perspective, secularism can be seen as a determined assault against religion, its symbols, its hold on people's imaginations, and its institutional apparatus. Alternatively, it can be seen as a blueprint for toleration and social harmony in societies deeply divided by their members' religious beliefs.

There is another understanding of the idea of the "secular," however, that is connected to one of the original meanings of the word. In this instance, the term denotes things of this world, as opposed to those of the hereafter, as well as the affairs of lay organizations and institutions, as distinct from—in the Christian case—ecclesiastical or monastic institutions. Whatever the ends to which the state and its power may be dedicated—be they self-consciously religious or openly secular—the means will involve the organization of human beings through coercion or persuasion in this world. It is this—the state's role as an organization of worldly power for the ordering of human society in this world—that imbues the state in its various cultural settings and throughout history with a certain secular logic. Every state, regardless of its particular character, is primarily a socially grounded organization of power in this world, not the next. Indeed, the force of this logic may lead to a preoccupation with the concerns of this world—with power over others, including coercive power, with advantage in relation to other people, and with access to material resources—regardless of the symbolic forms used to justify activity in these spheres. Where such justifications are themselves unabashedly secular, the lineaments of a full-fledged secularism are visible.

Even where this is not the case, it can be argued that such preoccupations tend to subject the uses of religious symbols and the authoritative religious institutions to a certain mundane logic, universal insofar as it stems from the exigencies of maintaining universally recognizable forms of state power. In seeking to understand the secularizing process, therefore, a distinction can be made. On the one hand, there is secularism as a consciously adopted strategy aimed at removing potentially irreconcilable religious differences from the domain of public conflict. On the other, there is the transformative secularist logic of the state as an organization of worldly power that demands certain reactions and adaptive transformations even from those who believe that the social order should approximate as far as possible the divine order. The effects of both of these secularizing dynamics have been unwelcome to many and have themselves been the cause of considerable political conflict—or at least have helped to shape political conflict and may have given it its distinct form.

In this chapter I shall seek, therefore, first to understand the dynamics, or the various "logics," associated with the state in the Middle Eastern context. The intention here is to examine some of the varied forms and mixed legacies that have produced particular kinds of state organizations in the Middle East, drawing out specifically the secular logic of the usages of state power. Second, I shall examine the ways in which governments of a number of Middle Eastern states have used distinctively Islamic themes in their legitimation strategies. In the third section, I will assess the implications of such strategies for the emergence of more radical or oppositional Islamist movements, looking in particular at the ways in which they have challenged the governments concerned and the ways in which the distinguishing forms of the state have, in turn, shaped these movements, even though they may ostensibly be rejecting the state itself. The intention, finally, is to understand the degree to which such movements constitute a challenge to the existing order or are contributing to a redefinition of that order in significant ways. Most, perhaps all, of the self-consciously Islamic political movements in the late twentieth century have incorporated into their program a strong critique of secularism and of the structure they call the "secular state." However, it seems possible that in engaging with the very notion of the state, they have themselves become implicated in the secular logic of its distinctive processes.

Secular Aspects of the State in the Middle East

Contemporary Middle Eastern states are hybrid creatures. On the one hand, they appear to comply with the formal definitions of the state determined by the dominant international order, modeled largely on the Western state tradition. Thus, the demarcation of a distinct territory, the claim that this delimits a distinctive political community, and the formal monopoly of the means of coercion in the name of that community by the government are all defining elements of the states themselves. Equally, many of these states are characterized by the existence of written constitutions that allude to the sovereignty of the people and that, in one form or another, prescribe the institutional arrangements under which such sovereignty can be realized in political practice. At the same time, most of the states concerned are marked by bureaucracies geared toward carrying out developmental and welfare functions. These are justified with reference to modern ideas of the welfare state and of the state's responsibility for the economic well-being of the associated society, broadly interpreted.

Nevertheless, regardless of the formal similarities that states of the Middle East share to a greater or lesser degree with those in other parts of the world, there are distinctive patterns of power that correspond more closely to indigenous conceptions of the state and of the effective ordering of power. These are not expressed in any straightforward and unified fashion. On the contrary, much of the recent political history of the Middle East has been marked by the encounter between different and in some senses antithetical state traditions. These traditions are not simply ideal constructions: They often underpin the normative orders that governments are seeking to implement through the structures of the state. In other words, different ideas about the proper framework for politics and the rules governing political behavior have real consequences. To a large extent these ideas and the forms of behavior appropriate to them have perforce been expressed on the terrain marked out by the dominant Western model of the state. This does not mean, however, that such a model has simply superseded more socially grounded ways of conceiving of and handling power. On the contrary, it could be argued that it has been subverted by the local state legacies.[1]

In this context, perhaps the most important local construct is that of the patrimonial state. Whether expressed through monarchical or republican forms, the basic structures of patron-client relations and the networks they create constitute the principal organization of power in all of the Arab states in the Middle East. Associated with the personalization of power, with authoritarian practices that maintain the hierarchies of power, and with the exclusions that lend to patronage its effectiveness, the specific character of the patrimonial networks in any particular state tends to reflect the main divisions within its associated society. At the heart of power is a community of trust, founded most frequently on the common origins of its members. Generally, these communities derive in large part from the same kinship group, which may, in turn, entail a common provincial origin, as well as a common confessional identity. However, as the cases of Egypt and Algeria demonstrate, these communities may also be founded on a number of different identities and interests.[2]

In such circumstances, the preoccupations of the ruler or of the ruling elite are twofold: first, that there should be cohesion within the inner core of the regime; second, that there should be acquiescence or acceptance within society at large of the dominant networks that control access to the resources of the state. To this end, a number of claims and ideologies have been pressed into service. It is in this context, therefore, that one should assess the relevance of Islam as a system of beliefs that may be interpreted and deployed in such a way as to reinforce the strategies of the ruling patrimonial elite. The latter seek social order and the resources that will allow them to implement an order favorable to their own community of trust. In many cases, these priorities may not coincide with the imperatives that come from a distinctively Islamic reinterpretation of political obligation.

It is in this realm of state definition and management that some of the contradictions and conflicts begin to manifest themselves—conflicts that have created the space in which many of the movements of Islamic protest have sought to operate, both ideationally and pragmatically. In the first place, the attempt to adapt to local conditions the imported model of the territorial nation-state, complete with its underlying assumptions concerning sovereignty, identity, and interests, has not always succeeded. Yet, even if it leaves something to be desired as a focus for identity and loyalty, this model of the state is a model of unquestioned power and, as such, has become extraordinarily seductive for elites and their challengers alike. Consequently, it cannot be given up easily but becomes the target of efforts to "indigenize" or "authenticate" it.[3]

Second, seeking to disguise indigenous systems of power and authority with the language appropriate to a conception of the state suggested by the Western model has brought with it tensions in a number of areas.

For instance, it is obvious that many of the regimes concerned have failed in the terms set by the very model itself, whether this be in the realm of ensuring citizens' rights, giving effective expression to popular sovereignty, fulfilling the developmental and welfare functions of the state, or, indeed, even in the most basic task of successfully defending the territories of the state. Furthermore, in promoting a legitimation of clannish power that is both populist and, at times, explicitly phrased in the idioms of religious discourse, many of these regimes have constructed the very framework for the critique of their own hold on power as well as suggesting the means whereby such criticism might become the basis of effective opposition.

Last, there is the question of the secular nature of the political enterprise in two senses. First, the explicitly secular nature of the Western model of the state makes certain demands of those who would organize power according to its criteria. Preoccupations of a structural kind, having to do with the successful management of the means of coercion, the administrative machinery of the state, and the defense of its territorial integrity, are matched by a moral language invoking the sovereignty of the people, the unity of the national community, and the greatest good of the greatest number. Second, understandable concerns about political survival and the proper ends of politics lead ruling elites to reinforce a more locally rooted secular tradition—that of kin or other socially connected groups that dominate the political order through control of the means of coercion. In both cases there is a secular logic at work that owes nothing to distinctively religious forms of thought, even if the language associated with such beliefs may sometimes be invoked in the attempt to acquire a greater degree of moral sanction.

The problem for the rulers of these states is that they do not wish to pursue the full-blown model of the Western state, since that would involve opening up their own systems of power to the scrutiny of a body of empowered citizens. Nor do they wish to claim that they are only ruling in the interests of their particular clan or communal grouping, even if this may approximate the truth. Instead, they deploy all the emotive themes they can to reinforce social control, while ensuring that they have under their immediate command all the coercive and informational machinery with which the modern state can furnish a ruler. In doing so, they suggest both the conceptual and the organizational apparatus with which self-consciously Islamic political groups may voice and act upon their criticism of the state. However, even if the tensions within the structure and the moral universe of the state may have encouraged such developments, it does not mean that the rulers of the state are without resources when it comes to facing up to the challenges provided by distinctively Islamist movements in politics.

"Islamic Politics" as Mirror of the State:
In Support of Government

The ruling elites of the Arab states have long sought to appropriate the legitimacy they believe is conferred among the mass public by nominal adherence to Islamic values. This practice has been much in evidence not simply throughout the history of Arab societies but also in the history of much of the Islamic world. The principal difference in the present century has been in the changed understandings of the size and constitution of the relevant political public. This change has, in turn, transformed the ways in which strategies of legitimation relying on distinctive Islamic values have been organized and presented. However, it has not reduced the centrality of the references to some conception of Islam in public discourse.

Whether in the Egypt of Nasser, the Algeria of the Front de Libération Nationale (FLN, National Liberation Front), the Jordan of King Hussein, or the Arabia of King Abd al-Aziz, the widely differing purposes of regimes and states have often been couched in the language of Islam, with those in power inevitably selecting those aspects of Islamic history or belief that spoke to their particular visions of the states they were seeking to construct. Thus, in Nasser's attempt to enthuse the Egyptians for his socialist measures, adopted increasingly as the path of development from the late 1950s onward, Qur'anic verses, sayings of the Prophet, and the whole panoply of Islamic jurisprudence under the control of the Egyptian president in the institution of Al-Azhar were pressed into service to expound upon the truly socialist nature of Islam.[4] Likewise, under the FLN in Algeria, where any distinctively Algerian identity was yet to take hold of people's imaginations and where the ambiguous legacies of their long relationship with and domination by the French were of prime concern, the distinctiveness of Islam as a marker of cultural separation from their erstwhile colonial masters was of prime importance in the nation-building strategies of an allegedly secular regime.[5]

Similar questions about the identities and loyalties of the population affected the Hashemite dynasty in Jordan. The potentially divisive impact of emerging Palestinian nationalism and the challenge to monarchical rule of secular Arab nationalism led to the cultivation by King Hussein both of his own image as a descendant of the Prophet and the licensing of the Muslim Brotherhood at a time when all other forms of political organization were banned.[6] Meanwhile, in Saudi Arabia, the Al Saud had maintained their long-standing alliance with the descendants of Muhammad Abd al-Wahhab in their conquest of most of Arabia, in the name both of the Al Saud and of the Wahhabi interpretation of Islamic obligation. This dual focus helped to unite under one purpose the scattered and diverse communities of Arabia.[7]

All of these strategies, with their very different ends, bring two questions to the fore: What is the deployment of Islamic symbols and themes
intended to achieve in particular settings, and why are there varied manifestations and interpretations of "Islam"? Clearly, there has been a common belief among the ruling elites in the efficacy, as well as the appropri-
ateness, of the emphasis on aspects of Islamic belief as one of the means of
winning popular approval for projects. As the founders of states, or as the
rulers of states only recently freed from European imperial domination,
those in power evidently felt the need to take some account of the belief
systems of the people whom they were seeking to bend to their will. Since
it was equally clear that they did not intend to consult these people in any
systematic way, the strategy of lending to the exercise of essentially patrimonial and authoritarian power a distinctive Islamic aura was certainly
meant to ensure obedience. However, it is possible that it was also intended to induce in people a feeling that the form of government was appropriate, that the newly defined or liberated state was in some sense
"theirs."

Underlying this objective, as might be imagined, was a project of social
control. This undertaking has had two particular effects on expressions of
Islamic support for the state authorities. First, it is clear that the "Islamic"
legitimation of government activities is but one strategy among many
open to and put into operation by the government. As the government's
priorities change, so too do the forms of Islamic endorsement of governmental acts. Since many of these acts are patently far from any distinctly
Islamic set of imperatives and relate—sometimes transparently—to the
exigencies of maintaining a patrimonial state, contradictions may ensue.
There is, of course, no contradiction that a well-organized, government-
subsidized establishment of Islamic commentators and ulama may not be
able to gloss over, but this problem will have implications for their authority—and thus for their future efficacy as rationalizers of the government's policies to the public.[8]

The second feature of Middle Eastern governments' uses of Islamic
themes in their strategies of governance is based in the fact that the overriding consideration for all regimes is that there should be no institutional
embodiment of an Islamic imperative that is independent of the state.
This concern has been demonstrated in the licensing of political parties
and organizations, the "nationalization" of all mosques, the funding of Islamic institutions of learning and the scholars who inhabit them, the cen-
sorship and control of all publications, and, if need be, the violent suppression of all alternative, independent interpretations of Islamic political
obligations. Within the limits of their capabilities these strategies have
been pursued by all Middle Eastern regimes in their efforts to maintain
tight control of the nature of the Islamic imperative that is being articu-

lated in society. Indeed, the variety in the interpretation of Islamic imperatives and the lack of established or recognized orthodoxy in Islamic societies give those with powers of patronage at their disposal enormous latitude in encouraging interpretations of Islamic law that might serve the political purposes of the patrons.

In other words, pressing "Islam" into the service of patrimonialism as patrimonial structures seek to manage the government of modern states could be said to be one of the main themes of late twentieth-century politics in the Middle East. It has taken various forms, some of which may be worthy of note here in order to give a sense of the ways in which a concern for particular interpretations of Islam has informed the strategies of rulers of nominally secular states. First, there has been the attempt to clothe the policies of the government in the language of Islamic belief. This endeavor has been evident in Libya, for instance, under Muammar al-Qadhafi. In al-Qadhafi's "Third Universal Theory" and in his other strategies of social control, the Islamic authentication of some aspects of his theory has been sought and asserted. The problem he faced was that the authentication itself was questioned by some of Libya's Islamic authorities as well as by obvious opponents, such as the Libyan Muslim Brotherhood, in the light of their interpretation of the traditions of Islam. Al-Qadhafi responded by simply silencing his critics and continuing to maintain that only his theory of government was the "true" interpretation of Islamic political obligation since, he alleged, it was based solely on Qur'anic sources.[9]

Second, in Egypt under Mubarak there have been various attempts to suggest that the government is particularly concerned with Islamic sensibilities. This project has manifested itself, for instance, in the trial by the state courts of a novelist and his publisher on charges of blasphemy—an indictable offense under Egyptian law. Both men were sentenced to prison terms, but, characteristically in the light of the kind of strategy being pursued, the president has delayed signing the order that would in fact send them to prison. This stalling has not prevented the government, however, from granting to a section of Al-Azhar, a state-funded institution, the power to censor all books published in Egypt in the name of "Islam." Meanwhile, although at a snail's pace, the Egyptian Parliament continues the task begun under President Sadat of bringing all Egyptian legislation into line with the *shari'a*.[10] Which interpretations of *shari'a* guidelines are to be the dominant ones, however, is a matter of constant debate and, as is clear in many instances, there are simply no guidelines in much of the *fiqh* for many of the legislative provisions of a modern state.

This brings one to another aspect of the ways in which Middle Eastern governments are seeking to utilize Islamic beliefs to bolster their rule and their states. This third aspect might be called the politics of identity or authenticity. Playing upon themes of Islamic history and on distinctively Islamic traditions of the society in question is one way of suggesting continuity between the regime and history, on the one hand, and the society over which the government rules, on the other. In most respects, this approach parallels and even follows the patterns of national self-identification. This has been evident in the ways in which the Saudi regime has sought to establish its claim to legitimacy and can be found in much of the rhetoric of regimes from Morocco to Oman.

In the case of Iraq under Saddam Hussein, interesting variants of this strategy have been observable. During the war with Iran, it was important for the Iraqi regime both to mobilize large numbers of Iraqis for the war effort and to ensure that they differentiated themselves from the Iranian enemy. Not only were the latter fellow Muslims, but also, as Shi'a, they shared the same sectarian identity as the majority of the Iraqis. Saddam Hussein's answer was to "nationalize" Islam by suggesting that only Arabs could have a true understanding of Islamic obligations—all non-Arabs were condemned to an understanding that was, at best, hazy and, at worst, simply wrong.[11] Whether this attempt convinced many Iraqis is a moot point, but it was obviously believed to be useful by the regime. Similarly, Saddam Hussein's use of Islamic themes, symbols, and observances during the crisis and war following the occupation of Kuwait was a notable part of a strategy aimed at undermining his regional enemies and mobilizing opposition against the dominant Western powers of the coalition.

In short, "Islam," as a set of symbolic markers, values, and beliefs, tends to be viewed instrumentally as something that should serve the purposes of the ruling elite. Although instrumental, this use of Islamic tenets may not be a wholly cynical endeavor since members of the ruling elite often share a view of the social order deeply imbued with their own sense of distinctively "Islamic" propriety. Whatever the actual foundations of their power, many Middle Eastern regimes clearly share a belief that, in the effort to mobilize or to pacify a mass public, some gesture in the direction of an "Islamic politics" is required. For these purposes, the ruling interpretation of this "Islam" is crucial. Whether such a restrictive project is feasible in the conditions of mass politics that have made this very public relevant, however, is questionable. In other words, the suspicion emerges that these regimes have encouraged forms of identity politics that they can no longer control through the established means of patronage. They must fall back increasingly on coercive strategies, as they see the themes of Islamic obligation being turned against them to indict them for failing to live by the very code they once tried to suggest the state should enforce.

"Islamic Politics" as Mirror of the State: Oppositional Activity

Every Middle Eastern government that has sought to use Islamic themes to shore up its own authority has found itself confronted by self-consciously Islamic groupings challenging it in the name of the very Islamic precepts it claimed to be upholding. Both the ends and the means of the political activity of the Islamic protest groups have been shaped in various ways by the nature of the state in which they were operating. Meanwhile, the constituencies for such groups have in general tended to lie amongst those whose situations have caused them either to question the customary rationales of the socioeconomic status quo or to react against the perceived loss of identity and community that the dominant political order seems prepared to countenance.

In all cases, there is nothing straightforwardly "traditional" about the movements that result. The forms of and justifications for political activity by the organizations of Islamic protest are very much those of mass, urban politics—of a modern understanding of the political and its proper sphere. This principle seems to apply with particular sharpness in four distinct areas: First, there are those movements concerned about the failing welfare functions of the contemporary Middle Eastern state, either because the resources to service an ambitious welfare state are no longer available or because they cannot keep up with population growth. Second, there are those that are seeking to use modern means of organization and even rationales adapted from a legalistic, liberal agenda to undermine the claims of authoritarian and patrimonial rule. Third, there are groupings preoccupied with the preservation, or perhaps better the reconstitution, of collective identity in a world where communities of this kind are being undermined by forces that are seen to be working through the state. Last, there are organizations seeking to use more direct, often violent methods in the pursuit of political power. The rationale governing their activities is based on the belief or assertion that once state power has been seized, the ideal of a truly Islamic order can be realized.

As far as the first manifestation of "Islamic politics" is concerned, Egypt has provided one of the best examples during the past fifteen years of Islamist groups setting themselves up self-consciously to attend to those areas where the welfare state appears to have failed. It is in this context that local clinics, attached to specific mosques and providing health services free of charge to those in need, have emerged in Cairo. A similar role has been played by groups providing photocopying facilities, transport, and housing to the large but indigent student community.[12] A very visible example of such activities occurred in connection with the 1993 earthquake in Cairo: Before the state organizations could get into gear, Islamist organizations were already on the scene, providing help, shelter, and food.

It is undoubtedly the case that many of these activities correspond to the well-established place of charitable works in Islamic tradition and belief. It is equally the case, however, that many of them are connected to organizations that favor a more explicitly Islamic dispensation of power in Egypt. Their involvement in an urban setting in highly visible welfare activities could be said to correspond to the notion of "propaganda by deed" once advocated as an oppositional strategy in other contexts by those seeking to undermine the authority of the state. More important, as far as the argument of this chapter is concerned, preoccupation of a systematic kind with the welfare of society as a whole, not simply with designated groups within it, brings in its wake a form of secular logic or argumentation. In the twentieth century it has become difficult to imagine such concepts as "social welfare," "social justice," or "social utility" without some reference, even if implicit, to the predominantly secular ideas of the social theorists of the industrial revolution in Europe, be they liberals, utilitarians, or socialists. This assimilation has become evident in the writings of figures as diverse as Sayyid Qutb in Egypt or Muhammad Baqir al-Sadr in Iraq, both of whom have inspired distinctive Islamic political movements. In both cases, although in different ways, the criterion of "social welfare" is employed to justify the advocacy of certain policies or, indeed, the particular interpretations of distinctively Islamic texts.[13]

In a practical sense, welfare activities of the kind alluded to above are designed more directly and instrumentally to reinforce the electoral strategies of organized groupings such as the Muslim Brotherhood. In Egypt, the space opened up by the government during the past ten years or so for electoral activity may be limited, but it has provided groupings such as the Muslim Brotherhood with an opportunity to play an electoral game. Cultivating potential constituents and giving the impression that Islamic organizations can play these welfare functions better than the state is obviously grist to the mill of an organization that campaigns under the slogan "Islam is the Solution."

Precisely because electoral politics can be said to be the antithesis of the established patrimonial systems of power, however, and because they promise to bring the public actively into the political equation, a significant number of Islamic political organizations in various countries have been eager to embrace them. In the few states of the Middle East where elections of any meaningful kind—even if limited—have been allowed, oppositional Islamic groups and parties have seized upon them as a means of expressing themselves and their ideas against the dominant power structure. Playing upon the frustrations of many with the record of unresponsive and irresponsible governments, they have capitalized upon the fact that they can present themselves as an alternative that is at one and the same time genuine and "safe." The electioneering of the Muslim Brotherhood, particularly in Jordan, indirectly in Egypt, and, a few years ago, in Algeria, demonstrated the tactic whereby the candidates of the Islamic parties put themselves forward as the candidates of change but relied heavily upon the public's apparent familiarity with Islamic slogans and beliefs for their power of persuasion.[14]

So, too, professional associations (doctors' and lawyers' syndicates and student unions, for example) have embraced Islamic electoral politics. In these fora in Egypt, for instance, the candidates of the Islamist movements have done consistently well. They have been able to capitalize on the resentments built up by years of mismanagement by government-appointed officers, as well as on the continued frustrations of these professionals in their dealings with government. The very specialized and limited role of the syndicates and the specific part assigned to the syndicates' leadership also reinforce the particular skills of these groupings.

As in the case of the welfare functions of the state, it is in the interest of the Islamist groupings to take over very specific functions and to be seen to perform them in an exemplary manner as a way of illustrating their larger claims. Their representatives have been eager to demonstrate their adherence to the rules of the democratic game. Whether or not they seek to justify such participation with reference to significantly reconstituted notions of *shura* (consultation) or *ijmma'* (consensus), they are aware of the fact that this is the terrain on which the restrictive circles of the ruling elites are at their most vulnerable.[15] The Islamists are also supremely confident that in a society composed largely of Muslims they will have the support of the vast majority of that society. Whether this confidence is justified remains to be seen. This will be an empirical or contingent matter. However, there is also a more serious problem in the fact that there is a secular logic to democracy. In the realm of majoritarian democracy, numbers, rather than virtues, count. Thus, a wholly secular criterion, based upon the enumeration of individual human beings, will in theory decide who or what rules the state and indeed the kind of state that is to be established. These individuals and their choices may be influenced by Islamic values, but in the final analysis it will be their numbers and not their religion that will decide the future of the political system.

The third area of concern for many of the groups seeking to establish a more distinctively Islamic order is to restore a lost sense of community or to protect in some fashion a community under threat. It is in this sphere of identity politics that Islamic political protest groups have been active throughout the Middle East, suggesting that the ruling regimes are threatening the communities of Muslims and the identities and values that such communities nurture. This critique has taken a number of forms, depending upon the nature of the state and the associated society. In many countries of the Middle East, the relationship between the ruling regime and outside powers, representing non-Islamic values, has been and continues to be denounced. Whether the target of denunciation is the Egyptian government or the Saudi government, the claim is both that the "true" identity of the community is being compromised by the specific alliances formed between the leaders and particular Western powers and that the leadership's seduction by the materialism and power of the West has robbed it of all claim to authority over a Muslim community.

Another manifestation of such identity politics could be said to be Hamas amongst the Palestinians. This problem is challenging not simply the Israeli authorities but also the mainstream nationalist movement of the PLO because of the alleged compromises it has made over the claimed "essential interests" of the Palestinians. The target here has become not simply a rival political organization but the very notion of secular nationalism. There is considerable theoretical ambiguity in this endeavor, however, deriving from the secular logic of nationalism and the nation-state. Historically, Hamas emerged among Palestinians affiliated with the Muslim Brotherhood who sensed that they were losing ground to the mainstream nationalist movement of the PLO and, furthermore, that the PLO was failing in certain important respects. Nevertheless, they were obliged, precisely because of the historical experiences of the Palestinians, to compete on the terrain of territorial nationalism itself. In other words, they did not simply announce that the very notion of Palestine was an irrelevance or an improper focus of loyalty, as other Islamic critics of secular nationalist projects have done. On the contrary, they sought to "Islamize" the idea of Palestine by declaring that it was an inalienable part of the *dar al-Islam*. Because they were, after all, operating among people who saw themselves as distinctively Palestinian, they identified the territory of Palestine as that originally demarcated by the British mandatory authorities.[16] Quite apart from the practical political problems they will face over the degree of compromise they may be willing to accept in the future regarding these borders, the question remains as to how it was that the purely secular notion of the territoriality of the state entered into the equation in the first place. Furthermore, it seems clear that once it had entered the equation, it began to exert a logic of its own—a largely secular logic that has markedly influenced the strategies of Hamas.

Fearing that compromises with the forces of secular politics will contaminate the identity of the community in question and the purity of the Islamic ideals it is intended to pursue, some groups have adopted the fourth option—that of violent opposition. Violence seems to serve both expressive and instrumentalist functions for a number of these groups. Whether on the symbolic or the practical level, it tends to illuminate what the state has become for members of these more violent Islamic groups. Some of the members of such groups have suffered violent treatment at the hands of the servants of the authoritarian state, and this experience may have helped to shape their attitude toward it. The concentration camps of the Nasser regime, for example, had this effect on members of the Egyptian Muslim Brotherhood—though some may have emerged convinced that they should not try to challenge the state on its own terrain, others saw violence as the only way of dealing with a fundamentally threatening and iniquitous state.[17]

These were the men who became the inspiration for the younger generation of Islamic militants. The latter have pursued the expressive strategy of attacking police officers, government ministers, the president, and other figures epitomizing state authority. It seems likely that they carry out such attacks for largely symbolic reasons, as much to do with the internal logic of their movements and their message as with any considered strategy of revolutionary change. Many of the same groups, however, have also attacked foreign tourists in Egypt, thereby serving the instrumentalist purpose of undermining the Egyptian economy as well as the expressive one of attacking those whom the Islamic groups believe to be partly responsible for the moral and identity problems of Egyptian society.

This pattern was repeated in Syria, Iraq, and more recently, in Algeria. In all three countries, to differing degrees, the symbolic and instrumental aspects of the violence deployed by the respective Islamic protest groups follow a logic suggested both by the structure of the state and the formations of the associated society. The use of violence has been acknowledged to carry a high price, however. One obvious price was most spectacularly and ruthlessly illustrated in the Syrian government's response to the Muslim Brotherhood insurrection in the city of Hama in 1982. Syrian government forces launched a full-scale assault against the city, leaving the center of the old town in ruins and causing an estimated 10,000 casualties. Likewise, the virtual civil war in Algeria is taking its toll on both sides, the Egyptian government's crackdown on Islamic militants has led to an unprecedented number of executions during the 1990s, and the Iraqi government's ferocity in suppressing all forms of active Islamic dissent matches that of the Syrian regime.

A more insidious and less obvious price of violence, however, has been reflected upon for some time by the Islamic political organizations in Egypt, particularly. This is the cost to the organization itself and to its principles if it seeks to maintain a paramilitary wing that, in the end, may begin to act on its own account, with little or no reference to the main body of the movement. The differences of opinion over the utility of violence tend to separate the present Muslim Brotherhood in Egypt from al-Jama'at al-Islamiyya. In part the attitude of the former could be said to originate in the unfortunate experiences of its "secret apparatus" during the period 1947–1954.[18]

It may also reflect a more long-standing unease in Islamic societies about the dangers of coercive strategies in politics. Coercion, in the sense of the successful organization of violence against the designated enemies of Islam, has been a constant theme in Islamic history since the time of the Prophet. In this respect, of course, Islamic history is no different from the histories of other great states and empires. However, the unease could be said to derive from the realization that powerful secular forces are at work in the organization of successful military enterprises. Military technology, administrative innovation, personal authority, the weight of numbers, the effectiveness of disciplinary procedures, favorable terrain, and a multitude of other wholly secular factors may contribute to military success. These may be supplemented, or in some instances countered, by the benefits to morale of religious faith. Nevertheless, there has been an enduring concern throughout much of Islamic history that those who are most effective militarily and politically may not be the most pious. The designation of the four "rightly guided caliphs" as the immediate successors to the Prophet in Islamic historiography has tended to suggest that in the early years of the Islamic state the secular logic of military, administrative, and political preoccupations was kept at bay by the personal qualities of the rulers. This very designation, however, also suggests that things became more controversial thereafter and that a logic other than a distinctly religious one began to shape the course of Islamic history, magnificent as some of its episodes might have been.[19]

Conclusion

States in the Arab Middle East can be said to be secular in two different senses. The first is a legacy of the indigenous secular tradition of patrimonial rule as the principal means of organizing political order. Adapting and reinterpreting this tradition under the changed circumstances of the twentieth century, states have had to come to terms with the different forms of secularism associated with the dominant Western model of the state. At the same time, the governments ruling these states have sought to use Islam in two ways. First, Islamic themes and symbols have been used to shore up patrimonial, authoritarian systems of rule, supposedly lending them a coloration that augments their authority among the predominantly Muslim members of the associated societies. Second, Islam, variously interpreted, has been used by these regimes to give a distinctive character to the identity of the state in order to correspond to the notion that the state represents and speaks for a distinct ethical community. This concern has its roots in the new conception of the political public and of the identity and representation of that public associated with the Western model of the state.

For those who wish to transform the state itself into a vehicle for the propagation and protection of their particular vision of an Islamic society and political order, a number of problems arise. First, there is the question of the degree to which they can expect to be effective in political societies without in some way relying upon the local "secular tradition" of patrimonialism and authoritarian rule. That is, they must face up to the ideological dilemma encountered by the advocates of an Islamic state since the death of the Prophet and, arguably, since the passing of his first four successors: how to make the message effective without succumbing to the logic of the dominant forms of power. Islamic history demonstrates that this problem was never resolved, even if compromises were worked out, often with impressive results. Second, there is the concern that in seeking to play the game of mass politics successfully within the framework of the modern state, they will succumb to the secularizing logic of democracy, of economic development, and of the territorial state. Precisely because both "secular traditions" correspond to systems of power, whether domestically or internationally, they oblige Islamist groupings either to come to terms with them in one way or another or to defy them openly and violently.

As many of the examples have shown, however, not only is such violence difficult to sustain, but it may also open up the group in question to the logic of the very secular organization of power that they were ostensibly seeking to combat. If unsuccessful, the violence is used by the patrimonial regime to underline its own invaluable role as guarantor of order in society, causing many who might otherwise despise the regime to cling to it as the sole bulwark of social order. This phenomenon has been visible in Algeria, Egypt, Jordan, Syria, Saudi Arabia, and Iraq—in all of which the government has attempted to use the more violent forms of Islamic protest as a means of bringing home to the population both the power of the regime and its role as guarantor of stability. Where violent strategies have been successful in causing distinctively Islamic groups to take over the state, the concern lies in another direction. The fear here is that the establishment of a state proclaiming itself to be Islamic will render "Islam"—whether as a system of beliefs or as a particular structure of authority—accountable to the mundane criteria of state success. It was for this reason that a number of the senior Shi'i clerics found Khomeini's vision of "Islamic politics" so disquieting—a disquiet borne out in the course of Iranian politics during the past fifteen years.

As with many other forms of protest politics, a certain ambiguity seems to be present in much of the Islamic protest in the Middle East. On the one hand, there is clearly a drive for efficiency or effectivity within the parameters of the states in which the oppositional movements operate. On the other hand, there is a fear that the more successful they are in organizing within the state or the closer they come to adapting the framework of the state to their ideals, the greater the number of compromises concerning the latter that they will have to make. It is at that point that the questions of authenticity and identity arise, with potentially disillusioning effects in the political world itself. In this respect, the example of postrevolutionary Iran may be instructive and has been watched with some anxiety by some of the more thoughtful Islamists both within the Shi'a tradition and beyond. Indeed, for those who have reflected upon this and other cases, it would seem that "Islamic politics" shares with many other ideologies the characteristics of any encounter between belief systems and the structures of state power. In this case, however, there are clearly grounds for arguing that the various secular aspects of the structures of state power in the Middle East will significantly shape the forms of self-consciously Islamic political activity. In seeking to appropriate the state and all its powers, Islamists may find themselves in turn subjected to the remorselessly secular logic of the state.

Notes

1. B. Korany, "Alien and Besieged, Yet Here to Stay: The Contradictions of the Arab Territorial State," pp. 47–74 in G. Salamé (ed.), *The Foundations of the Arab State* (London: Croom Helm, 1987).

2. G. Salamé, "'Strong' and 'Weak' States: A Qualified Return to the *Muqaddimah*," pp. 205–240 in Salamé (ed.), *The Foundations of the Arab State* (London: Croom Helm, 1987).

3. See R. Owen, *State, Power and Politics in the Making of the Modern Middle East* (London: Routledge, 1992), chapters 2 and 3.

4. A. Abdel Malek, *Egypt: Military Society* (New York: Random House, 1968), pp. 219–221; R. Dekmejian, *Egypt Under Nasir* (Albany, N.Y.: SUNY Press, 1971), pp. 132–134.

5. A. Lamchichi, *L'Algérie en crise* (Paris: L'Harmattan, 1990), pp. 307–315.

6. K. Salibi, *The Modern History of Jordan* (London: I. B. Tauris, 1993), p. 175.

7. J. Kostiner, *The Making of Saudi Arabia, 1916–1936: From Chieftancy to Monarchical State* (Oxford: Oxford University Press, 1994), pp. 72–79.

8. G. Kepel, *The Prophet and Pharaoh* (London: Al-Saqi Books, 1985), pp. 91–102.

9. Mohammed Tozy, "Islam and the State," pp. 102–122 in I. W. Zartman and W. M. Habeeb (eds.), *Polity and Society in Contemporary North Africa* (Boulder: Westview Press, 1993).

10. N. Ayubi, *The State and Public Policies in Egypt Since Sadat* (Reading, U.K.: Ithaca Press, 1991), pp. 233–240.

11. Saddam Hussein, *Religious Political Movements and Those Disguised with Religion* (in English) (Baghdad: Dar al-Ma'mun, 1987), pp. 8, 14.

12. N. Ayubi, *Political Islam* (London: Routledge, 1991), pp. 195–200.

13. Muhammad Baqir al-Sadr, *Iqtisaduna* (Beirut: Dar al-Kitab al-Lubnani, 1982), pp. 260–264. Qutb's realization of some of the implications of this for the authority of the sources of the *shari'a* seems to have led to significant changes in his approach to politics and social questions evident in his later writings. See C. Tripp, "Sayyid Qutb: The Political Vision," pp. 165–175 in A. Rahnema (ed.), *Pioneers of Islamic Revival* (London: Zed Books, 1994).

14. F. Charillon and A. Mouftard, "Jordanie: les élections du 8 November 1993 et le processus de paix," *Monde arabe Maghreb Machrek* 144 (April/June 1994), pp. 44–51; J. Esposito and J. Piscatori, "Democratization and Islam," *Middle East Journal* 45, no. 3 (Summer 1991), pp. 427–434.

15. Esposito and Piscatori, "Democratization," pp. 434–438.

16. Perhaps due to unease about the implication of this, Islamic Jihad has adopted—at least in theory—a rather different and less territorially specific program. See Z. Abu-Amr, *Islamic Fundamentalism in the West Bank and Gaza* (Bloomington: Indiana University Press, 1994), pp. 27–40, 96–104.

17. Kepel, *Prophet and Pharaoh*, pp. 27–35.

18. Mahmoud Abd al-Halim, *Al-Ikhwan al-Muslimun: ahdath sana'at al-Ta'rikh*, Part 3, *1952–1971* (Alexandria: Dar al-Da'wa, 1985), pp. 63–69; R. Mitchell, *The Society of the Muslim Brothers* (London: Oxford University Press, 1969), pp. 73–79, 144–162.

19. E.I.J. Rosenthal, *Islam in the Modern National State* (Cambridge: Cambridge University Press, 1965), pp. 12–20, 85–101.

4

Pax Islamica: An Alternative New World Order?

DAVID GEORGE

Protagonists of Islamic fundamentalism[1]—self-styled Islamic opposition movements, states, and regimes—appear to be preoccupied by two problems, both of which are internal to those contemporary states and societies with predominantly or exclusively Muslim populations. The first of these is the problem of secularism. Islam claims to be an inclusive, immutable, final, and imperative guide to human life on earth. Failure to live up to its ideal standard—a dereliction of duty on the part of Muslims that is widely believed to be the ultimate cause of the decline of Muslim countries and a precondition for modern disasters (such as the 1967 war) they have suffered—is attributed to the penetration of the Muslim world by corrupting secularism. Under its impact, Islam has become separated from government, politics, economic activity, education, culture, and morality, a divorce (or even a diremption) that marginalizes the religion by substituting human norms of behavior for the God-given rule of conduct. Although the source of secularism is normally associated with an alien, hostile, secular, and even "toxic"[2] West, the blame for this complex but calamitous state of affairs is nonetheless laid primarily at the door of the indigenous governments.

Thus the second and connected issue is the problem of Muslim governments. Whatever happens to be the immediate, particular cause for concern—say, one of the sundry forms of moral corruption—it can be blamed on the government, since it may be claimed, with some plausibility, that the Muslim government has failed to discharge its fundamental duties of protecting believers, defending and extending the faith, and securing full implementation of divine law throughout society. Such governments are

likely to be further charged with one or more offenses against divine
law—impiety, infidelity, apostasy, and injustice (or tyranny)—by Islamic
opposition groups. Moreover, fundamentalist critics cite the common failure of Muslim governments to secure not just the spiritual but also the
material well-being of their citizens. Blaming government for a host of
problems is not unique to Muslim countries—the idea that government
should be able to provide jobs, decent housing, and minimal health care,
as well as deal quickly and effectively with both natural and man-made
disasters, is widespread in the late twentieth century. Nevertheless, it
does provide an additional and very big stick with which to beat the government. Thus, for example, Islamist opposition movements criticized
government sluggishness and incompetence in the face of floods in
southern Tunisia in 1990, an earthquake in Egypt (especially in Cairo) in
1992, and Israeli mass bombardment of border villages in southern
Lebanon during the summer of 1993. At the same time, such misfortunes
provided golden opportunities for these movements to show their com-
petence and compassion by providing the victims with speedy, effective
relief.

The logic of this situation is that a change of government, whether
achieved through elections, persuasion, or violent overthrow, would be
not just a recipe for good government but also for ending secularism
within both state and society. The fundamentalist goal of a transfigured
Muslim state and society, namely, an Islamic order wherein divine law
(shari'a) is comprehensively restored and God's purpose for mankind
thereby fully served, can only happen when worldly, unregenerate rulers
are replaced by pious and just governments drawn from the ranks of the
Islamic opposition.[3]

Islam and International Relations

A preoccupation with the two internal problems of secularism and inept
governance has meant that a third, external, and essentially radical secular challenge is scarcely recognized by Islamic fundamentalists.[4] This
challenge is the one posed to every Muslim state by the modern international order.[5] Whether that order is considered in terms of the international system of states or in terms of a global economy, its distinguishing
feature is its radical, indeed perfect, secularization. Unlike the challenge
of secularism within Muslim states, there is no shari'a or other Islamic element to oppose within the international order, for in it all religion has
been eliminated. And the requirement of the international order that all
its component states and economies conform to its purely secular princi-

ples and practices is, in substance, its compelling challenge to Muslim states and their economies.

Modern states exist only as parts of this international order and by virtue of its secular law they are corporate, legal personalities. As components of the international system of states, then, Muslim states, qua states, are no less secular than their non-Muslim counterparts. By the same token, an Islamic state is a contingent impossibility, a sheer contradiction in terms; Islam and the secular are mutually exclusive. Thus, if the ultimate goal of Islamic opposition groups and regimes may be described as the full restoration of Islam, whatever the changes made within the state and domestic economy, the end is unattainable so long as the current international order continues to exist. Islamic fundamentalists are therefore faced with a challenge every bit as daunting, and maybe even more so, than that involved in, say, overthrowing an unjust, tyrannical ruler or attempting to undo the corrosive effects of modernization and westernization. For what is required to ensure the success of the Islamic enterprise is nothing less than the replacement of the present world order by an alternative Islamic one—an authentic *pax Islamica*.

For the most part, this external challenge to Islam is either overlooked or neglected in the academic literature.[6] Where it is not, it is understood in terms of the threat posed by nationalism and the nation-state,[7] or by the territorially based state,[8] or in terms of the difficulties involved in Islam becoming *the* factor in the determination, formulation, and implementation of the foreign policy of Muslim states.[9] Although each of these issues calls into serious question Islam's place in the modern world, none completely eradicates it. They are, in this sense, lesser challenges than the fundamental one posed by the secularism of the international order.

Nationalism, it has been said, is "the supreme manifestation of political secularism."[10] Certainly, the place of Islam in Muslim countries was threatened and undermined by the nationalist challenge, especially by the radical Arab version during its period of ascendancy from 1948 to 1967. But that was an internal affair. Externally, nationalism offered a principle for reconstituting the international order, a doctrine and norm saying that the only legitimate state is a nation-state, that is, a state with boundaries coinciding exactly with those of a nation (understood as an ethnic or cultural group) and where national self-government is the only lawful form of government.[11] Every Muslim government and state in the world today, without exception, is illegitimate on this strict criterion, whether nationhood is defined in terms of language, history, ethnicity, popular culture, or religion. But this is also true of many—perhaps even most—other states and governments in the world, which are either multinational, like the United States, the United Kingdom, or Spain, or else subnational, like Germany and China.

Modern states, like Saudi Arabia or Syria, need not be nation-states then, but they must be territorial states, and that, it has been said, is incompatible with the ideal (or the idealized) Islamic polity.[12] But this formulation surely cannot be right, because every Islamic polity, from "the politically autonomous community"[13] established at Medina onward, was territorially based, in the sense of being limited to a defined area of the earth's surface over which a Muslim ruler held sway and caused the *shari'a* to be implemented.[14] By contrast, the Islamic community (*'umma*) was not tied to a specific territory: Its members were united by a common faith and bound by the ligaments of a divine law that had no territorial jurisdiction because it was a personal law. The Islamic community might be governed by one, a few, or the many, but the Muslim ruler's autocratic and usually despotic power was exercised over all the inhabitants of a determinate territory, Muslims and protected unbelievers alike. This territory—or, where there were several Muslim autocrats, the totality of such territories—constituted the domain of Islam (*dar al-Islam*). Beyond it lay the lands over which no Muslim ruler held sway, the zone of unbelievers. Some members of the Islamic community might live in this zone, the domain of war (*dar al-harb*), but as they continued to be bound by divine law, the writ of the *shari'a* ran here too.

The boundary line between the two domains was thus drawn by the presence or absence of Muslim power over a territory and its population. An identical principle of power determined the fragmentation and subdivision of *dar al-Islam* into a number of territorially based polities, yet without transforming the *shari'a* into a body of state law with an exclusively territorial jurisdiction. (Historically, divisions of territory within the domain of war were of little or no importance to Muslims.) To say that every Muslim polity from the beginning has been a territorial political community, therefore, is to say only that it has been ruled by a Muslim potentate whose autocratic sway extended over a limited, more or less ill-defined area and all its inhabitants. These territorially based polities should not be confused with the modern state, where municipal law has an exclusive jurisdiction within precisely demarcated territorial boundaries. The fundamental problem for Islam, then, is neither the nation-state nor the territorially based state but rather the modern state as such, that is, the modern sovereign state based on municipal law that is exclusively territorial in its jurisdiction, an integral component of the modern international state-system.

This brings us to a related external problem for Muslim and self-styled Islamic states—the possibility or impossibility of an Islamic foreign policy. Writing some thirty years ago, Fayez Sayegh observed that although the marks of Islam were pervasive and clearly discernible in the internal policies and national institutions of the Muslim regimes of his day, Islam had been banished completely from their foreign policies. No less astonishing, he went on, "is the replacement of Islam by extraneous principles and values." He concluded, "In matters pertaining to international affairs in general and neutralism in particular, the reasoning of the contemporary generation of Muslim leaders is indistinguishable from that of non-Muslims."[15] Sayegh perhaps overstated his case, but it is true that Muslim states act no differently toward each other than they do toward non-Muslim states. Thus, for example, the international principle of noninterference in the internal affairs of other states was recognized in such agreements as the League of Arab States Pact (1945), the Baghdad Pact (1955), the Charter of the Organization of the Islamic Conference (1972), and the Arab Maghreb Union Treaty (1989). Similarly, secular national interests are vigorously pursued against other Muslim states, even by avowedly Islamic regimes. For example, the Islamic Republic of Iran went to war in 1980 over territory disputed with Iraq and refused to enter into peace negotiations until Iraq withdrew from that territory, and Sudan's Islamist regime has had a lengthy dispute with Egypt over the Halaib territory on Sudan's northeastern border.[16] Despite Sayegh's claim, Islam today may, it seems, assume a dimension in the foreign policy process of Muslim states, though one more concerned with the manner of its implementation, perhaps, than with its determination and formulation.[17] If so, many questions will need to be resolved. Exactly what is to count as an application of Islamic principles and values to foreign policy, for example? And, beyond the uncontroversial promotion of Muslim solidarity and mutual aid, how far should such policies go? Will they involve simply forging bonds through such bodies as the Organization of the Islamic Conference or forming an Islamic bloc within the community of nations, or will they involve collaboration in attempting the Islamic liberation of Jerusalem, as well?

Happily, it is not necessary to consider the matter any further. For present purposes, it is enough to note that in the matter of external relations, as in the case of the internal preoccupations, Islamic objectives must be accomplished through the instrument of the modern state—an irremediably secular institution. Although the foreign policy of Muslim states may be more or less inspired, legitimated, and rationalized by Islamic principles, it can never be exclusively so. If an Islamic foreign policy can be defined as one where all determining influences on policy are internal to Islam, in which the formulation and making of policy are based entirely upon Islamic considerations, and for which policy implementation and justification are conducted wholly in terms of Islamic values and principles, then such a policy is simply impossible within the context of the contemporary international order and its intrinsically secular (state) components. Precisely because it is the policy of just such states toward other modern states, the foreign policy of Muslim states will be, at most, a Muslim policy, that is, a variable mixture of Islamic and non-Islamic elements. A purely Islamic foreign policy—one untainted by an iota of the secular—cannot occur outside an Islamic world order any more than the project for a full restoration of Islam can be realized outside the *pax Islamica*. And, with this point, the third (external) secular challenge to Islam is finally reached.

The Modern International Order

The modern international order is based on an absolute separation of religion from politics and economics, one that far outstrips any form or degree of secularism occurring within the state. Within the Muslim state, Islam and its law still have a part to play, however small it may have become under the impact of secularism.[18] In the international order, however, it has no part to play at all, because that order rigidly excludes religion. Moreover, the current international order requires an absolute conformity to its purely secular principles by all its component states and economies. Nor is this all. The international order originates in the West and is dominated by non-Muslim, Western powers and by.Western nongovernmental organizations such as multinational business corporations. In short, the current world order is upheld by a formidable combination of non-Muslim powers. And, as if this were not enough, the New World Order canvassed by former U.S. President George Bush will, if it ever comes to pass, accentuate both the secular character (especially its legal element) and the Western (especially American) domination of the international order.

George Bush made clear his intention to bring a moral dimension to international affairs chiefly through a renewed emphasis on secular human rights (which would include a right of apostasy) and the democratization of the internal political systems of states (for instance, by instituting elections to popular assemblies, which would have more extensive powers than a simple entitlement to be consulted [*shura*]). In each case, the West was both the source and exemplar for what was said to be morally required. The core component of Bush's proposal, however, was his call for the United Nations, under U.S. leadership, to maintain world order by upholding and enforcing international law. Law and order enforcement would include the imposition of sanctions and a selective use of military force—following Weinberger's 1984 criteria for U.S. military intervention. Such force would be placed at the disposal of the UN by the remaining global military power, the United States, and to a lesser extent by its NATO allies and any other states that could be induced to contribute.

Within the current international system, and more so in its possible future modifications, then, Islam has not been marginalized or even partially eclipsed: Instead, its universalist claim to provide a comprehensive guide to human life is completely ignored and its presence has been totally eradicated. Consequently, human (international) law has completely replaced the *shari'a* as a basis of external relations between states. Furthermore, the effect of this complete exclusion of Islam from the international order is to relegate it to the domestic or municipal level entirely; Islamic law now becomes part of a body of internal state law, along with non-Islamic law, and has a similar, purely territorial, jurisdiction. Effectively, the *shari'a* is now wholly subordinated to international law; in the event of conflict between the two, the requirements of this man-made law override those of divine law.

All this was true of the world order that existed before September 1990 when George Bush announced his proposal. What his New World Order did was highlight the central place of man-made law within the international state-system and its implicit superiority to all other law, including the *shari'a*. And this, it would seem, is a far more grave cause for concern on the part of Islamist groups, states, and regimes than any current constraints resulting from U.S. and Western domination of the international system—as well as a complaint they have in common with the rest of the Third World. Conceivably, that dominance might be removed at some point in the future, but at most that would only enhance the position of Muslim states vis-à-vis Western ones *within* the international order; both would continue to be full, integral parts of the international state-system and of the global capitalist economy. Subservience to the essentially secular international order would thus remain, and with it the impossibility of achieving a full and final *pax Islamica*.

A Secularized System

The modern international system superseded the Islamic one roughly 400 years ago, and its secular character is most readily seen in contrast with that system. As has already been noted, Islam's traditional system was based upon a bifurcation of the world into two parts—the domain of Islam and the domain of war. The latter was a sphere over which no Muslim potentate ruled and that had not yet embraced Islam or submitted to its *shari'a*. From the Islamic point of view, relations between the two spheres were regulated by Islamic rules (*shari'a*) relating to the conduct of holy war (*jihad*), whereby a truce or peace treaty could suspend jihad hostilities for up to ten years: Human law and man-made moral principles had no place in the norms of the Islamic international system. Moreover, recognition of non-Muslim rulers or of other non-Muslim authorities, such as that involved in concluding a truce or treaty, could only be de facto, never de jure. To give de jure recognition would imply Islamic acceptance of non-Islamic regimes as equal juridical entities under the Islamic legal system. Unless such rulers and their subjects in the domain of war either embraced Islam and conformed fully to its legal and moral standards, or, alternatively, became tolerated, protected, poll-tax paying, religious communities, they lacked any status under Islamic law. To use Majid Khadduri's phrase, they were its object, but not its subject.[19] In short, they were not legally recognized entities. Nonrecognition, confrontation, and jihad would remain the key features of the Islamic world order until eventually the whole of *dar al-harb* was absorbed into *dar al-Islam*. At that point, the full and final *pax Islamica* would be realized. In the meantime, the two domains opposed one another in what medieval Christendom knew as *guerra fria* (Cold War).

This Islamic system ended when Muslim rulers abandoned the *shari'a* as the rule of external relations in favor of a body of secular international law.[20] Muslim and non-Muslim political communities now recognized one another as legitimate politico-legal entities—not, of course, in terms of religious law or principle, but on a purely secular, and mainly legal, basis. Mutual recognition involved two things. First, each political community treated all the others as its legal or formal equal in terms of international law. This principle gave each community an independent or sovereign jurisdiction over its territory and its inhabitants. Furthermore, each territory and its population were to be regulated by domestic state law—whether that law was religious was immaterial—and was subject to the principle of noninterference in its internal affairs. Thus, mutual recognition in terms of *jus gentium* meant that each recognized entity—a modern state—acquired its essential legal identity. Each had become a *universitas* or *persona ficta* (a corporate legal person), that is, a legal artifact with an essentially secular, fictive personality (or legal character) derived from its legal parentage, the no less secular law of nations. Second, mutual recognition meant that permanent jihad was effectively abandoned in favor of permanent and peaceful coexistence. Relations within the new system of sovereign states would be conducted henceforth in terms of such entirely secular principles as the balance of power; mutual accommodation; the pursuit of dynastic, and subsequently national, interests; and unprincipled *Realpolitik* and almost always on the basis of the time-honored conventions, customs, and courtesies of diplomacy (a code of behavior of exclusively Western provenance).

From the inception of this system during the seventeenth century to the present day, and despite the formal equality and independence of its parts (the modern states), power has been distributed within the system in a way that operates to the not inconsiderable disadvantage of individual Muslim states and their citizens. (Varying degrees of economic and other kinds of dependence are closely correlated with this relative impotence.) It is important to note, however, that the two issues, the essential or constitutive secularity of the international system and the distribution of power within it, are conceptually separate, though often muddled together. Such confusion is probably responsible for Islamic fundamentalists' (and others') failure to perceive the nature of the external challenge to Islam, especially that posed by Bush's New World Order, in its true terms—as a radical rejection of the *shari'a* in favor of human law—in addition to its more obvious enhancement of Western, especially American, political and military domination of that world order. Old and (would-be) new world orders are intrinsically secular and therefore completely antipathetic to the religion of Islam. Specifically, with their basis in human law and custom, both diametrically oppose and supplant the *shari'a* as the rule of human conduct in international relations.

An important consequence of this secularist substitution of laws, a part of the absolute separation of religion from politics at the international level, is the relegation of religion's status within the state. At most, Islam and all other faiths are reduced to the status of purely state religions; at the least, they become the exclusively private concern of their citizens. Either way, this exclusion of Islam from the public sphere of the international order amounts to privatizing religion, a matter of restricting it to a purely domestic concern. Not only is the relegation of Islam to the private sphere of its component states completely foreign to Islamic history before the seventeenth century, but also the very public/private distinction upon which it rests is utterly alien to traditional Islam. The next question, therefore, is this: In what ways, and to what extent, have Islamic fundamentalists reacted to this total exclusion of Islam from the international system?

Islamists' Challenges

There have been relatively few reactions by Islamic fundamentalists to the secularization of the modern international order. Indeed, it would be unrealistic to expect Islamic opposition groups to be much exercised by the issue, given their current preoccupation with problems internal to state and society. For the same reason, it would seem, self-styled Islamic regimes, for the most part, fail to notice the problem. In any case, relatively few Muslim states identify themselves as Islamic states, and fewer still have both the will and the might to mount an Islamic challenge—however ineffective—to the current international order. Not surprisingly, Islamic fundamentalists have tended to take the softer option of challenging the dominant position of the Western states, especially the United States, relative to non-Western, especially Muslim, states. But there have been a few cases of a more fundamental challenge to the secular basis of the system itself. Four of the more significant examples, two by Saudi Arabia and two by Iran, will be noted here.

Saudi Arabia implicitly challenged the international order and its law during the second Gulf war when the question arose of what to do if Saddam Hussein were captured. To those who argued he should be tried for crimes against humanity before an international tribunal similar to the Nuremberg one, leading Saudis stated he should be tried before a *shari'a* court, presumably in Riyadh.[21] If this was a project to bypass secular international law, the second Saudi challenge, which occurred in May 1993, was, in effect, a circumvention of human rights enshrined in the UN Charter (to which it is a signatory) and the Universal Declaration of Human Rights (to which it does not subscribe), which formed a part of Bush's projected New World Order. In this case, a self-appointed Committee for the Defense of Legitimate Rights wrongly equated human rights with positive legal rights of Saudi subjects under the *shari'a*.[22] Perhaps not surprisingly, given its close ties with the West and especially with the United States, the Saudi challenges were not against Western domination (especially U.S. hegemony) within the international state-system but against the system per se.

The same cannot be said of the two root and branch challenges by Iran. First, the 1979 seizure of the U.S. embassy in Tehran, and the subsequent hostage crisis (a "struggle between blasphemy and Islam," according to Khomeini), which lasted until 1981, violated several key rules of international law and custom, including diplomatic immunity. That same principle was violated in May 1987 when a senior British diplomat, with full diplomatic privileges, was kidnapped in Iran and beaten up following the arrest of an Iranian diplomat, without diplomatic privileges, in the United Kingdom, for a minor offense and for more serious criminal offenses involved in trying to avoid arrest. As one commentator observed, the behavior of the Islamic Republic of Iran "was not thought to be contrary to the *shari'a*. In traditional Islamic thinking there was no such entity as diplomatic immunity."[23]

Iran's second principled challenge was the *fatwa* against Salman Rushdie. Khomeini's ruling struck at the very basis of the international state-system, whereby the citizens of a sovereign state are subject only to the jurisdiction of the territorial state law or, where relevant, to secular international law. From the standpoint of the international order, the *fatwa* was simply Khomeini's official incitement to murder a private British citizen and probably an act of international terrorism. From an Islamic standpoint, it might be viewed as an application of the divine law to someone who is bound by it, an apostate member of the Islamic community, or, more radically, to a person who is not a past or present member of the *'umma* but just one of God's creatures and so subject to divine law.

Such challenges are at present no more than "straws in the wind." More of them, probably even more diverse and perhaps still more far-reaching, might be expected in the future, if and when greater numbers of Islamic opposition groups succeed in winning governmental power. For then the present goal of the fundamentalists—a fully Islamic state and society—will be found to be unattainable within the current world order, since every member state shares its intrinsic secularism. In the short and the medium term, however, it is likely that Islamic fundamentalists—in or out of power—will continue to be preoccupied by concerns internal to the state and society to the neglect of the secular international order and of its legal creature, the modern sovereign state.

Be that as it may, the theoretical challenges to the current international order made by two Islamist authors, and the alternatives to it that they envisage, merit consideration. Here some insight may be gained into the vexing question of whether something more than contemporary, piecemeal challenges to the international state-system is in prospect. That possibility was ruled out as recently as 1984 by Ali Karaosmanoglu when he argued, "We cannot speak today of an Islamic conception of world order relevant to foreign policy or of a Muslim conception of international politics that differs from the Western one."[24] If, however, a reorganization of the international order has been placed on the Islamist agenda, will it be an attempt to restore a more or less idealized past—that is, the abode of Islam and the abode of war theorized by classical Islamic jurists?[25] Or, to adapt R. M. Burrell's distinction,[26] could the effort be aimed at applying Islam's eternal principles to the creation of a basically new, Islamic world order, a *pax Islamica*? To answer these questions, we must examine the doctrine of Ayatollah Khomeini and the normative theory of Professor AbdulHamid AbuSulayman, rector of the International Islamic University in Malaysia.

Toward a *Pax Islamica*

Khomeini's critique of the current international order and his ideas about the *pax Islamica* are well known.[27] He employed a binary concept that has been in common currency in revolutionary circles since its invention in

1789 by the Abbe Sieyes. Thus, he took the double dichotomy of oppres-
sors/oppressed, exploiters/exploited, but gave it a Shi'i coloration, referring to the Qur'anic concept of the oppressed as "weak" (Q4:75, *mustazafin*) and to the oppressors as "proud and mighty" (Q16:22–23,
mustakbirin). In Khomeini's ideal, but provisional, new world order, the
downtrodden, oppressed masses overthrow their corrupt oppressors and
exploiters country by country, take back their God-promised rightful heritage, and rule over an ever-increasing portion of the earth in accordance
with divine law and true religion until the advent of the hidden Imam as
the Mahdi. The Islamic revolution in Iran was just the first step in this
process. Thereafter, the revolution would be exported to the rest of the
world, not by the sword of armed jihad, but by the jihad of heart, tongue,
and hands, that is, by unarmed struggle, the force of example and propaganda.

Khomeini's vision of the provisional *pax Islamica* saw the oppressed
and exploited of the earth locked in a bitter and nearly interminable
struggle with their oppressors and exploiters for power, justice, and the
eventual triumph of Islam. It was a provisional, or interim, Islamic world
order, since the full and final *pax Islamica* could not begin until the occultation of the twelfth Imam ended and he returned on earth as the Mahdi.
With this inauguration of the final, Islamic *saeculum*, absorption of the
remnants of *dar al-harb* by *dar al-Islam* would be completed; the *shari'a* and
purity of faith would be fully restored; all wrongs would be righted and
divine justice prevail; and all state boundaries would be dissolved with
the unification of the universal Islamic community in a single, global
polity. Islamic world government by the Imam-Mahdi would ensure the
peace of Islam on earth.

Superficially, the Islamic new world order envisaged by Khomeini appears to be a reversion to the traditional dichotomy of *dar al-Islam* and *dar
al-harb*, with, perhaps, a special emphasis on the hostile, confrontational
relationship between the two domains. On closer inspection, however, it
turns out to be quite different in three respects. In the first place, the oppressed are not identical with Muslims and their oppressors are not the
same as unbelievers. Members of Muslim social, economic, and political
elites are included in the ranks of the oppressors—usually through their
connection with one of the two superpowers, such as in the case of the
Shah. Altogether, there are three categories of oppressors: the Eastern and
Western blocs, organized around the superpowers; the rich, proud, and
mighty, who crush the meek, humble, and weak everywhere; and all enemies of the (potentially) global Islamic revolution. Opposing them, the
oppressed and exploited include not only the nonoppressive members of
the Islamic community but also that much larger category of Third World
peoples that Frantz Fanon so memorably termed "the wretched of the

earth." Furthermore, the conjunction of exploitation with oppression, and its strong economic connotations, distinguishes Khomeini's idea of *mustazafin* (oppressed and exploited) from the Qur'anic concept of *mustad'a-fun* (weak and oppressed). Khomeini's definition of *estez'aaf* (oppression) appears to have three parts: political oppression; socioeconomic deprivation and exploitation; and a quasi-structural element relating to circumstances that, directly or indirectly, inhibit an individual's cultural and educational development.

In the second place, the demonization of the oppressors, namely, the Satanic superpowers and their corrupt and corrupting accomplices, who are held responsible for all the evils of the international order, goes far beyond traditional Islamic nonrecognition of political authorities in *dar al-harb*. Indeed, it seems to have no counterpart in the traditional juristic system.

A third difference between Khomeini's new world order and the traditional Islamic world order is that, in Khomeini's vision, the worldwide struggle between the oppressed and their oppressors is not conducted according to *shari'a* provisions for warfare and truce. Indeed, Khomeini did not envisage armed jihad as the way to reconstruct the world on new Islamic foundations. Given that the oppressed are identified as powerless, it could hardly be otherwise. But if the provisional new world order envisaged by Khomeini is not one based on the *shari'a* throughout, that is, in both its liberated and nonliberated areas, then, in the strict sense, it cannot be a fully Islamic order. The salient fact about the Islamic world system that antedated the modern international state-system was that all relations between *dar al-Islam* and *dar al-harb* were conducted in conformity with rules of Islamic law and principle. Should the ostensibly peaceful, revolutionary struggle between the oppressed and their oppressors promised by Khomeini qualify as an Islamic modus operandi, however (and there must be at least an element of doubt about this), it is difficult to see how it could be imposed upon the oppressors. And if its imposition is impracticable owing to the current extent of global economic integration and the overwhelming Western domination of the present world order, an Islamic new world order—one regulated exclusively by Islamic law and principles—does not and perhaps cannot exist at present.

Khomeini had no intention of upholding territorial state boundaries and the international suzerain state-systems that went with them. Like the French revolutionaries of the 1790s or the Bolsheviks and their immediate successors, he aimed to subvert not just individual states but the whole international state-system. On this reading of his argument, Khomeini was not in the business of trying to restore a more or less idealized past. Nor was he attempting the alternative postulated by Burrell, namely, to apply Islam's eternal principles to the creation of a wholly new

Islamic international order. Instead, his scheme gives a central place to the activist, revolutionary, and inherently secular double dichotomy mentioned earlier—oppressors/oppressed and exploiters/exploited. However much they are disguised in Islamic garb, their secular European origins are unmistakable. Moreover, a necessary (though not a sufficient) condition of an Islamic world order—namely, that it is *shari'a*-based in its entirety—is seemingly absent from his projected scheme.

Like Khomeini, AbuSulayman (and his collaborator al-Faruqi) is highly critical of the West's failure to provide a world order of peace and justice despite its ideal of a universal human community.[28] He is no less critical of the simultaneous promotion of conflict in the Third World by the two superpowers and their European allies, though he does not demonize them.[29] Since the West repeatedly failed in its quest for universal community, he says, a new, law-based, Islamic world order of peace, justice, and brotherhood must be established instead. In place of the international state-system and the national particularism it generates, there must be a single federal or confederal world government with a single international law and courts to enforce it. Non-Muslim minorities would live in a *millet* system as protected religious minorities with a right of appeal to the supreme courts. There would also be free movement of goods and persons; personal liberty ("all individuals and peoples are free to live according to their deepest beliefs and to maintain their freedom to cooperate on the basis of understanding and respect") within the limits of not harming others; equality before the law and in education and employment (not first- and second-class citizenship); and openness of all associations to the suitably qualified.[30] At no point is this discussion of the full and final *pax Islamica* connected to the inauguration of a new age by the advent of an expected Mahdi.

AbuSulayman insists that before this ultimate *pax Islamica* comes into being, Islam's basic values and concepts "can provide an essential framework for relations among nations in the contemporary world,"[31] thereby achieving an interim framework of peace and cooperation. Attaining this peace, as well as guarding and maintaining it, is the exclusive responsibility of Muslims, he argues, and they must do it "according to their ideology and religion."[32] This discussion involves him in an extensive inquiry into what he terms the methodology of Muslim jurisprudence (*usul al-fiqh*) and its reform. The sources—the Qur'an and Sunna—are thus no longer subject to the traditional sterility of *talfiq* (piecing together) and *taqlid* (imitation), with the resultant stagnation of Muslim thought.

After undertaking prodigious labors on *usul al-fiqh*, AbuSulayman examines four exemplary episodes from the sources (including the treatment of prisoners of war after the battle of Badr) to generate a provisional Islamic framework for international peace and cooperation. The resulting irenic structure, it has to be admitted, is disappointing. It has three main features. First, military jihad as the basis of relations between Muslims and non-Muslims is abandoned in favor of jihad understood as personal and social exertion for justice, suppression of evil and promotion of the good, and above all, peace. Second, he favors the adoption of diplomatic reciprocity and alliances with non-Muslim states, a proviso that appears to entail a mutual recognition of states. Third, he recommends an implementation of the principle of positive neutrality on the part of Muslim states.[33] Added to these three elements are the fundamental Islamic principles and values that should inform all policy in this area, such as *tawhid* (interpreted as the unity and equality of mankind, in addition to God's divine unity), justice and mutual support, and nonaggression and the complete absence of tyranny, corruption, and excesses.[34]

AbuSulayman attempts, essentially, to apply his interpretation of Islam's eternal principles to the establishment of a new and peaceful international order within a world divided into Muslims and unbelievers. The interim *pax Islamica* is intended as a contemporary irenic counterpart to the traditional juristic division of the world into *dar al-Islam* and *dar al-harb*. Insofar as it is based on Islamic law, principles, and values throughout, it must count as a genuinely Islamic proposal, though its similarity to current, secular, international practice may raise some doubts about its Islamic authenticity. What is most striking to the sympathetic observer, however, is that none of the three elements in his proposed framework represents a wholly new departure from present-day relations between Muslim and non-Muslim states. Classical jihad has long been abandoned in practice as the basis of relations between Muslim and non-Muslim countries. For example, when the last Caliph to proclaim the jihad, the Ottoman Sultan, did so in 1914, it was against the Christian powers of Britain, France, and Russia. The Caliph, however, waged jihad in alliance with two other Christian powers, Germany and Austro-Hungary, an impossible course of action in the pre-Westphalian, Islamic international order. Again, alliances with infidel states and diplomatic reciprocity—the second element of the framework—have been a feature of the current international order since the Ottoman Empire was integrated into the international state-system that emerged after the Treaty of Westphalia (1648). Lastly, the principle of positive neutrality has been a feature of the contemporary world since the inception of the Third World nonaligned movement at the Bandung Conference of 1954.

The fact that these elements already exist—admittedly without the Islamic values and principles that AbuSulayman argues should permeate them—demonstrates that his Islamic new world order is a viable one. But that same fact might lead one to question the likelihood of the anticipated peace. The three parts of the Islamic order, in their current, secular form, have conspicuously failed to promote peace and justice in the world to date. Whatever the shortcomings of AbuSulayman's proposal for a new Islamic world order, the fact remains that, like the doctrines of Khomeini, it represents a rare recognition of the intrinsic incompatibility between the secularism of the current international order and Islam. It is, in addition, a unique and ambitious attempt to construct the theoretical basis for an alternative Islamic new world order—a *pax Islamica* that, after some four centuries of separation, aims to reunite religion and politics finally at the international level.

Conclusion

This chapter may be summarized in five key points. First, the consideration that has led radical Islamist groups to take up an oppositionist stance within contemporary Muslim states—secularism and its attendant separation of religion from politics and other areas of social and personal life—is a significant feature of the present world order. As such, this order is, in principle, also vulnerable to their challenge. There is a second reason for that vulnerability, namely, that the fundamentalist project of founding an Islamic state and society cannot fully succeed so long as Muslim states remain components of the present international system and therefore share its intrinsic secularism. Neither reason, however, is sufficient to warrant the conclusion that there *must* be an Islamic challenge to the current world order, and even less that it will be an attempt to overthrow it in its entirety. Those are matters that can only be settled in the light of empirical evidence. And, given the current preoccupation of Islamists with bringing about fundamental changes within Muslim states, evidence for this external challenge is not extensive. Third, what little evidence there is suggests tentatively that the challenge has already started, both in practice and, to a lesser extent, in theory. (This challenge, it was argued, should not be confused with the quite separate one directed against Western, particularly American, domination within the current international order. Of this other Islamist challenge, there are a great many examples.) The emerging Islamist challenge to the present world order at the level of practice is directed not against its peripheral aspects but against central features of the contemporary international order. At the theoretical level, the writings of Khomeini and AbuSulayman demonstrate the ambition of replacing the present world order by a new Islamic one. Fourth, since the wholesale secularism of the modern international system against which the nascent Islamist challenge is directed remains and might even be intensified, there is no good a priori reason for supposing the challenge will be discontinued in the future. Finally, whether it will take a pacific form, as both Khomeini and AbuSulayman envisaged—that is, unarmed struggle instead of military jihad—is, perhaps, more dubious. Armed challenges to Muslim governments currently being waged by Islamist opposition groups in the Arab world could well be transferred to the international arena and directed against not only the dominant Western states but also against key components of the international system itself. Indeed, this *may* already have begun. But if an Islamic transformation of the international system should become a more prominent objective of the Islamists in the future than it is at present, it does not follow that this goal would be pursued by the single method of jihad. If the present diversity in the modus operandi of the Islamist oppositions is any guide, it is more likely to become one of many means employed to pursue the Islamic end.[35]

Notes

1. Using this term is regrettable for the reasons adduced by J. L. Esposito, *The Islamic Threat: Myth or Reality?* (New York, 1992), pp. 7–8. A.K.S. Lambton's brief account of Islam and religious fundamentalism is the point of reference in his essay "The Clash of Civilisations: Authority, Legitimacy and Perfectibility," in R. M. Burrell (ed.), *Islamic Fundamentalism* (London: Royal Asiatic Society, 1989), pp. 33–34.

2. The accusation of toxicity, "Westoxification," was originally made by Jamal Al-e Ahmad in *Gharbzadeghi* (Tehran, 1962), passim (English translation: *Occidentosis: A Plague from the West*, translated by R. Campbell [Berkeley, Calif., 1984]). For an example of Khomeini's use of the term, see M.M.J. Fischer, "Imam Khomeini: Four Levels of Understanding," in J. L. Esposito (ed.), *Voices of Resurgent Islam* (New York, 1983), pp. 168–169. H. Omid examines its application to the Iranian *'alma* by Ahmad and Ali Shariati in "Theocracy or Democracy? The Critics of 'Westoxification' and the Politics of Fundamentalism in Iran," *Third World Quarterly* 13 (4), 1992, 677–683. "Westoxification" now seems to have been superseded by "cultural assault" in the Iranian revolutionary lexicon—for example, in "Cultural Assault, Its Nature and Dimensions," *Keyhan International* (Tehran), May 26, 1994. (I am indebted to Hossein Aryan for this last reference.) P. J. Vatikiotis argued that the separation of politics and religion and a concomitant marginalizing of Islam are not a modern phenomenon but one that began in the tenth and eleventh centuries (apart from in Egypt). P. J. Vatikiotis, *Islam and the State* (London, 1987), pp. 58, 69.

3. Although the goals of the various Islamist opposition groups have here been described in general terms, this should not be taken to imply that specific details are uniform. On the contrary, ideological diversity, notably over what constitutes an Islamic state, goes hand in hand with diversity in the methods used by the (equally diverse) Islamic movements.

4. Vatikiotis argued that the Islamic movement is not absorbed by problems in the rest of the world but only by those in Islamic society: "Captiously defined, the

Islamic revolution today is once again, as in the past, trying to resolve an internal problem: the place of Islam in the modern state, and its role in politics; or, in other words, the relation of Islam to political power. To this extent it is essentially a social phenomenon," P. J. Vatikiotis, "Islamic Resurgence: A Critical View," in A. S. Cudsi and A. E. Dessouki (eds.), *Islam and Power* (London, 1981), p. 171. This is even true, for example, of the Islamic World Order postulated by Musa Saleem in his study *The Muslims and the New World Order* (London, 1993). The Islamic World Order is said to comprise a system, a set of moral values that include justice, moderation and balance, and fear of God (*taqwa*) (pp. 217, 220). These values and the God-fearing conduct with which they are associated are genuinely universal and thus merit inclusion in a world order. However, viewed simply as a system, Saleem's Islamic World Order is wholly internal to the state; it is neither international nor global, because the postulated system simply consists in founding Islamic governments and institutions by means of jihad (p. 221).

5. Erwin Rosenthal (following Ibn Khaldun) drew a precise distinction between the Islamic state, where government and the administration were regulated by the *shari'a*, and a Muslim state, where Islam and divine law continued to be important but were separated from government, and to which there corresponded a functional division between government and the religious institution. Rosenthal here used the term "state" in its generic sense, where its range of application extends to the feudal realms of Christendom, the Greek *poleis*, and the Islamic polity at Medina. The possibility of an Islamic state today was rejected by Rosenthal, though for reasons other than those offered in this essay. E.I.J. Rosenthal, *Islam in the Modern National State* (Cambridge, 1965), p. 26. See also W. M. Watt, *Islamic Fundamentalism and Modernity* (London, 1988), p. 90.

6. See E. Sivan, *Radical Islam: Medieval Theology and Modern Politics* (New Haven and London, 1985), passim.

7. J. P. Piscatori, *Islam in a World of Nation-States* (Cambridge, 1986), pp. 76–116, and Vatikiotis, *Fundamentalism*, pp. 35–83.

8. Piscatori, *World of Nation-States*, pp. 40–75.

9. A. Dawisha (ed.), *Islam in Foreign Policy* (Cambridge, 1983), passim. Also, R. O. Olayiwola, "Islam and the Conduct of Foreign Relations in Nigeria," *Journal of the Institute of Muslim Minority Affairs* 9 (2), 1988, 356–365.

10. Vatikiotis, *Fundamentalism*, p. 76.

11. E. Kedourie, Nationalism, 4th ed. (Oxford, 1993), p. 1.

12. A.K.S. Lambton, *State and Government in Medieval Islam* (Oxford, 1981), p. 13; also Lambton, "Clash of Civilisations," p. 40.

13. M. Cook, *Muhammad* (Oxford, 1983), p. 55.

14. According to Lambton, "The *dar al-islam*, the abode of Islam, was wherever Islam ruled and was not linked to a limited and defined territory." "Clash of Civilisations," p. 40.

15. F. A. Sayegh, "Islam and Neutralism," in J. H. Procter (ed.), *Islam and International Relations* (London, 1965), p. 73.

16. A.S.M. Sidahmed, "Sudan and Egypt: Tension Eases—But for How Long?" *Middle East International*, July 23, 1993, 17–18.

17. Dawisha, *Foreign Policy*, passim.

18. Vatikiotis argued that the *shari'a* was restricted in its application "to personal matters and certain commercial transactions," *Fundamentalism,* pp. 58, 69.

19. M. Khadduri, "The Islamic Theory of International Relations and Its Contemporary Relevance," in Proctor, *International Relations,* p. 25.

20. Abandonment of the *shari'a* as the rule of external relations in favor of secular international law by the Ottoman Empire occurred unmistakably at the Congress of Carlowitz (1699) when the Sultan agreed to a peace treaty with the Hapsburg Empire and the Venetian Republic framed in terms of contemporary *jus gentium.* Britain and Holland, moreover, presided as mediators at the peace congress. See M. Keens-Soper, "The Practice of a States-System," in M. Donelan (ed.), *The Reason of States: A Study in International Political Theory* (London, 1978), p. 30.

21. I take the Saudi stance at its face value. However, it should be acknowledged that Islamists elsewhere dismiss the Saudi demand as empty rhetoric in the light of their deep, Islamic misgivings over Saudi conduct during the Gulf crisis. I am indebted to Dr. A.S.M. Sidahmed for drawing this to my attention.

22. The Committee for the Defence of Legitimate Rights was immediately hailed in the Western media as a human rights watchdog to monitor abuses of human rights in the kingdom. "In any other country a human rights group would be normal," a spokesman was quoted as saying (*The Guardian,* May 8, 1993), but the initial communiqué of the committee made it clear that the rights it aimed to defend were those secured by the *shari'a* (*The Times,* May 10 and 11, 1993). Senior Saudi officials similarly equated human rights with the provisions of the *shari'a* when commenting publicly (and adversely) on the new committee. Dr. Ghazi Al-Gosaibi, the Saudi ambassador to the UK, stated that the *shari'a* courts (and not the Committee) were the guardians of human rights in his country (*The Guardian,* May 14, 1993), and the Saudi interior minister, Prince Nayef Abdul Aziz, was reported to have said that the issue of human rights did not arise in Saudi Arabia because Islamic law was fully implemented: "We rule by virtue of our Islamic principles. We have a higher respect for human rights than any other country in the world" (*The Guardian,* May 17, 1993). However, human rights, whether taken legally or morally, are neither identical nor equivalent to the provisions of the *shari'a.* From a legal point of view, human rights are components of secular international law, some of which—like the two human rights covenants of 1966—have been posited by the United Nations. Not only do they have an entirely human and secular legal basis, but also in important areas they are discrepant from the provisions of the *shari'a.* Human rights law, for example, allows for a person to change religion (apostasy), prohibits slavery, and accords an equal status to women and men as bearers of rights. None of these measures are present in Islamic law. Morally too, there is a difference. Human rights, like moral rights, are grounded in abstract human personality and are nonderivative: Entitlements under the *shari'a* are derived from correlative obligations laid upon others and both are grounded in the will of God.

23. Watt, *Fundamentalism,* p. 73. Watt's claim about the *shari'a* is controversial. Details of the second violation of Iranian diplomatic immunity are taken from Watt, *Fundamentalism,* pp. 96–97. Probably the earliest example of its violation of the diplomatic code occurred on February 17, 1979, when the new revolutionary

regime in Iran closed the Israeli embassy and presented it to PLO leader Yasser
Arafat, who was visiting Tehran at the time.

24. A. L. Karaosmanoglu, "Islam and Its Implications for the International System," in M. Heper and R. Israeli (eds.), *Islam and Politics in the Modern World* (London, 1984), p. 114.

25. "The division of the world into the sphere of Islam and the sphere of war is
by no means a thing of the past. In so far as traditionalist Islam grows in strength
it could come into the forefront of world politics." Watt, *Fundamentalism*, p. 16.
Watt is right to stress this scenario as a possible outcome, though a moderate
skepticism about its likelihood is legitimate. If, indeed, the world corresponded to
the dichotomy of Islamic jurisprudence in the past, and the early formulation of
an intermediate status between *dar al-Islam* and *dar al-harb* for certain territories
and populations (*dar al-ʿahd* and *dar al-sulh*) in the history of Islamic jurisprudence
suggests there were difficulties, then the applicability of the Islamic dichotomy
could have been aided by the prevailing high degree of physical segmentation or
separation of communities that has long since disappeared in the manifold
processes of global integration. In a globalized world, the possibility of *dar al-
Islam* existing side by side, but independently, of *dar al-harb* is, on the face of it, remote.

26. R. M. Burrell, "Introduction: Islamic Fundamentalism in the Middle East—
A Survey of Its Origins and Diversity," in R. M. Burrell (ed.), *Fundamentalism*, p. 5.

27. This section is based on F. Rajaee (ed.), *Islamic Values and World View: Khomeini on Man, the State and International Relations* (Lanham, Md., 1983), pp. 73–92,
and R. Khomeini, *Islam and Revolution: Writings and Declarations* (London, 1985),
passim.

28. A. A. AbuSulayman, *The Islamic Theory of International Relations: New Directions for Islamic Methodology and Thought* (Herndon, Va., 1987), pp. xiii–xix.

29. Ibid., pp. xix–xxi.

30. Ibid., pp. x, xxii–xxix.

31. Ibid., p. ix.

32. Ibid., p. x.

33. Ibid., pp. 116–126, 133.

34. Ibid., pp. 126–129.

35. In February 1993, the World Trade Center in New York was bombed, allegedly by Islamic militants associated with Sheikh Omar Abdel Rahman, a reputed leader of the militant Egyptian opposition group al-Jamaʿa al-Islamiyya
(the Islamic group). Other associated Islamic militants were allegedly involved in
a conspiracy in June 1993 to bomb what one of them termed "the world's government," that is, the United Nations headquarters in New York, and to assassinate
the UN secretary-general.

Part Two

Case Studies

5

The Roots and Future of Islamism in Algeria

CLAIRE SPENCER

The rise of a popularly based Islamist movement in Algeria in the late 1980s was a source of surprise to many observers of contemporary Algerian politics. Since independence from France in 1962, the Algerian state had been associated with a secularized, modernizing, and socialist path of development. The main catalyst for the government's change of political direction toward democratization from late 1988 was not itself Islamist in nature: The urban riots of October 1988 were above all a protest against unemployment, economic hardship, and the rigors of reforms that affected the young and poor more than they affected the vested interests at the center of the one-party state.

The elaboration of a new multiparty constitution in early 1989 nevertheless favored the formation of political groupings around Islamist precepts. In the short period between its legal formation in 1989 and its thwarted electoral success in December 1991, the Islamic Salvation Front (Front Islamique du Salut, FIS) was the main beneficiary of the popular protest aroused in October 1988. More than other Islamist groups, the FIS not only galvanized the opposition of the young and unemployed to the existing single-party government and legislature but also revived forms of Islamic expression rooted in earlier periods of Algerian history. Far from being an externally inspired movement, Algerian Islamism has continued to coalesce modes of social and political opposition particular to Algerian society. Although the Islamist opposition was limited and hidden from view for most of the 1960s and 1970s, its rapid resurgence has underlined its significance as a recurring feature of Algerian political life, both prior to and post independence.

For the purposes of this analysis, Islamism may be defined as the use of Islam to social and/or political ends.[1] Seen in this light, the movements, social organizations, and political parties that have espoused Islamist goals in Algeria cannot be deemed to represent the entirety of Muslim or Islamic life in Algeria and have indeed frequently been divided amongst themselves, particularly over the use of violence to achieve their ends. Until its prohibition in February 1992, the FIS predominated over other Islamist parties through the ability of its leaders to draw several trends of thought and activism together under a single, mobilizing, populist umbrella. Moderates and radicals found a place there, along with those committed simply to undermining the governmental hegemony of the single party, the National Liberation Front (Front de Libéracion Nationale, FLN). Under the conditions of the 1989 constitution, no other party, Islamist or secular, acquired the same level of popular support.

Since early 1992, the suspension of the constitution and the prohibition of the FIS as a legal political party have changed the dynamics of the Islamist movement within Algeria. In the past, the FIS represented and encompassed a wide range of opinions and approaches; however, the dismantling of the public organizational networks of the FIS undermined its cohesion and balance. As both moderates and radicals were forced from the public arena of Algerian politics (many through arrest, imprisonment, and voluntary exile), the focus of Islamist activism devolved to clandestine and militant groups engaged in violent opposition to the military-backed government and the statements of its dispersed leadership. Only a few "moderate" Islamist groups, such as the Hamas party of Shaykh Nahnah, have been allowed to continue functioning in the public arena, on condition that they do not oppose the military regime.

In the period from the cancellation of elections and the substitution of the presidency by a five-member High Council of State until a single president was appointed again in January 1994,[2] the targets of Islamist militancy shifted and increased in number and severity. Originally two groups, the Armed Islamic Group (Groupe Islamique Armé, GIA) and the Armed Islamic Movement (Mouvement Islamique Armé, MIA), were held responsible for attacks against security posts, barracks, and public places throughout 1992. In the course of 1993, these groups mounted increasingly organized ambushes of security forces and extended their campaign of assassinations to individual citizens who, like the writer and journalist Tahar Djaout, were deemed to be too vocally anti-Islamist, or, like Djilali Lyabés, an ex–Minister of Education, were too closely associated with educational reforms that proponents of Islamism did not favor.[3]

Since November 1993, foreigners resident in Algeria have also been targets of the Islamist militants, on the grounds that their presence signals, at very least, their passive support for the residual government.[4] From early 1994, however, the distance between the GIA and the MIA became more apparent as the MIA changed its name to the Islamic Salvation Army (Armé Islamique du Salut, AIS) and claimed affiliation with the FIS as its military wing. The FIS leadership has increasingly condemned excesses of violence, particularly where children and women have been the victims, but their statements have remained ambiguous over the use of violence against those more directly associated with the military-backed regime.[5] The most horrific killings have subsequently been more closely associated with the radicals of the GIA, who are alleged to have claimed responsibility for a number of individual murders.

In a situation depicted as one of protracted civil war, in which some 50,000 or more people have lost their lives since January 1992, it is unclear to what extent FIS sympathizers have become disillusioned with the use of violence as a means to social and political change. The larger-than-expected turnout of 75 percent of the electorate who voted in the presidential elections of November 1995 went against the calls for an electoral boycott by the FIS leadership. Until then the statements of Islamist leaders, both within Algeria and from exile in Europe, had been uncompromising in their rejection of dialogue on the terms hitherto tentatively proffered by the Algerian government and army.[6]

In the summer of 1994, progress appeared to be under way when a series of discussions with legal political parties, convened by President Zeroual, left the door open to the participation of representatives of the FIS in a process of national dialogue. The conditions stipulated that the FIS agree to renounce violence and accept the provisions of the 1989 constitution, including a respect for political pluralism. In September 1994, the two main FIS leaders, Abbasi Madani and Ali Belhadj, were released from prison to house arrest following the receipt by the president of letters from Madani suggesting that the FIS was prepared to accept these conditions. Subsequent to their release, however, Madani required that a full meeting of the FIS executive council be convened in order to formulate a negotiating position. Because of residual doubts over whether this meeting would also include representatives of militant groups, contacts between the presidency and the FIS stalled by the end of October 1994, thus returning the initiative to military hardliners who had always opposed any form of accommodation with the FIS.[7]

The violence has not, however, been attributable to Islamist militants alone, in that official military repression of Islamist networks has involved summary executions and indiscriminate raids on neighborhoods known to harbor Islamist sympathizers, according to an Amnesty International report published in October 1994.[8] Less explicable cases of individual violence may in turn be due to a generalized breakdown in law and order, in which opportunistic reactions to the prolonged state of emergency have played as much of a role as the pursuit of Islamist aims.

It is also supposed that the GIA may have been infiltrated by the security forces, seeking to discredit the wider Islamist movement.[9]

The consequences of this situation for the future of a broad-based Islamist movement in Algeria would appear to be subject to a number of contradictions. Since the prohibition of the FIS, the mainstream movement has become internally divided over its objectives and strategies. On the one hand, the impetus and initiative for direct action has fallen to those on the extremes of the movement, who, like members of the GIA, have evolved stances ill-suited to political compromise or the control of an Islamist political leadership. On the other hand, proponents of gradualist change have been caught between a position of passive resistance in the face of official, and violent, repression and a reluctance to condone the violence of the extremists. With much of the earlier leadership in prison, or exile, it is difficult to assess how many of the statements issuing from France, from Germany, or from within Algerian prisons and places of hiding continue to enjoy the active support of those who voted for the FIS in December 1991 but who also took part in the presidential elections of November 1995.

Forging a consensus on the role to be played by Islam in politics constitutes one of the main dilemmas of Algerian politics today. In this respect, the responses of Islamism represent not only a failure of the secularized political process since independence but also a long-standing challenge to oversimplifications of Algeria's national identity.

The Historical Roots of Algerian Islamism

In an examination of the multifaceted phenomenon of Islamism, it is important to look beyond the immediacy of events in Algeria to the historical context within which this movement gained momentum. In view of the speed of developments in Algeria, the temptation to concentrate on recent events has nevertheless been strong. Within a year of the confirmation of its legal existence in July 1989, the FIS claimed 3 million active adherents out of a voting population of 12 million. In June 1990, the FIS gained the majority of seats in the local elections.[10] This success was largely urban-based, and FIS candidates hardly featured at all in the Berber region of Kabylia or the southern provinces. In the first round of national elections in December 1991, however, the voting strength claimed by the FIS was largely vindicated, as the FLN witnessed the crumbling of a support base it had long taken for granted.[11]

The cancellation of the general elections before the second round of voting in early 1992 closed a chapter in the history of the FIS. The subsequent recourse to violence of some of its members is not, however, without precedent in the history of Algerian Islamism. In the early 1980s, at a time when few people identified Algeria as a hotbed of Islamist activism, a small group of militants gathered behind the leadership of Mustafa Bouyali to form the Algerian Islamic Armed Movement (Mouvement Islamique Armé Algérien). From the maquis of the hills surrounding Algiers, Bouyali and his followers launched a series of attacks against security posts to gain arms, ostensibly to fight for the creation of an Islamic state by force. Their guerrilla activities, it is true, had a certain resonance for Algerians who had fought in a similar fashion against French forces in the War of Liberation from 1954 to 1962. Beyond his small band, however, Bouyali enjoyed little popular support, and in late 1987 he was caught and killed in an ambush.[12]

In the interim, it was a different form of Islamist movement that gained the most strength. The first activities of the movement headed by the FIS were born not of violence, but of a concentration of efforts to provide for the needs of those in overcrowded city quarters suffering most from the neglect of central governments. The group's relatively young and vocal leaders offered, through the mosques, a variety of social services of the type withdrawn by the government for economic reasons or over-stretched by the burgeoning populations of cities like Algiers. Also through the mosques, young preachers such as Ali Belhadj (arrested and imprisoned in June 1991) were able to protest against the degradations of urban life through the propagation of a new vision of Islamist social and political morality.

The oppositional elements contained within the FIS's message, however, were not so new. In reality, appeals to Islam have always played a role in contesting the legitimacy of the given status quo in Algeria's political history. At different times, a specifically Islamist opposition has been expressed in a variety of ways—that is, different trends within the same spectrum of political and social ideologies have drawn their strength from appeals to the values of Islam. At different times, these trends have intertwined and coexisted, but in the main they have consisted of three approaches.

The first is the intellectual or ulama-based trend of reformism that was characteristic of the Salafiyya movement, which grew throughout the Middle East from the turn of the century. In Algeria, as in other states of North Africa, Egyptian reformers, such as Muhammad 'Abduh and later Sayyid Qutb and Hasan al-Banna, were highly influential in the early years of what became the nationalist, then independence, movements against French rule. In 1931, an Algerian Ulama Association (Association d'Oulema Algérienne) was formed under the leadership of Abdelhamid Ben Badis, whose aims, at least initially, were to avoid any direct political involvement.[13] In the period preceding the formation of the FLN in 1954, however, this reformist and essentially inward-looking trend of Islamism proved necessary to the reevaluation, then reinforcement, of an Islamic identity within Algerian nationalism, expressed first in distinction, then in resistance, to the assimilationist pressures of French rule.

As the independence movement gained strength, so a second trend became apparent—the growth of increasingly violent opposition to France. The historical outcome of this development, as well as the main legacy within Algerian politics, was the War of Liberation from 1954 to 1962. This eight-year-long guerrilla war was bloody on both sides and left a strong mark on Algeria's political culture, even among younger generations who were not directly involved. The FLN, which launched this struggle, both incorporated and subsumed the majority of existing nationalist opposition groups and parties. Through the formation of its armed wing, the National Liberation Army (Armé de Libération Nationale, ALN), it also came to marginalize those who resisted the armed offensive, both within Algeria and in exile in France.[14] The FLN's program, published on the day it was formed on November 1, 1954, called for "the restoration of the sovereign democratic and social Algerian State in the framework of Islamic principles."[15] In other words, far from being the secular, socialist movement it arguably later became in government, the FLN contained a strong Islamic component in its program of armed resistance that coexisted with other strands of Algeria's national identity.

Another legacy of the War of Liberation within Algeria's political culture can be identified in traditions of resistance to and defiance of authority within Algeria's political culture, even under conditions of apparent authoritarian rule. The revolutionary vocabulary of the official state ideology assisted in keeping this spirit of defiance alive. It also gave rise to a high degree of moral zeal, which in the period of Algeria's greatest economic growth beginning in the late 1960s was expressed more through assertions of national self-determination and independence from external influences than in specifically Islamic terms. Nevertheless, alongside other forms of opposition to the authoritarian presidency of Boumedienne (1965–1978) and the corrupt presidency of Chadli Benjedid (1979–1992), small Islamist groups continued to preach the Islamic roots of the Algerian revolution.[16]

The third Islamist trend might almost be seen as a synthesis of the reformist and activist trends represented by the FIS at the height of its strength. The main thrust was what Gilles Kepel has called the pietist, or legalist, wing of popular reformism.[17] Its goal has been social change from the grass roots, that is, a mass and populist movement originating in the lowest echelons of society. The overall aim has been to change the moral basis of society from below through a reassertion of basic values perceived to have lapsed under the weight of secular modernity, a failure responsible for the prevailing atmosphere of uncertainty, disappointed expectations, and immorality in public life. It was this approach that demonstrated the revival of a community-based spirit, which by the early 1980s continued to exist only in the rhetoric of the FLN. The provision of housing and other forms of social welfare by the FIS and its financial supporters in the disillusioned middle classes did more than fill gaps where the government had abandoned urban populations; it also restored a sense of dignity to younger generations and fueled a propensity toward greater activism.

In public statements, the FIS leadership stressed first of all a peaceful evolution toward social justice in accordance with the principles of Islam. Beyond this, the compatibility of *shura* (consultation) and *ijmma'* (consensus) with democracy was consistently left vague, along with the finer details of economic policy. The rationale—not necessarily internally flawed— was that the regeneration of Islamic modes of behavior in both public and private life would lead to the eventual resolution of these issues along the lines of the thinking of Hasan al-Turabi of the Sudanese National Islamic Front.[18] Unlike other movements, however, the FIS had clear political objectives in seeking positions of power and public office to further its mission.

Despite an external appearance of coherence, the FIS was not monolithic from the outset. To parallel its more peaceful activities within the community, the FIS always contained elements of what some Algerian observers have called "friendly fascism":[19] in other words, the use of coercion, intimidation, and even violence to encourage adherence to the movement. The use of threats against women reluctant to adopt the *hijab*, or Islamic dress, for example, became more prevalent in the run-up to the local elections of June 1990. In other ways, expressions of violence both reflected the sense of moral zeal engendered by the opposition and served as a response to officially perpetrated brutalities against opponents of the regime.

At its height, the movement had two main spokesmen: Abbasi Madani, a British-educated moderate, who represented the FIS for external audiences, and Ali Belhadj, who stirred popular opposition against the FLN-led status quo from the mosques and poorer quarters of Algiers. Despite its successful incorporation of both legalist and rejectionist modes of action, the FIS cannot attribute its success entirely to its organizational strengths. A combination of actions put into motion since the early 1980s and opportunities seized at the appropriate political moment gives a clearer picture of how the FIS came to displace its Islamist rivals.

The Political Conjuncture from 1989

The political moment came for the FIS in late 1988, when the democratization process set in train by President Chadli Benjedid in 1988 gave rise to the formation, eventually, of around sixty movements or parties. Several of the newly formed groups openly embraced Islamic values, yet none gained the national appeal of the FIS. One of the more prominent formations, the Movement for an Islamic Society, or Hamas, founded by the popular preacher Mahfoud Nahnah in December 1990, postdated the FIS and appealed more to the traditional intellectual reformists. In the period following the suppression of the FIS, Sheikh Nahnah spoke out against violence and sought dialogue with the government, but in so doing he became associated with the illegitimacy of the military-backed regime. Another, the Movement for an Islamic Renaissance (or al-Nahda), led by Abdullah Djaballah, has likewise remained small at the national level, drawing most of its support from its regional base in the east of Algeria.

By their very nature, which is conservative and more closely aligned with reformism than militancy, these groups have never appealed to the diverse social groups represented by the FIS. Their limited resources and organizational networks also encouraged opponents of the FLN to vote for the FIS in 1991. Moreover, from their precarious position of official recognition, these groups have joined other opposition parties in demanding a role for the FIS in any discussions aimed at resolving the political crisis. In the presidential elections of November 1995, Shaykh Nahnah nevertheless received 25 percent of the vote, in second place behind the official military-backed candidacy of Liamine Zeroual, who received 61 percent of the votes.

Of the so-called secular parties, the Front of Socialist Forces (Front des Forces Socialistes, FFS) and the Assembly for Culture and Democracy (Rassemblement pour la Culture et Démocratie, RCD) have been largely bound by their constituencies amongst the Berber populations of Algeria, representing 20 percent of the Algerian population. Whereas Said Sadi of the RCD has been more forthright about separating religion and politics in a secular and liberal vision of the Algerian state, Ait Ahmed of the FFS promotes an inclusive vision of national reconciliation. These two approaches reflect the diversity of political opinion in Algeria.[20] Other political formations have been too closely associated with factions within the FLN to appeal to a broad audience. Partly because of the youth of FLN leaders at independence, many have remained within circles of power for thirty years or more, and much of the opposition expressed since the late 1980s has been against the accumulated wealth and benefits of those close to the regime. Attempts since 1989 to create support for the party of Algeria's first president, Ahmed Ben Bella (1962–1965), also failed, not least because his long years in exile from the heart of Algerian politics put him out of touch with the concerns of younger generations.

The success of the FIS was built on stronger foundations. Not only did its leaders present radical alternatives, directed at the mass of the population, but they also had the means to propagate their message swiftly when the moment arose. Since the mid-1970s, a campaign of privately and publicly sponsored mosque-building had been facilitating the expansion of clandestine Islamist groups.[21] Initially condoned by Boumedienne as a social and political counterweight to the leftist opposition groups that arose in the late 1970s (particularly in university circles), under Chadli Benjedid accelerated plans to build Islamic universities in Algiers and Oran, along with other centers of Islamic learning, directly benefited Islamist groups.

The key to their success by the late 1980s was the access of new social groups to these centers of learning, which expanded the domain of higher education to include "the humble, the peasants and the sons of peasants."[22] In spite of the policies of Arabization promoted by President Benjedid in the early 1980s, it was the first generation of Arabophone graduates who found themselves denied positions within the established regime, which generally based patronage on family connections, especially for those educated in French, which prevailed as the main language of education in the early years of independence of the Algerian republic. Their limited employment prospects also coincided with a period of international developments that emphasized divisions and setbacks within the Arab and Muslim world, to the perceived benefit of the West.[23] Only the Iranian revolution of 1979 stood out as an act of defiance within a Middle East seen to be increasingly controlled both economically and politically by the West. Drawn in simplistic terms, the Islamists' condemnation of Western secular models of development struck a chord with large numbers of Algerians, who equated the FLN's hold over the state with its espousal of Western (and hence anti-Algerian) interests.

In the early 1980s, the public activities of Islamists continued to be controlled in cases deemed to present a challenge to the regime. Abbasi Madani, for example, was arrested and imprisoned from 1982 to 1984 for openly presenting an Islamist political platform at a public meeting.[24] Under the conditions of political liberalization that prevailed from the late 1980s, however, under Chadli Benjedid and most notably under Prime Minister Mouloud Hamrouche (1989–1991), the government turned a blind eye to the excesses of FIS activists. Part of the explanation can be found in the desire of Hamrouche and Benjedid to provoke a reaction within the FLN to strengthen support for their own program of reforms. Failing that, this laissez-faire approach was an ill-conceived attempt by Benjedid to distance himself from the FLN and fashion the presidency as a political arbiter. In reality, the real arbiters came from

within the upper echelons of the army, who lost no time in forcing Benjedid to resign when they canceled the general elections in January 1992.

A final factor contributing to the rise of the FIS can be found in the universalist leanings of Algerian political culture since independence. From
1962 to 1989, the FLN provided the political facade behind which the
leadership and direction of the state were decided through factional
struggles and the adjudications of the army. Like many single parties, the
FLN subsumed for public consumption the professed aims and ambitions
of the independent Algerian state. This activity took the form of an independent, egalitarian development ideology, whose beneficiaries were to
be the Algerian nation, under the ubiquitous rallying cry of *le peuple algérien*.

Because this ideology was all-encompassing, it was essentially mean-
ingless for the majority of Algerians. Nevertheless, most tolerated it while
economic prosperity lasted until the late 1970s. In programs for the rapid
industrialization of Algeria and the nationalization of the hydrocarbon
sector, President Boumedienne also defended the international dignity of
independent Algeria as a state dynamic in both its internal and external
enterprises. In contrast, from 1979, the regime under Chadli Benjedid was
rapidly perceived as having lost the sense of national destiny encapsulated by Boumedienne. Instead, he squandered the benefits of independence on a small coterie of party officials and the marginally less tainted
military establishment.

Chadli Benjedid's assumption of the presidency also coincided with a
period of increasing domestic economic pressures and a fall in oil and gas
revenues, which had buoyed up the development efforts of the 1970s. Of
perhaps more significance, he presided over a period in which Boumedienne's ideological blueprint for development, the Algiers Charter of 1976,
was reassessed in ways that effectively undermined the global vision of
the earlier official ideology. This loss of direction, combined with a growing number of corruption scandals, had two main effects. On the one
hand, it deprived the FLN of its guardian role, its vision, and to a large
degree its legitimacy. On the other hand, it heralded a series of economic
reforms that were considerably less egalitarian in their impact than any of
the state-centered development strategies of the Boumedienne era. As a
result, corruption grew at a pace with public disaffection with the official
political establishment.

The riots of October 1988 provided the first major demonstration of the
extent to which a political void had appeared between the government
and Algerian society since the first economic reforms of 1986. In their an-
archistic rejection of the symbols of the FLN-backed regime, the riots also
marked the first time that the younger, postindependence generation of
Algerians had made their political presence felt on such a scale. Until

then, the fact that more than 50 percent of the Algerian population by the late 1980s was under twenty years of age had been barely felt in the political arena.

By opening up the political system after 1988, Chadli Benjedid made a final and public admission that the historic mission of the FLN had failed. Yet few of the parties that emerged in 1989 represented precisely what was then missing, namely, a new and reinvigorated mission for the Algerian nation. On one level, at least, the FIS fulfilled an almost subconscious desire on the part of many Algerians to revert to the historic (and mythologized) days of the FLN, when the factionalism of the 1950s had given way to the demands of a greater national cause. For those who had been born into the relative affluence of the Boumedienne era, the desire for a single, state-driven vision was almost as strong as for those who had fought in the War of Liberation.[25]

Of all the parties created in the late 1980s, it is noteworthy that only two—namely, the FIS and the FFS, which had existed in embryonic form since the armed insurrection led by Ait Ahmed in 1963—grasped this need to replace the FLN with another front.[26] The leading members of both fronts, Ait Ahmed and Abbasi Madani, had been actively engaged in the ranks of the FLN in the period prior to independence, Ait Ahmed as the leader of the FLN's paramilitary wing, the Special Organization (Organisation Spéciale, OS), the precursor of the FLN.[27] In 1989, however, Abbasi Madani's party enjoyed a distinct advantage in promoting an ideology that replaced the redundant symbols of national unity previously utilized by the FLN. The altogether more complex vision of a modern democracy promoted by the FFS has appealed more immediately to the sectional interests of Berbers and middle-class liberals than to the disillusioned young, who are impatient for more revolutionary and immediate change.

Conclusion

Despite attempts to marginalize different elements within the FIS, the broad-based movement has continued to exist as a political network of some complexity, given the geographical dispersion of its main leaders. In addition to its considerable organizational strength and strategic planning, the exclusion of FIS representatives from the public political arena has served to obscure the extent of divisions within the movement over issues central to the future of democracy and the state in Algeria. FIS leaders in exile and in prison have not been slow to use their outlawed status to play down these divisions or to claim, with some coherence, that only when the executive council of the FIS is allowed to meet can clearer policy positions be defined and agreed upon. Statements of individuals cannot, therefore, be seen as binding on the larger membership or supporters of the FIS.

In the meantime, the stated aim of the Algerian military authorities has been to return to democratic government, starting with the presidential elections of November 1995. The confirmation of Liamine Zeroual as elected president—a post he had held through army appointment since January 1994—has been interpreted as a sign that the majority of Algerians are above all tired of the continuing violence. According Zeroual a certain personal legitimacy to re-start negotiations with all opposition parties seems to have been the primary aim of the electorate. The continued and official use of violence to "eradicate" the extremist proponents of Islamism has after all done little to facilitate the emergence of longer-term civilian alternatives to military rule.[28] The ambiguous links of the FIS with radical Islamist groups have provided official justification for the exclusion of the most prominent Islamist opposition group from direct participation in the process of national dialogue. Yet as conditions for dialogue, appeals to a respect of the 1989 constitution and nonviolence sit uneasily alongside the record of the security forces over the period since January 1992. Even though President Zeroual has disassociated himself from those who took the decision to cancel the 1991 elections, the regime continues to encompass many of the same political and military figures who suspended the constitution in favor of a state of emergency in early 1992. It thus remains to be seen whether Zeroual commands the support of all military factions to allow for a more legitimate civilian role in politics.

In the absence of this, the moderate and non-Islamist opposition parties that have so far engaged in dialogue with the presidency have been in danger of jeopardizing the integrity of their position if seen to acquiesce too far with the policies of the regime. For this reason, most have insisted that dialogue cannot proceed without some accommodation with and representation of the FIS as represented in the joint platform signed in January 1994 in Rome by eight opposition parties, including the FLN and FFS, and alongside the FIS.[29] The logic underlying this demand is that, having been denied the fruits of electoral victory in 1991, the moral and political alternatives presented by Islamism have yet to be put to the test. In the meantime, the political victimization of the FIS by those in power, the retaliatory measures of the security forces against communities alleged to be harboring terrorists, and the torture of individual suspects in detention have militated against the effect on residual FIS supporters of alleged Islamist atrocities. Until a distinction is made between the moderate and radical elements of the FIS, a large portion of the population is likely to remain unrepresented and unconvinced of the moral fallibility of the FIS's political program.

Underlying these perceptions is the clear moral illegitimacy of the state, to which the untried vision of the FIS may still remain a powerful alternative in the minds of many, particularly the young. Ironically, it is the long-standing and generalized disrespect for the rule of law that has continued to favor military, rather than political, solutions to the crisis in Algeria. However, neither the military nor the Islamists—and much less, more moderate opposition groups—can benefit from an indefinite perpetuation of this situation. The dilemma facing Islamists of all but the most intransigent persuasions is that only through a return to a position of legality can the moral imperatives of reformist Islamism be strengthened in Algerian society. In confronting this task, however, the FIS has lost the main mechanisms—namely, the control of local government posts and the mosques—to continue with the gradualist strategy and moral mission that proved so popular. For many ordinary people, morality was the key to their adherence to the FIS. Despite countervailing governmental excesses, this moral mission has now been undermined, not so much by the attacks of radicals on security forces as by indiscriminate violence against innocent civilians not directly linked to the regime.

In assessing the future of political Islam in Algeria, it should not be forgotten that Islam is the religion of all Algerians, Arabs and Berbers alike. There continues to be considerable resistance to and rejection of the misuse of its values. Despite the storm of publicity over the FIS, the movement never won universal approval among the Algerian electorate, 40 percent of which failed to register votes in 1991. Opposition to the FIS has not just existed in the secularized opposition, women's groups, and Berbers. Algerians have a long history of both active and passive resistance to all forms of political coercion, both external and internal. If the pietist, populist trend of Islam is to regain its strength, it will have to be reformulated to eliminate the violence and abuses that characterize the "secular" regime to which most original FIS supporters were opposed. It should also be encouraged to do so, by its inclusion in a serious form, within official political circles once again. Otherwise, the conclusion of an old man overheard in an Algiers street at the height of the FIS's popularity in 1990 will continue to hold true. Representing the feelings of many moderate Algerian Muslims, he said of the Islamists: "Their mosques are full, but their hearts are empty."[30]

Notes

1. Bernard Lewis argues that despite associations with protestantism, "Islamic fundamentalism" is a "less deceptive" term than "Islamism," which gives the impression that "these movements are something typical, normal and central; that it is Islam, the Muslim religion, the Muslim civilization . . . [w]hich is not the case."

Rather, Islamist movements are "movements of crisis, are not universal, but almost always limited to a region, to a period, according to circumstances." See "Un entretien avec Bernard Lewis," *Le Monde*, November 16, 1993 (author's translations).

2. After the end of its extended "transitional" period of rule on January 31, 1994, the High Council of State was dissolved in favor of the return to a single presidency. The appointment of Defense Minister General Lamine Zeroual as president was perceived as an open admission of the military's assumption of power. See David Hirst, "Algeria's Laboratory of Conspiracies," *The Guardian*, January 31, 1994; Robert Fisk, "General Assumes Presidency," *The Independent*, January 31, 1994.

3. Both were killed in spring 1993. See Séverine Labat, "Les assassinats d'intellectuels," in Reporters sans frontières, *Le Drame Algérien* (Paris: Editions La Découverte, 1994), pp. 184–186.

4. See Shyam Bhatia, "Allah's Warriors Strangle Algeria," *The Observer*, January 23, 1994. In an atmosphere in which Islamic groups have rarely claimed responsibility for these attacks, some have raised the question of whether they are not deliberate attempts by other extremists to discredit the Islamists. See David Hirst, "The Second Liberation," *The Guardian*, January 29–30, 1994.

5. For example, Rabah Kebir, the FIS spokesman in Germany, condemned a bomb attack at a cemetery in Mostaganem (Eastern Algeria) on November 1, 1994, in which five children died. Another FIS leader in exile, Abdelbaki Sahraoui, later accused the Algerian government of planting the bomb to discredit the FIS. See Summary of World Broadcasts (BBC Monitoring), Third Series, ME/2143 MED/19, November 3, 1994; ME/2144 MED/14, November 4, 1994.

6. See *Le Matin* (Algiers), November 16, 1993.

7. See the speech of President Zeroual of October 31, 1994, Summary of World Broadcasts (BBC Monitoring), Third Series, ME/2142 MED/17–20, November 2, 1994.

8. Victoria Brittain, "'20,000 Killed' in Algeria's Civil War," *The Guardian*, October 25, 1994. In August 1994, President Zeroual expressed his readiness to investigate documented human rights abuses. See Summary of World Broadcasts (BBC Monitoring), ME/2147 MED/14, November 8, 1994.

9. See, for example, reports of an increase in bank raids, in *El Watan* (Algiers), November 16, 1993.

10. See Jacques Fontaine, "Les élections locales algériennes du 12 juin 1990," *Maghreb-Mashrek*, July-September 1990, pp. 124–140.

11. Allegations of electoral abuses, such as the disappearance of around 900,000 ballot papers, and the invalidity of around 1 million votes cast, have not been fully investigated since the cancellation of elections, from which 40 percent of the eligible electorate abstained in the first round. See *The Times* (London), editorial, January 13, 1992.

12. See M. Al-Ahnaf, Bernard Botiveau, and Franck Frégosi, *L'Algérie par ses Islamistes* (Paris: Karthala, 1991), p. 28.

13. This disavowal of political intent can also be seen as a strategy to avoid repression by the French authorities. See ibid., p. 21.

14. Witness the career of one of Algeria's earliest nationalists, Messali Hadj, who attempted to form an organization to counter the FLN, the Mouvement National Algérien, which ultimately failed. This revered nationalist leader was superseded by a younger generation of men who formed the FLN. See Benjamin Stora, "Messali Hadj (1898–1974)," in *Dictionnaire biographique de militants nationalistes algériens* (Paris: L'Harmattan, 1985), pp. 60–64.

15. Quoted in Clement Henry Moore, *Politics in North Africa: Algeria, Morocco and Tunisia* (Boston: Little, Brown, 1970), p. 87.

16. The first Islamist groups became apparent in Constantine, in the east of Algeria, after 1970. See Ahmed Rouadjia, *Les frères et la mosquée: enquete sur le mouvement islamiste en Algérie* (Paris: Karthala, 1990), pp. 146–149. Although the *salafiyya* school of Islamist reformists have written little, they draw their inspiration primarily from the works of Sayyid Qutb and Abul Ala Maududi. See Séverine Labat, "Islamismes et islamistes en Algérie," in Gilles Kepel (ed.), *Exils et Royaumes: Les appartenances au monde arabo-musulman aujourd'hui* (Paris: Presses de la Fondation Nationale des Sciences Politiques, 1994), pp. 44–46.

17. Gilles Kepel, "Le mouvements de 'réislamisation,'" *Liber* (supplement of *Le Monde*), September 1990.

18. See the summary of statements made by Dr. Turabi at the University of South Florida in May 1992 under the title "Islam, Democracy, the State and the West," *Middle East Policy*, Vol. 1, 1992, No. 3, pp. 49–61.

19. Interviews in Algiers, July 1990.

20. See Catherine Simon, "Algérie: un geste à l'égard des islamistes," *Le Monde*, January 21, 1993.

21. A detailed study of the relation between the construction of mosques and the growth of Islamism has been undertaken by Rouadjia in *Les frères et la mosquée.*

22. In the words of Rachid Benaissa, interviewed in April 1998 by François Burgat in his *L'islamisme au Maghreb: la voix du Sud* (Paris: Karthala, 1988), p. 101.

23. These developments included the Camp David accords of 1979, the internal divisions of the Arab League after the expulsion of Egypt, the invasion of Lebanon by Israel, and the Iran-Iraq War beginning in 1980. See Burgat, ibid., p. 93.

24. Ahnaf, Botiveau, and Frégosi, *L'Algérie par ses Islamistes,* p. 27.

25. See Amin Khan, "Chronique d'un cas de malchance dans l'historie," in *Algérie, 30 ans: les enfants de l'indépendance* (Paris: Editions Autrement, 1992), pp. 97–105.

26. See Clement Henry Moore, *Politics in North Africa*, p. 206.

27. Ibid., p. 84; Stora, "Messali Hadj (1898–1974)," p. 269.

28. The term *éradicateur* is used openly to describe those in the political and military establishment who seek to eradicate the Islamists. See Hirst, "The Second Liberation."

29. See Simon, "Algérie."

30. Cited by Francis Ghilés (of the *Financial Times*) in a personal interview, December 1990.

6

Egypt: The Islamists and the State Under Mubarak

MAHA AZZAM

The development of the Islamist movement in Egypt represents a political and ideological struggle between one of the leading states in the Middle East and the most widespread opposition movement in the Muslim world in recent decades. Furthermore, it sheds light on authoritarianism and democratization in Egyptian society. This struggle has been a complex one, starting with the growth of the Muslim Brotherhood in the 1930s and 1940s and followed by their experience of persecution during the Nasser years, the greater accommodation granted them during the Sadat era, the growth of more militant groups since the 1970s, and increasing attempts to repress them in the 1980s and 1990s. The relationship between Islamist groups and the state from 1981 to the present has been multifaceted. First, there is the political dimension, which involves the nature of the Egyptian regime and that of the Islamist groups themselves, the limited attempt at political liberalization, and the issue of the implementation of the *shari'a*. Second, there is the economic situation and the extent to which it contributes to the spread of Islamist support and influences government responses to them. Third, there are the social and ideological trends, which reflect perceptions of the path that society should pursue and views of Egypt's regional and international role.

The Political Dimension

Given the breadth of the Islamic political spectrum, such general terms as "radicals" (referring mainly to al-Jihad and al-Jama'a al-Islamiyya)[1] and "moderates" (referring to the Muslim Brotherhood and other Islamists against the use of force as a means of spreading Islam) are used here to point to differences between the main political poles within the Islamist movement. As is the case with most political movements, however, there is a degree of fluidity as well as diversity among the various tendencies. First, there are groups, namely the Jama'at al-Islamiyya,[2] whose politics have straddled both camps.[3] Second, although many members of the Muslim Brotherhood and some independents are generally sympathetic to the more militant Islamists, the radical al-Jihad group is highly critical of the Brotherhood on grounds of its overall policy of nonconfrontation with the government and its denunciations of the use of violence as a means of opposition. Both strategies are perceived by al-Jihad as an endorsement of the existing status quo.

The history of the Islamist groups in Egypt has been one of exclusion from political power due to government policies or particular ideologies or activities. Constitutional parliamentary politics during the 1930s and 1940s failed to draw the Muslim Brotherhood into any kind of official participation as a political party, although it played a central role in the political dynamics between the Palace, the Wafd, and the British. Despite the relatively free political atmosphere of the time, the Brotherhood was viewed with suspicion and fell prey to the political intrigues of its opponents, which were manifested in the assassination of its founder, Hasan al-Banna, in 1949.

The experiences of a constitutional parliamentary system in the first half of the century, whether in Egypt, Syria, or Iraq, were overshadowed by dictatorial state systems that, in one form or another, came to power in the second half of the century. The Muslim Brotherhood's attempts during the 1980s to accommodate itself within the existing political system and to avoid confrontation with the government was to a large extent a response to the experience of persecution suffered under the Nasser regime and reflected a fear that the organization could not sustain a renewed attack.

Like all Islamists, both radical and moderate, the Muslim Brotherhood is committed to the implementation of the *shari'a*. Unlike the radicals, however, members of the Muslim Brotherhood believe that it is advantageous for Islamist groups to operate as a political party whenever possible. The limited democracy in Egypt during the 1980s was viewed as offering a guarantee of basic civil rights without which the Islamic call (*da'wa*) was bound to suffer.

The parliamentary elections of November 29, 1990, had a low turnout, resulting in another assured victory for President Mubarak's National Democratic Party (NDP). A boycott by the three main opposition parties—the Wafd, the Liberal Party, and the Socialist Labour Party (SLP)—as well as by the allied, but technically illegal, Muslim Brotherhood, undermined the image of "greater" democracy that the government had been trying to foster ever since the elections of 1984. The opposition's stated reason for the boycott was that it would only participate in free and fair elections. The authorities tried to play down the boycott despite the opposition's intention to fight a legal battle contesting the legitimacy of the Assembly. Among the boycotting parties was the Muslim Brotherhood, which in the election of 1987 shifted its alliance from the Wafd to the SLP and the Liberal Party, forming a coalition that came to be known as the Islamic Alliance (al-Tahluf al-Islami). This bloc formed the main opposition to the NDP, winning sixty seats, of which thirty-eight (compared to seven in the 1984 election) went to the Muslim Brotherhood. Forming the Islamic Alliance was the most serious step taken by some elements in the contemporary Islamist movement in Egypt and enabled them to function as a political party. Whatever the shortcomings of the experiment, the Brotherhood viewed it as less harmful than not participating and therefore marginalizing itself from the then prevalent climate of political liberalization.

In contrast, al-Jihad and al-Jama'a al-Islamiyya have consistently viewed the existing system of government as illegitimate and rejected the idea of compromise and participation. Among the key ideological concepts that place the radicals in a different category than the Muslim Brotherhood, for example, are their concept of *hakimiyya l'allah*,[4] meaning that sovereignty lies only with God, and *jihad*, which is described as the missing pillar (*al-farida al-gha'iba*)[5] in Muslim devotional practice. Muslims are called upon to pursue jihad against a ruler deemed to be an unbeliever (*kafir*) either by virtue of his not implementing the *shari'a* or through a host of other failings, including moral decadence and economic corruption (*fasad*) or making peace with the Jews. Although these concepts have provided religious legitimacy for the resort to violence and the dismantling of the existing political order, a political and theological chasm over their interpretation has also persisted.

A polarized situation between the radical Islamist groups and the government continued to develop. The Muslim Brotherhood itself, however, found little room to maneuver given the unwillingness on the part of the government to allow the democratic process to proceed unhindered. Although the degree of criticism permitted by the government, most notably through the organ of the *Sha'bb* newspaper, has been unknown since 1952, overall government control of the media, the enforcement of emergency laws since 1981, and human rights abuses have seriously curtailed basic democratic freedoms.[6] By functioning within the limited parameters the state had conceded to them, however (namely, the opportunity to participate in elections under the umbrella of another party), the Muslim Brotherhood and its supporters were gradually questioning the government's legitimacy by their constant call for the application of the *shari'a*.

The call to have the *shari'a* applied as the principal source of legislation in conformity with Article 2 of the constitution of 1971, as amended in 1979, unleashed a major debate on the Islamic credentials of the state.[7] The government argued that in Egypt most laws were already in conformity with the *shari'a*. The concern of the Islamists, both moderate and radical, was that the constitution should be amended so that the *shari'a* would become the sole source of law.

The government's attempt at "national dialogue" during 1994 with some opposition figures, labor leaders, and academics has lacked credibility. The government has emphasized economic issues as the core of the problem and has sought acknowledgment that more time is needed in order to improve the economic situation, while barring discussion on constitutional reform.[8] At the same time, part of the government's motive was to seek condemnation from the opposition and independent figures of the wave of militant Islamist activities. The government's attempt to develop a dialogue with its opponents does not represent a retreat from its determination to eradicate the radical Islamist groups but is mainly an attempt to pursue a different policy of control and containment.

Despite the obstacles confronted by the Muslim Brotherhood and the Jama'at al-Islamiyya in their legitimate participation in the political arena, they have nevertheless functioned through various secondary political channels, such as professional syndicates and student unions. They have increased their popularity by combining the adept use of some democratic procedures with the operation of a network of social services that includes schools, clinics, and banks. The Muslim Brotherhood's dual call for the respect of basic liberties (*hurriyat*) and implementation of the *shari'a* remains a powerful one that finds a resonance in society. There has been a growing demand for the respect of civil liberties voiced by both secularists and Islamists with professional syndicates, student groups, lawyers, and writers speaking out about human rights abuses. For the Islamists, both radical and moderate, these abuses seem to be mainly directed at them. The main demands being made by the Muslim Brotherhood and moderate Islamists in general are their rights to freedom of speech against the government, protection against torture, access to due process of law, an end to corruption, and the implementation of the *shari'a*.[9] They believe that political pluralism is a guarantee of these and a legitimate process through which the *shari'a* can be implemented; therefore, at this stage their commitment to democratization is greater than that of the government.

The Islamists have not only formed a positive stance toward political pluralism but have also been influenced by the political processes and ideological currents that shaped the contemporary political environment of Egypt and the region. They have been part of the nationalistic and socialistic experience and have implicitly appropriated some of it and disregarded the rest. Overall, they represent a reaction to the lack of political participation and accountability, military defeat, poor economic development, and social and cultural influences that have beset Egypt over the second half of this century. The government is particularly vulnerable to acts of political violence because of the questionable basis of its legitimacy, the absence of genuinely representative political institutions, serious failings in respect to the rule of law, and the failure to bring about sufficient economic progress. The absence of full participation for the Islamist current in the mainstream of Egyptian politics has contributed to · violent tactics by both the government and the radical Islamists in their search for greater control of the political arena.

The Security Dimension

The limited attempts at a degree of political liberalization on the part of the Sadat and Mubarak regimes has failed to quell the demands of moderate Islamists for more serious recognition or to stop the spread of militant activity. The resort to violence by Islamists as a legitimate means of combating the Egyptian regime has since the 1970s taken on dimensions that constitute a threat to the regime. Acts of violence have increased, both in terms of the number of incidents and the number of locations affected. Not only Cairo but also a growing number of towns and villages in Upper Egypt have been involved. Whereas the Jihad group initially focused on the head of state as the main target of assassination if judged to be an unbeliever (*kafir*), as in the case of President Sadat, in the 1990s targets have included tourists, senior government figures, and security personnel as well as civilians believed to be government informants. There have been limited cases of institutional targets where small bombs were placed outside banks charging interest. The threat of attacks on resident foreigners (as distinct from tourists) and investors, announced in faxed messages in February 1994, were never carried out. The threat, however, represented a clear escalation of the security situation in the country as a whole. There might be an element of emulation of the Islamists in Algeria, despite the Algerian Islamists' relative advantage in terms of numbers, ammunition, terrain, and level of ruthlessness. In many cases, those targeted have had some direct connection with the measures of combating al-Jama'a and al-Jihad, either as security personnel or as heads of military courts that have sentenced Islamists to death.

The violent campaign of the Islamists against the government, particularly in Upper Egypt, is intertwined with the common practice of vendetta (*tar*). For example, if an Islamist from Asyut is killed by the security forces, the whole family or village seeks vengeance from the family of the individual who killed him or ordered his killing, irrespective of the political context of the incident. There have been similar cases (although less prevalent) in Upper Egypt, where families of government personnel killed by the Islamists have also demanded vengeance, again outside the political context. A feature of the general atmosphere of violence and vendetta has been Coptic/Muslim clashes, particularly in Upper Egypt. The Jama'at have frequently targeted Copts as a way of attacking the regime; however, there has usually been a local cause behind intersectarian strife, such as disputes over land or building rights. The government, for its part, uses these clashes in its propaganda to warn of the danger of sectarian conflict as an aspect of Islamist activity.

The strategy of al-Jama'a al-Islamiyya and al-Jihad to extend the range of targets has resulted in a greater challenge to the regime than has previously been the case. The campaign has had a serious effect on tourism and has undermined the regime's credibility both domestically and internationally. It is unclear whether it can control these extremist elements, regain stability, and maintain law and order.

The regime presents its role as that of combating terrorism and views the activities of the Islamists primarily as a security threat. It believes that the growing Islamist trend can be explained as a response to economic difficulties that it is seeking to alleviate but that cannot be rectified overnight. However, the concern with the security dimension, which is shared by other regimes in the region, remains prominent and has involved the coordination of security measures through interior ministerial levels.

Al-Jama'a al-Islamiyya and al-Jihad as well as moderate Islamists claim that the escalation of violence is a response to the violence of the state. The government's clampdown on Islamist activities has included the banning of student activities organized by Jama'at al-Islamiyya in the universities, the appointment of government preachers (from the Ministry of Religious Affairs and Endowments) to mosques, restrictions on the appointment of Muslim Brotherhood candidates to head professional syndicates (whose elections lately have been regularly postponed), and the decision to appoint rather than elect the mayors (*'umad*) of Upper Egypt's 4,000 villages. In its campaign to eradicate the groups, if necessary by a "shoot to kill policy," the government believes it reached a turning point with the shooting of Talat Yasin Hamman, a key figure of al-Jama'a, in April 1994 (and of his successor, Ahmed Hasan Abdel Galil, in November). By tracking them down, the security forces claim to have gained a great deal of information about al-Jama'a, and claim to have penetrated the group. Following these successful strikes against the radicals, the government, on the whole, felt confident that it could quell the challenge to its security. Confrontations continue to occur, however, between armed Islamists and the security, police, and armed forces. There have been high levels of security alertness in the country from Asyut to Minya and other parts of Upper Egypt, including Sohag and Ina, accompanied by curfews in some villages.

The acts of violence perpetrated by some of the Islamist groups have served as ammunition in the regime's anti-Islamist propaganda war, which has portrayed the Islamists as misguided and their ideology as a misunderstanding of the true tenets of Islam. The Islamists are presented as seeking to establish a puritanical, backward-looking, and uncivilized society concerned only with religious detail. The regime has instilled fear in the public mind by drawing parallels with Iran and giving examples of Islamic-sanctioned punishments (*hudud*) from Sudan. This message has been transmitted through the government-controlled media and lately through the cinema. The regime has succeeded in spreading the term "terrorists" as a reference for the radical Islamists. The response in society at large toward acts of terrorism has been one of anger and antagonism toward the groups, both because of the human cost and the loss in tourist revenue. The regime itself is also unpopular, however. The public seems less concerned (as far as such attitudes can be gauged) when a member of government is targeted than when a member of the public is the victim. Similarly, following President Sadat's assassination, there was little evidence of public grief.

The high level of security alertness reflects the seriousness of the threat the government faces (despite its rejection of this notion). There were almost daily clashes between the government and the Islamists throughout 1994. The challenge is not yet insurmountable; nevertheless, the acts of violence are potentially destabilizing given the fact that the government cannot rely on its own popularity, has not opted for accommodation of its religious opponents, and has not pursued the democratic option. Although at times there has been a lull in the violence, it resurfaces. In the Egyptian context, the use of violence by al-Jama'a al-Islamiyya and al-Jihad is tactically part of a broader strategy, however ill formulated, for a change of the existing regime and the reform of society politically, economically, and socially. On the one hand, the gradual and moderate spread of Islam by the Muslim Brotherhood, combined with the confrontational and violent politics of some Islamist groups, has provided a real challenge to the regime. On the other hand, it has resulted in the regime attacking extremists in particular and Islamists in general.

During 1994 the government launched an attack on the Muslim Brotherhood for what it claims is its ideological inspiration of the militant groups; it pointed to the Brotherhood's "fundamentalist thought" (*fikr usuli*) in its use of the writings of Ibn Taymiyya and Sayyid Qutb.[10] This attack was part of the government's expansion of its anti-Islamist offensive, which has included increased arrests, allegedly running into thousands, of anyone suspected of Islamist sympathies or activities. These actions, which include systematic abuses of human rights,[11] are in turn likely to continue to fuel antigovernment activity.

The relationship between the government and the Islamists needs to be seen in relation to individual groups as well as in terms of the government's overall policy toward the Islamist challenge. The government has frequently pursued a policy of suppression over one of accommodation in its belief that it can suppress the problem over time through strict security measures and an improvement in the economic situation. This choice reflects a lack of commitment to political liberalization, a rejection of an alternative ideological trend in the political process (something of which the Islamists themselves are frequently accused), as well as the manifest inability of the Islamists to force change on the regime.

Should the government face an intensification of violence by the Islamists, coupled with growing criticism from the opposition in general and international pressures for reform, it would have a number of options open to it that fall broadly into three categories. The first is a continuation of its present policy of hunting down Islamists, which would create an increasingly polarized situation and possibly an eventual escalation of violence. Second, it could accommodate some moderate Islamist elements in government and put greater government emphasis on Islamization through further implementation of the *shari'a*. Finally, it could begin to open up the political process in order to maintain a hold on power while winning the support of non-Islamist forces that might then make the Islamists appear a less attractive alternative for ordinary Egyptians. The present polarization only demonstrates the respective weaknesses of both the regime and the Islamists. Although the successive governments in Egypt have survived since 1952, keeping the state-system intact, the present regime faces the most serious and widespread ideological and political challenge since the coup, despite the absence of a direct bid for power by the Islamists. The latter, for their part, remain weak in terms of resources. They are disunited and lack the leadership that could provide direction for the Islamist groups and appeal to others in society.

The Economic Dimension

The general economic context of relations between the state and the Islamists needs to be set against the background of economic liberalization (*infitah*) begun during the Sadat period. Economic liberalization is generally viewed, on a popular level, as responsible for the increased disparity

between rich and poor, the increase in unemployment (currently estimated at 20 percent),[12] and the spread of corruption (*fasad*), with this last
element forming the focus of repeatedly expressed public discontent. The
government itself is viewed as corrupt, and it is widely acknowledged
that corruption has permeated all levels of society. Accepting bribery, for
example, has become a necessary means for many of augmenting a meager salary in order to make ends meet. *Fasad* (corruption) has become a
catchall phrase for Egypt's economic predicament. The government itself
has attempted to win credibility by exposing cases of corruption in high
places, but on the whole, this strategy has only further cemented the public's belief that corruption exists at the highest levels of state.

Economic liberalization produced a class of entrepreneurs who benefited from the new economic climate and established rapidly expanding
businesses. These included a category of "Islamic investment" specialists
whose investment companies (*sharikat tawzif al-amwal*), developed in the
1980s, attracted the public by offering unusually high rates of return (typically 20 to 30 percent) while insisting that their funds were invested in
accordance with Islamic principles. The early success of these companies
benefited political Islam, mainly because they made financial contributions supporting Islamist candidates for parliament and helped fund Islamic publications. However, their collapse (many appear to have been
money pyramids) and the subsequent loss of investors' money, amidst allegations of corruption against some of the major companies, such as al-
Rayyan, al-Saad, and al-Sharif, was exploited by the government to taint
Islamists in general with corruption.

These investment companies flourished in an unregulated market, and
the government's moves against them were partly motivated by the wish
to protect private investors. The government was also motivated, however, by the desire to quell the growing contradiction, pointed out by U.S.
commercial bankers, between the mounting debt of the Egyptian government and the vast sums deposited in the commercial banks as a result of
profits accumulated by investors in these companies.[13] The investment
companies were able to offer, if only temporarily, an alternative to government institutions and appeal both to a cross-section of investors motivated by profit as well as to nationalist and Islamist figures who saw
these enterprises as fulfilling Islamic tenets and investing national savings in the country.[14] Despite their eventual failure, they reflect the appeal
of combining Islam with finance primarily for profit but also for religious
legitimization.

There are also those professionals who made their money in the Gulf
states or through successful practices in Egypt and who donated money,
and frequently their time, to "Islamist" welfare projects. These projects
have enabled the Islamists to gain support among the poor and needy

and have been seen by many as providing essential services on a day-to-day basis in areas where the government has failed to offer solutions as well as in times of crisis, as, for example, during the earthquake in 1992.

Despite the government's connection with corruption and inefficiency, many beneficiaries of its economic and political policies are committed to its survival. *Infitah* spurred a degree of social mobility and increased income opportunities that tied many to the establishment as represented by the Mubarak regime. The economic situation remains fragile, however, and the government is under constant strain to please entrepreneurs who have supported the system as well as to improve the general living standards of Egyptians in the hope of stemming the appeal of the Islamists. The Egyptian government, like the Algerian government, has been unable to cut subsidies for fear of invoking riots that could be exploited by the Islamists. Because the Islamists are generally untainted by corruption, their ideological message could help rally support for necessary austerity measures (although, should they come to power, they too would likely find it very difficult, despite initial popularity, to cut subsidies). One of the main weaknesses of the Islamists is their inability to place the economy at the top of their agenda and provide a clear economic program of reform and development. Thus, the public lacks hope and confidence in those who are meant to provide an alternative. It is because of Egypt's overwhelming economic reliance on U.S. aid, and the fear that the assumption of power by Islamists would jeopardize existing U.S.-Egyptian relations, that the regime continues to have an advantage. Although an improvement in the economic situation might temporarily strengthen the hand of the regime, it is unlikely to quell the demand for greater accountability and further Islamization not only by the deprived or marginalized in society, but also by many urban middle-class elements.

The economic situation has strongly affected support for the various Islamist groups. In order to place this influence in perspective, it is necessary to assess some of the social and cultural dynamics of Islam in present-day Egypt.

The Social Dimension: Religion and Worldview

The centrality of Islam to Egyptian society is not new. Since the 1970s, however, there has been an increased expression of religiosity in society at large. This trend has manifested itself through an increase in the number of worshipers, mode of dress, the vast number of publications dedicated to religious subjects, and the general cultural and intellectual environment, which is saturated with Islam as faith, language, law, and history. In Egypt, as elsewhere in the Muslim world, there is an appropriation of the old and the new occurring under the banner of Islam. What is worrying for the state is that this appropriation includes politics and that the line dividing religious practice and political activity is not a difficult one to cross for many Muslims.

Among the Islamists' main advantages is that they are in touch with a religious current that has spread throughout Egyptian society. They have been able to foster and direct this current through their organizational ability and dedication, and there is no rival opposition group to match them. The stress on devotional practices and cultural purification from all that is "un-Islamic" is shared by various Islamist groups, and this focus provides a framework of action for their followers and has contributed to the Islamization process. The most profound contribution, however, has been that of the Muslim Brotherhood, which from the time of its founding has placed an emphasis on education (*tarbiyya*) and on the individual becoming a better Muslim. This emphasis has borne fruit, insofar as the basic belief and practice of Islam have been reasserted and spread among a new generation and throughout a cross-section of society.

Although most regimes in the Middle East have used religion in different ways as a means of legitimization, since the 1970s there has been a concerted effort on the part of the Egyptian government to assume Islamic credentials. It has attempted to do so by using the media and the Azhar to promote what the government views as an accurate and moderate interpretation of Islam. By assuming this policy the government has indirectly participated in the further Islamization of society; nevertheless, it is clearly still perceived by its Islamist detractors as secular and un-Islamic.

At present the government has opted for more openly enhancing the secular trend and undermining the Islamist alternative rather than attempting to ride the Islamic current, as it had done in the past. For example, over the past two decades, there had been mounting pressure from the Islamists, and more generally from society, for women to wear the *hijab* (veil). The government now appears to be making a concerted attempt to discourage the *hijab* by excluding women who wear it from study missions and by generally discriminating against them, wherever possible, in state-controlled employment. This attitude of defiance is likely to create greater animosity and polarization not only between the Islamists and the state but also between the broad spectrum of religious Muslims and those who want to strengthen the secular character of Egyptian society.

Nevertheless, the multifaceted process of Islamization continues and encompasses a wide range of political views, including some that are actively opposed to the regime, some that are critical of it, and some that support it. Likewise, the secular current has within it opponents of the regime as well as the mainstay of its support. Despite a degree of convergence between secularists and Islamists opposed to the government over certain political issues such as the rule of law, the Arab-Israeli peace process, the Gulf War, and Bosnia, Islamists nevertheless tend to interpret contemporary political challenges involving Muslims as being directed at them specifically because they are Muslims. Part of the ideological challenge facing the Egyptian state and other Muslim states is the emergence in society of the search for an alternative identity based exclusively on Islam. This identity is presented by Islamists as being better equipped to defend Muslims, as was the case, they argue, historically.

There has been no clear articulation by the Islamists of Egypt's role regionally and internationally, beyond a general notion about the need for unity between Muslim states in order to promote greater justice for Arabs and Muslims. Islamists and members of the public generally believe that it is not the Muslims who are anti-Western, but the West, and at present, particularly, the United States, that is undermining the development of Muslim states. The state, for its part, seeks to pursue growth and development through closer political and economic cooperation with the West as well as with Israel. It is this latter vision that represents a regional trend that is being supported politically and partly financially by the United States and the European Union. The state has presented it as forming a new overarching economic and political reality that will undermine the Islamist trend. Although this view of an alternative has gained momentum with the peace process, it is greatly undermined by a legacy of economic failure and corruption associated with the regime, disillusionment with the political process, and the ideological alternative being offered by the Islamists.

There is growing polarization between the increasing number of Egyptians who are seeking a more "Islamic friendly" society in which to live that would not contradict their religious values and those who want to maintain and promote a less religiously oriented society. In today's Egypt, the moderate interpretation of Islam is what was once considered extreme, and there has been a shift in corresponding notions of what constitutes "moderate" and "extreme." Such classifications have different features at different times and therefore need to be constantly reviewed in order to assess what they represent at a particular period.

In a society where the moral fabric is under strain because of increases in corruption, crime, and drug abuse, Islam is perceived by many as offering an ethical code of behavior and a means of countering this social malaise. The Islamists see themselves, and an Islamic society, as the guardians of an "Islamic" code of behavior in all spheres of life. They have therefore been active in certain parts of the country, attempting, for example, to put an end to prostitution and drugs.

Although religion has always been central to Egyptian society and culture, there has nevertheless been a gradual "revolution" that has involved, in terms of numbers and outward expression, an unprecedented stress on Islam as the focus of identity. The choice of Islam as the lynchpin of identity and values among an increasing number of people from different economic and social strata has been the single most important step toward the Islamization of society, although not as yet of the state. The ideological and political challenge this poses for the state brings with it two options: accommodation of its opponents or a continuation of its present policy of control and containment, both of which are unlikely to stem the demand for greater Islamization of state and society.

Notes

1. The Jihad group became apparent with the assassination of President Sadat in 1981, an act for which they were held responsible as an organization. The group is still committed to armed struggle against the regime and the establishment of an Islamic system of government. The name "Jihad" was given to the organization by the authorities; members merely refer to it as "al-Jama'a al-Islamiyya." This issue of the organization's name became more confusing, however, when, in the 1980s, the group splintered into two groups, the Jihad and al-Jama'a al-Islamiyya. Both espouse similar aims and tactics but seem to differ over the issue of leadership. Today's Jihad, and its military wing, Tal'a al fath, reject the leadership of Omar Abdel-Rahman, although he was originally reputed to be the leading figure for the Jihad group, which turned to the *fatwa* (religious ruling and legitimization) for Sadat's assassination.

2. The Jama'at al-Islamiyya (not to be confused with al-Jama'a al-Islamiyya) is a creation of the 1970s, when members first appeared on university campuses and began to gain control of student unions throughout the country. They contributed a great deal to the initial assertion of Islam among the young in post-Nasserist Egypt. By the 1980s, their influence had spread beyond the campuses and involved welfare work. Overall they became synonymous with Islamist political assertion, and both moderate and radical social and political activities were attributed to them. Although the activities of the Jama'at throughout the country generally followed a similar pattern, activists nevertheless tended to follow the instructions of their particular amir (leader). Thus in one context, for example, Assyut, they would pursue more violent activities than in other areas.

3. Issam al-Aryan, leader of the Jama'at in the Cairo University faculty of medicine in the late 1970s, was elected to parliament in 1987 as a candidate for the Islamic Alliance.

4. The idea of *hakimiyya* is derived from the writings of the main theoreticians of the contemporary Islamist movements, Qutb and Maududi. See S. Qutb, *Ma'alim fil-Tariq* (Landmarks Along the Path) (Cairo: Dar al-Shuruq, 1980); S. Abu'l A'la al-Maududi, *The Process of Islamic Revolution* (Lahore: Islamic Publications, 1980).

5. Muhammed 'Abd al-Salam Faraj, "Al-Farida al-Gha'iba," reprinted in *Al-Ahrar*, December 14, 1981.

6. Amnesty International, London, "Egypt: Grave Human Rights Abuses amid Political Violence," May 1993; "Egypt: Military Trials of Civilians: A Catalogue of Human Rights Violations," October 1993; "Egypt: Human Rights Defenders Under Threat," September 1994.

7. I. Altman, "Islamic Legislation in Egypt in the 1970's," *Asian and African Studies* 13 (1979), 209.

8. *Al-Hayat*, May 30, 1994.

9. Something of this emphasis was reflected in the Islamic Alliance's ten-point program with which it contested the election of April 1987 and which contained the following points: (1) faith in God as the basis of solving economic problems; (2) an end to the state of emergency, restoration of civil liberties, and the guarantee of fair elections; (3) the *shari'a* as a comprehensive system of government and way of life. According to the *shari'a*, "The Copts are citizens whose rights and duties are like those of Muslims." Impact International, London, July 22, 1988, p. 10.

10. Ibn Taymiyya (1263–1328) was a medieval theologian of the Hanbali school who issued a *fatwa* ruling that the Muslim Mongol rulers in Marden (modern Turkey) were not to be considered Muslims because they applied a mixture of *shari'a* and Mongol laws (the Yasa). Islamists draw parallels with modern governments that only partially apply the *shari'a*.

11. A case of human rights abuses by the state is that of Islamist lawyer 'Abdel Harith Madani, who died in police custody in April 1994.

12. *The Economist*, April 9, 1994.

13. S. Zubaida, "The Politics of the Islamic Investment Companies in Egypt," *British Society for Middle Eastern Studies Bulletin* 2 (1990), 156.

14. Ibid., pp. 159–160.

7

Climate of Change in Jordan's Islamist Movement

BEVERLEY MILTON-EDWARDS

Democracy does not consist merely of
institutions. It is a tradition and a way of life
that characterises society.
                              —**King Hussein of Jordan**

Since the introduction of the process of "democratization" in Jordan, the political climate of the kingdom has changed. The political reforms introduced by King Hussein since 1989 have resulted in a reordering of relations within the kingdom's largest political grouping, the Islamist movement. The opportunity of increased access to the corridors of parliamentary power was first offered by the king through a general election in 1989. This poll resulted in a major victory for the Islamists.[1] At the time, many voiced fears that the "tide of fundamentalism" had finally reached Jordan. Yet these fears were allayed three years later, when the kingdom held its first multiparty election in decades. Although the Islamist movement polled well, the process of political reform prevented it from translating this victory into parliamentary seats. Thus, in 1993 its share of parliamentary seats dropped from 36 to just 16. The climate of political change heralded by the democratization process has not improved the political fortunes of the Jordanian Islamist movement. Instead, the political popularity and success it enjoyed in 1989 has been eroded and undermined. There has been evidence of a policy within the king's court to ameliorate the threat posed by the movement, and a number of reforms and other incidents provide evidence to support this theory.

The Islamist victory at the polls in 1989 indicated the strength of one of Jordan's oldest political movements and its ability to marshal support from the people, although a number of other factors prevented this event from marking the start of an "Islamic fundamentalist revolution" in Jordan. In many respects, the notion of "fundamentalism" was never part and parcel of Jordan's Islamist movement; however, the label was frequently applied to the Islamists in the years following their 1989 victory. By 1993, the notion that "Islamic fundamentalism" posed a very real political threat to Jordan was being highlighted through a series of show trials in the kingdom and there was a policy of hostility from the palace.

Islam Is the Solution

The 1989 election was not called on a whim. King Hussein's policy of political reform had been carefully considered and was part of a deliberate policy to transform Jordan while at the same time maintaining the supremacy of the monarchy over the political system.[2] The king had been well aware of the power that the kingdom's Islamist movement, particularly the Muslim Brotherhood (al-Ikhwan al-Muslimeen), had attained over the decades. Unlike other branches of the movement in the region, the Muslim Brotherhood had enjoyed a fruitful political relationship with the Jordanian regime and its monarchy. It had always been described as the "loyal opposition." Talking about the Brotherhood's relationship with the king, veteran Muslim Brother Yusuf al-Athm noted: "In Jordan we have a lot of breathing space, we are not agitating against the king because he is wise, he will not destroy us. The Ikhwan are part of his people, they will help him. Our enemies are with the police and the *Mukhabarat* [Jordanian security service]."[3]

Loyalty to the king, however, did not always guarantee loyalty to the political system, and a recalcitrant Islamist movement was easier to handle if it was co-opted by that system. The election in 1989 wove the group into the fabric of the legislature, bringing them into the policymaking process and governance with important effects. This result, in turn, created a division of ranks within the Islamist movement itself, with some groups inside the political system and others outside and excluded from it. Once the Islamists were represented in parliament, the king was able to gain a firmer control over the Muslim Brotherhood by linking it to political reform and other issues, such as foreign policy. This relationship paid high dividends during the hiatus created within the kingdom during the

Gulf crisis, when both monarch and Muslim Brotherhood were criticized internationally for their support for Saddam Hussein.[4]

Power Relations

As some Islamist groups in Jordan became fully entrenched in the system and new oppositional groups emerged, the balance of power within Jordan's Islamist movement changed. New groups and figures have arisen that are radicalized and contentious. Others have spoken out against the new system of power relations as well as against corruption and the democratization process. In addition, there has been evidence of growing resentment within the movement against the predominance of the Muslim Brotherhood.

Political Islam in Jordan is not a one-dimensional affair or constrained by a monolithic relationship with theological doctrine and practice. Political Islam and the groups identified with it are heterogeneous and embrace a number of interpretations of the teachings of the holy Qur'an and the tradition of Prophet Mohammad. Some of Jordan's Islamist groups, such as the Muslim Brotherhood, have moved with the course of political change within the kingdom over a forty-year period, their position, for the most part, reflecting the prevailing policy of the monarchy. Others, like the Islamic Liberation Party (Hizb al-Tahrir), have always opposed the regime and refused to recognize the king's claim to rule. They have been refused permission to organize as a political party and have suffered politically as a result.

Diversity, then, characterizes the myriad of Islamist groups, including Hizb al-Tahrir, al-Jihad al-Islami (Islamic Jihad), Jaysh al-Muhammad (Muhammad's Army), and others in Jordan today. Although all groups work toward the same declared goals—an Islamic state that implements *shari'a* law and resurrection of the Caliphate—the groups offer an infinite number of ways and means to achieve this goal. Since the elections in 1989 and the identification of some Islamist groups with the policies of the regime, it has been increasingly difficult for those groups who oppose the policies of the regime as un-Islamic to get along with their "Muslim brothers." This schism has widened, exacerbated by the regime's charges against some groups and not others and the failure of those groups within the system to effect what could be considered as meaningful and directed Islamic change. Contradictions and fissures are now sometimes aired in public, indicating that new cadres of Islamist activists have arisen to challenge the prevailing political order as well as the leadership of traditionalist Islamic groups like the Muslim Brotherhood.

Reaching a Point of Departure

The Muslim Brotherhood is one of Jordan's oldest and most enduring political actors. The group, which was founded in the 1940s with King Abdullah's blessing, has enjoyed a close relationship with the monarchy. This relationship has sometimes been characterized by periods of disagreement over specific political issues, such as the Baghdad Pact in the 1950s and Jordanian-Syrian relations in the 1980s, but these differences have not damaged the rapport between Jordan's political secular monarchy (which claims direct lineage from the Prophet Mohammad) and the Muslim Brotherhood, which is a reformist rather than a fundamentalist antiregime movement. Thus, the Jordanian Islamic resurgence is different from that of countries like Egypt, Syria, or Algeria because it has always been linked to the regime (the monarch) rather than growing out of opposition against it. The biggest change since 1989 for the Muslim Brotherhood has been that the "loyal opposition" has invested a large part of itself into the resurrection of parliamentary life under the king's policy of "democratization."

The new Islamist groupings and alliances that have emerged since 1989 are largely the product of a younger generation of Islamic activism in the kingdom. Their leading figures grew up under the traditional influence of the Muslim Brotherhood and were inspired by a number of disparate groups foreign to the Jordanian experience of Islamism in its political form. This background has given them a unique ideological and religious viewpoint. Although it is still accepted that "Islam is the solution" (the election slogan of the Muslim Brotherhood in 1989), these new groups question exactly who will provide the solution.[5] More particularly, they oppose the prevailing system of politics, arguing that it is corrupt. The movement then has reached a crossroads. The old guard is having to acknowledge the younger generation and its new perspective. And whereas the old guard had identified itself with the regime, the new cadres are "oppositional" in nature.

The very names of these groups and alliances evoke the vision that these activists share: Mohammad's Army, which derives its name from a religious reference to the Khaybar events; Islamic Jihad, the Islamic Liberation Front; and the Muslim Mujahideen. Rather than evoking images of reform, education, and preaching, these names call for armed struggle[6] carried out in the name of Allah. These groups believe that the Islamic struggle in Jordan is not yet over. A number of them seek radical change. Their experiences at the hands of the regime are interesting and illustrate the dilemmas the regime faces in handling this new religious force in the kingdom. Mohammad's Army underwent a trial, for example, in 1992 that brought into focus the varied impact of the new Islamic groups as well as their inspirational sources and their relationship with the regime. The nature of the trial and others that followed cast serious doubt on the democratization program declared by King Hussein and drew criticism from all quarters. In addition, the trials revealed the regime's hostility against the new Islamic trend.

Mohammad's Army and the Afghan Experience

Mohammad's Army was formed in Jordan in 1988 by Afghan returnee Samih Abu Zaydan, a former disillusioned member of the Muslim Brotherhood. The idea for the organization emerged during a meeting between Zaydan and the Palestinian Islamic activist Abdullah Azzam while they were both serving in the Arab brigades in Afghanistan.

The influence of the Afghan experience on these two men cannot be underestimated. The Arab brigades in Afghanistan, which the author Godfrey Jansen estimates at some 5,000 volunteers,[7] brought together Islamic activists from throughout the Middle East, including Jordan. This association allowed them to compare experiences and explore ideas and ideologies in an environment based on the ethos of holy struggle, or *jihad*. The images of the mujahideen, evoked in thousands of articles in Islamic magazines and newspapers distributed from Algeria to Indonesia, increased the rhetoric of the Afghan approach to Islamic politics. The power of this rhetoric was apparent in the Arab brigades, composed of volunteers willing to die for the cause. In addition, the war became associated with an Islamic argument that centered on Afghanistan as the first step in the liberation of the whole of the region from Western-inspired secular tyranny. In the Occupied Territories, Islamic leaders would often declare that the road to Palestinian freedom and the liberation of the holy city of Jerusalem started in Afghanistan. When it came to the export of revolution, the Afghani case was proving as potent, if not more so in some cases, than the Iranian example to the Sunni Muslims of the region.

For the leader of the new Jordanian group, the Afghan setting was important for a number of reasons. Among other things, his experiences in the war help to explain the direction he took on his return to the kingdom. Serving in Afghanistan was an important bonding experience for members of the new movement. Veterans were not going to allow themselves to be "pensioned off." They returned with a specific agenda in mind, and as the author Ehud Ya'ari states, "They [saw] Afghanistan not as the final Islamic victory, but as a springboard for the next step forward."[8] At another level, Afghanistan provided these men with an opportunity to learn how to use weapons and explosives. Some of the returnees had engaged in armed combat during their time in Afghanistan.

Their knowledge of such matters when they returned to Jordan in the late 1980s was considerable and dramatically affected the potential of the group.

The prevailing political situation in Jordan upon their return, however, did not appear to affect the direction that the group was heading in. The political situation, despite the election in 1989 and other reforms under the umbrella of "democratization," remained, for recruits to the fledgling Mohammad's Army, relatively unchanged. The victory of their Islamic counterparts at the polls did not signal a swift or direct move to an Islamic state system and must have been doubly frustrating for those, like the leaders and members of Mohammad's Army, who, it is alleged, believed in the need for radical change.

Through their experience in Afghanistan, these men had seen real change and an Islamic victory. Success in Afghanistan through the work of the Islamic mujahideen had come through armed struggle and jihad. Meanwhile, in Jordan the Muslim Brotherhood and its parliamentary allies were declaring that change had to be incremental and reformist. Muslim Brother deputy Abdel Aziz Shabaneh summed up the mood within the movement when he declared, "We want gradual legislation, not a revolution. We are with the people—the nation—now we are in parliament."[9]

Thus it comes as no surprise that the leaders of Mohammad's Army eschew the path of political change in Jordan. Instead, Abu Zaydan recruited men and formed armed cells, each headed by one member. The group remained underground and secret. For the first two years, the members of the group concentrated on recruitment, training, and funding. Money was solicited through worshippers at mosques throughout the kingdom. The funds, according to court transcripts made available after the capture and trial of Mohammad's Army, were used to purchase various firearms for illegal objectives inside Jordan. The purchase of this weaponry made the intent of the organization clear. The group's ideological objectives would be achieved primarily through armed jihad in Jordan. The reestablishment of the Caliphate and an Islamic state would be brought about through revolution, not through incremental reform of existing state structures.

By January 1991, the core of the group, numbering fewer than twenty cadres, were alleged to have undertaken their first attacks against targets considered inimical to the interests and ideological motives driving the group. The choice of targets reflected some interesting insights into the theological and ideological motives driving the organization. Stores selling alcohol were a target, for example. Although the Muslim Brotherhood had also targeted liquor stores, it had chosen parliamentary legislation as its method of introducing change. The Christian community in Jordan also became a target of Mohammad's Army. This was a new and worrying development for the Christian minority, which had continually sought assurances from the regime regarding the protection of their rights. Previously, Islamist groups had not singled out Christian figures, but in this case a Greek-Orthodox priest, Kamil Haddad, was the victim of a rocket attack by the group. The final target of the group before their arrest in the summer of 1991 was a Jordanian intelligence officer involved in the investigation of the organization. Taken as the sum total of the activities of the group, these choices seem confused. Why did the army not target prominent political figures, or anti-Islamic personalities? These issues were not explored during the trial or in the media.

The arrests, interrogation, and subsequent trials of the men alleged to have been involved in the organization caused something of a sensation in Jordan. Initially, more than 100 people were arrested and questioned by the Jordanian security service. In September 1991, following allegations of ill-treatment and torture, most of the detainees were released. However, eighteen men were sent for trial in the state security court, presided over by three military judges. Observers were concerned that the arrests and trial were not being handled by the civil authorities and argued that the court procedures did not protect the democratic rights of the individuals.

The trial raised many issues surrounding the activities of the Islamic movement in Jordan. It alarmed the mainstream Muslim Brotherhood, who saw a covert warning from the regime. When the trial began, one Muslim Brother, Deputy Hamzah Mansur, was quoted as saying, "These people [Mohammad's Army] have been dragged here so that the Islamic current will be put on trial." Islamic independent deputy Laith Shubailat argued that the affair was part of a policy "that seeks to create the climate and mobilise public opinion against the Islamic movements, which constitute the main obstacle in the face of capitulation to the enemies. We declare that whoever concedes to work to weaken this Islamic tide and plot against it puts himself in a position of hostility to his nation."[10] The trial was criticized as unconstitutional and contrary to the spirit of democratization that was supposed to be prevalent in the kingdom.

On November 25, 1991, the court, headed by Judge Colonel Yusuf al-Fa'uri, "sentenced eight men to death after finding them guilty of plotting to illegally change the country's constitution, possessing explosives and arms, attempting murder and terror acts, belonging to an illegal group, collecting funds for illegal organisations and using fake car licence plates."[11] In addition, all the defendants were convicted of illegal membership in Mohammad's Army. The verdicts against them gave some indication of the threat the group was perceived as posing to the political stability of the regime and sent a message to the Islamic movement from the palace regarding the issue of real political power in the kingdom. Less than a month later, on December 24, King Hussein, in a beneficent goodwill gesture, is-sued a royal decree commuting the sentence to life imprisonment.

The formation and activities of Mohammad's Army had been a worry-ing development in the Jordanian system. It indicated that not every Is-lamist group in the kingdom would subscribe to the policy of co-optation. As in past decades, some groups would continue to reject the Jordanian regime and operate illegally and underground. In addition, opposition, despite "democratization," was being handled in a less than democratic manner, and thus those identified as opponents were treated with little regard for the constitution or the rights of individuals. The fact that the Jordanian security services were still empowered to round up and detain hundreds of civilians without firm evidence or charges was a worrying aspect for the promoters of the fledgling democracy. Whether the phe-nomenon of Mohammad's Army also alerted the Jordanian state system to the impact of the Afghan returnees is debatable. Certainly, at the time there was a groundswell of opinion throughout the region that the Afghan returnees were linked to the troubles in Algeria and Egypt. Yet, the returnee phenomenon in Jordan is a small-scale affair compared to their impact in other Arab countries. Nevertheless, the trials, allegations of torture, and severity of the sentences indicated that the regime would hold no truck with such activities.

Mohammad's Army also alerted the regime and its most prominent po-litical figures to the notion that Islamic opposition to the political changes taking place would be varied and posited on different theological and po-litical debates. Criticism from inside and outside the system was not the preserve of one group or directed at a specific target. The case of the Armed Vanguard of Islamic Youth (Shabab al-Nafeer al-Islami) was espe-cially disturbing. This trial, following on the heels of the Mohammad's Army debacle, added credence to the argument that the palace was changing its policy toward Islamic opposition groups. It was almost farci-cal in terms of the nature of the charges and the underlying agenda. The reverberations of these trials and others to follow were apparent during the 1993 multiparty elections, where the number of Islamist candidates, and in particular, Islamist independents, declined, opening the field to the mainstream Islamic Action Front (Jabhat al-'Amal al-Islami), which, for the most part, represented the Muslim Brotherhood.

The Armed Vanguard of Islamic Youth

The trial against the leaders and members of Mohammad's Army re-sulted in a startling twist within the kingdom. One of the trial's most out-spoken opponents, Parliamentarian Laith Shubailat, and his colleague

Deputy Sheikh Ya'qub Qarrash, found themselves targeted by the security services. Both men, highly individual in style, were popular figures on the parliamentary scene. Elected as Islamist independents, they formed the Dar al-Qur'an (The House of Qur'an) alliance in the House of Representatives after their 1989 victory at the polls.

Both men were prominent in Jordanian politics, yet their backgrounds and agendas were quite different. Laith Shubailat was first elected to the Jordanian parliament in 1984 after rising through the political ranks of the Jordanian Engineer's Association to become its president in the late 1980s. As the parliamentary representative for the third district of Amman, Shubailat had proved himself the most popular deputy in the kingdom, receiving the highest number of votes for a single candidate in both the 1984 and 1989 elections. An educated and articulate man, Shubailat was recognized as one of the most important figures of the Islamist movement outside of the traditionalist Muslim Brotherhood. He often toured the country to speak at universities and professional association meetings.

Ya'qub Qarrash is a Palestinian who was deported by the Israeli authorities for his activities in the Islamist movement in Jerusalem in 1980. Before his decision to stand in the 1989 election, Qarrash had been imprisoned on four occasions by the Jordanian secret service. He had become involved with the Sufi movement and had aligned himself with the Shadhaliyya tariqa (Sufi Brotherhood). Nevertheless, he still held and expressed radical opinions about the need for a jihad to liberate the Palestinians from Israeli occupation. His decision to stand in the 1989 election was both pragmatic and political: "If there was a chance of democracy and all I had to do was pay 500 dinar [the candidate registration fee] to speak to the people, then I would give them something different from the Muslim Brotherhood to hear about."[12]

Shubailat was described by one Jordanian newspaper editor as being the "leader of a new generation of *sufis* in Jordan." Both Shubailat and Qarrash had become members of the Dar al-Qur'an Sufi society in Jordan, led by Sheikh Hazem al-Ghazaleh, who is also involved in the Shadhaliyya tariqa of Sufi Islam.[13] It is asserted, however, that "despite the coincidence of both of his disciples being charged, neither the Sheikh nor the rest of the group had any relationship with the Vanguard business."[14] Nevertheless, Shubailat and Qarrash were two of the tariqa's most important figures. Sheikh Qarrash affirmed his close tie to Sheikh al-Ghazaleh, noting, "He is our mentor. There is a mentor and a chosen student (murid); I am that chosen student."[15] During the 1989 election, both stood as members of the Dar al-Qur'an society.[16]

On August 27 and 31, 1992, first Qarrash and then Shubailat were arrested by the Jordanian authorities. Along with two others, owners of a furniture store, Shubailat and Qarrash were charged with the possession of explosives and weapons, slander against the monarch and the parliament, and "trying to undermine Jordanian-Iraqi relations." Speaking about the charges, Qarrash commented, "I wasn't surprised at what happened. I'm a Palestinian and this is my fate and I will always be vulnerable. But Laith was surprised. He's a Jordanian and his system turned against him."[17]

Shubailat and Qarrash were accused by the Jordanian authorities of undertaking hostile activities through their leadership and command of the Vanguard of Islamic Youth. Qarrash was also accused of leading another group called Jabhat al-Tahrir al-Islami (The Islamic Liberation Front). The trial against the Vanguard of Islamic Youth started on September 29, 1992. Once again, the court was under the jurisdiction of the state security and there were three military judges, led, again, by Colonel Yusuf Fa'uri. Defense attorneys for Qarrash and Shubailat challenged the constitutionality of the court, the manner of the charges, and the credibility of witnesses. At one point, the defense attorneys resigned following the testimony of a "secret" prosecution witness, allegedly from Syria, who spoke of an Iranian financial link with Shubailat. Shubailat and Qarrash also went on a hunger strike to protest the proceedings, and they refused the court-appointed defense after their lawyers left the trial.

The trial led to a great deal of disquiet among the members of the kingdom's Islamist movement. The tide seemed to have finally turned against them, with government policy directed at particular targets. Within weeks of the commencement of the trial, it was announced that a case was being brought by the state security court against another Islamist group. One man, Ibrahim Sirbil, a Palestinian originally from Hebron, was arrested and accused of forming an illegal group named "Islamic Jihad–al-Aqsa Battalions."

The trial also elicited widespread protest from political figures in the kingdom. It was soon commonly accepted that the raison d'être for the state prosecution was the uncompromising stand Shubailat had taken on the investigation of corruption in the kingdom. Shubailat was serving on the parliamentary committee to probe the misuse of funds and was committed to his task. A statement was issued during the trial, signed by representatives from political, parliamentary, and professional organizations, urging his release. Muslim deputies in parliament met in several highly publicized gatherings to discuss the trial, and media interest in the case was intense. Concern centered on the implication of the trial for the "democratic process" and its validity in Jordan. Pleas were issued to the king to bring a halt to the trial, and tensions were raised in the kingdom.

The verdict announced by the state security court was a shock. Shubailat and Qarrash were found guilty of all charges except trying to overthrow the regime. Death sentences were passed by the judge and then immediately commuted to twenty years' hard labor for both deputies. Protest from all political quarters within the kingdom was immediate, and again the king was urged to intervene. Thus, in a move generally accepted as one designed to defuse political tension and end speculation about a campaign against the Islamist movement, the king announced an amnesty two days after the verdicts. Prime Minister Sharif ben-Shakir appeared on television reading a letter from the king on the eve of his birthday in which the king emphasized the need to urge the "black sheep of the kingdom to return to the flock." The text of the letter said, "We have decided to issue a general amnesty for those jailed and detained, affirming at the same time our full pride, absolute support, and our backing and protection for the fair judicial authority."[18]

A day later, on November 15, Shubailat and Qarrash were released along with other imprisoned Islamists, including ten men from Mohammad's Army, Mohammad Sirbil from the Islamic Jihad, and convicted members of the Islamic Liberation Front and Hamas. The Islamist movement responded with great praise for the king, commending his wise and kind decision and respect for the "Islamic trend" in the kingdom. It was almost as if a collective sigh of relief were heard throughout the Islamist movement after the months of worrying about the regime's attitude toward their activities. Talking about the experience, Qarrash said, "The sentence was no surprise. After all those lies [in the court] this was the biggest lie of all. Since the pardon though, I feel stronger, although I am very angry at what happened to me. I'm angry at my brothers in parliament, at the government, and the *Mukhabarat*."[19]

Both Shubailat and Qarrash were careful with their words when it came to the king, praising him for his benevolence. Shubailat, in an interview with the Arabic daily *al-Quds al-Arabi,* cited the king as the most democratic person in the country and criticized the "Islamic movement" for its stand on the promotion of "true" democracy.

The end of the trial, the amnesty from the king, and the release of Shubailat and Qarrash did not, however, bring the matter to an end. A number of issues lingered. There were concerns over the nature of a judicial system described by its monarch as "fair." It emerged after the trial that the affidavit of the "secret" Syrian witness in Germany revealed that the man, an Iraqi, had been forced to testify by the state prosecution. He had been drilled by top figures related to the trial, including prosecution lawyer Major Hijazi, in his fabricated testimony against Shubailat and the Iranian connection. A debate was scheduled in parliament to discuss the trial, and international human rights organization Amnesty International criticized the state security court's denial of the right of appeal. The trial focused the attention of Jordan's political figures and citizens on the true meaning of democracy and threats to the regime in Jordan. As Shubailat asked in his newspaper interview, "Who shook the regime? Was it Laith Shubailat, Laith Shubailat's trial, or the farce of the military court's procedures?"[20]

Pragmatic Politics

The events of 1992 and the trials, as well as the prospect of a forthcoming election year in 1993, had a tremendous impact on the Jordanian Islamist movement. The trials sent a message to the "independents" that they would be tolerated only if they worked within the framework laid out by the palace and that the palace would dictate the pace of reform and change. Although the king had issued an amnesty in what was widely recognized as an attempt to diffuse further political tensions, at the same time he honored the state security judge, Colonel Fa'uri, and the prosecutor, Major Hijazi, with royal medals. The significance of this act could not have been lost on the independent wing of the Islamist movement. Nor did 1992 see an end to state trials against members of the Islamist movement. The new year would also include a new assault, this time on the ranks of the already marginalized and illegal Islamic Liberation Party (ILP).

The events motivated the Muslim Brotherhood to undertake a series of changes. The shifts signaled, despite the Brothers' remarks to the contrary, that they were willing to further entrench themselves within the framework of the prevailing political system and work for its stated goals—even if these appeared to contradict "Islamic goals." In addition, the changes highlighted the centrality of the Muslim Brotherhood in the kingdom's "Islamic trend." The trials of 1992 had reflected badly on the organization and led to fears within its ranks about its future role within the regime. These fears were amplified when the Muslim Brotherhood compared its own position to that of fellow brethren in Egypt and Algeria that year.

Thus, in December 1992 the Muslim Brotherhood announced that changes were afoot in the organization and that it would be heading into 1993 with a new appeal and a new approach to the issue of representation in politics. The Brotherhood announced its complete commitment to the regime, the king, and the "democratization" program. Citing its maturity, its experiences in parliament, its lessons in "growing up," and "flexibility," a spokesman for the organization said, "There is a marked change in our attitude towards what appears not to be Islamist. We now believe we cannot judge by appearances and that the Jordanian society is basically Muslim at heart if not in appearance."[21]

Stepping back from a confrontational approach toward the issue of civil liberties within the kingdom, the Muslim Brotherhood also made clear that it had its sights firmly set on the general election expected in November 1993. Speaking about the type of candidates expected from the movement for a future election, a high-ranking figure was quoted in the *Jordan Times* as saying, "We used to choose representatives according to their commitment to Islam and Muslim doctrine. Now we will choose the representative most able to deliver Islam to the people at this time. You will see at least a fifty per cent change. Experience has brought change among the Brothers."[22] These sentiments reflected the reality of the successful co-optation of the Muslim Brotherhood since 1989 and signified increasing dissension within the ranks of the Islamist trend. The Muslim Brotherhood had announced that the goal of an Islamic state would be temporarily shelved and that they identified with the goal of the Hashemite kingdom and its monarch. The Brotherhood has always been recognized as a pragmatic actor, and once again pragmatism overtook principle.

The new trend and new era announced within the Muslim Brotherhood was boosted with the successful registration of the Muslim Brotherhood–backed Islamic Work Party (Hizb al-Amal al-Islami, or Jabhat al-'Amal al-Islami [Islamic Action Front, IAF], as it became known) in December 1992, which had been made possible by a new law on the formation of political parties that had been passed in July 1992. Led by Islamist parliamentarian Ishaq Farhan, the IAF was supposed to act as an umbrella organization for a number of Islamist groups. It was apparent from the first, however, that it was controlled by the Muslim Brotherhood and that the place of "other" Islamists was minor and incidental. Within weeks of the registration of the IAF, the Muslim Brotherhood dominated the consultative committee (al-Shura) and independents were complaining about a lack of representation despite promises from the Muslim Brotherhood to the contrary. Independent Islamists only won 18 seats on the 120-seat committee, and thus had a 15 percent minority representation.

On December 28, seventeen prominent independent Islamists sent a letter of resignation to Farhan stating they were leaving "to allow the party to remain, as many others have described it, just another face of the Muslim Brothers."[23] The feelings of independents toward the Muslim Brotherhood were emphasized in the text of the letter, which said, "Since the movement [the Muslim Brotherhood] did not uphold its pledge to stick to the great goal of uniting the Islamic efforts in this country, and since its practices have come out in contradiction to its statements, this party will not be able to recruit new elements and in fact will not even be able to keep its non-Brother elements because they will feel as if they are rowing on a strange sea and are only vehicles to reach certain objectives."[24]

The resignations and marginalization of the Islamist independents made it clear that the IAF was none other than the party of the Muslim Brotherhood. Why the Muslim Brotherhood did not just register as a party in its own name and choose the facade of the IAF instead is revealed on a close inspection of the law on the registration of political parties. The legislation states that all new parties must be open to the scrutiny of the Jordanian intelligence services and that they are not allowed to receive funding from outside Jordan or be linked to political parties abroad. The Muslim Brotherhood has always maintained close political and economic links with its namesakes abroad, and the formation of the Islamic Action Front was a way in which to get around this legislative loophole.

The IAF made it clear that it was the main Islamic contender for the election. The only other "Islamic" registered party included Christians and women on its executive committee. This meant that the Muslim Brotherhood had a strong leading edge. The pluralism of choice that should have been offered to Islamic voters was just not apparent under the new "multi-party" system. Islamic independents (individuals) were likely to provide the only real alternative. Yet after the assault on independents in 1992, the Islamic Vanguard trials, and the marginalization of independents in the IAF, there was intense speculation over whether independents like Shubailat and his colleagues would stand again for parliament.

Gearing Up for an Election

Despite the initial setbacks and internal fissures experienced by the IAF in the latter part of 1992, leading figures in the Islamic movement approached the elections scheduled for November 1993 with confidence. Although the fringes of the Islamic movement had been battered and frayed, the mainstream Muslim Brotherhood eagerly awaited the opportunity to prove their popularity at the polls.

A number of domestic and regional developments, however, undermined the electoral confidence of the movement and ensured the further marginalization of the radical wing of the Islamist movement. These developments weakened the position of the Islamic movement as a whole and of the Muslim Brotherhood and IAF in particular. The first occurred in June 1993 when it emerged that the Jordanian security services had arrested ten members of the ILP and uncovered a plot to assassinate the king during a military parade for new recruits to the army. The plot, it was alleged, had been hatched by members of the Islamic Liberation Party in an attempt to topple the regime. Again, the trial of Islamist activists made front-page news in the kingdom. Following the tradition of similar cases, the trial was conducted, after the accused had been interrogated by the security services, in a military court. The defendants were all held incommunicado at the General Intelligence Department (GID) in Amman and were denied access to lawyers or family visits. The accused alleged that their confessions were extracted under duress and torture.

The trial, which would last for four months, was depressingly familiar to those observers who had followed the cases against other Islamists in the kingdom. The defendants announced they wanted to retract their confessions, and the testimony of witnesses was called into question after it emerged that they had "privately admitted that their testimonies were not truthful."[25] As in the other trials, it seemed inevitable that harsh sentences would be levied against the Islamist defendants.[26]

By autumn the king was revising the election law to change bloc-voting to a one-person, one-vote system. The decision, which was not the result of parliamentary legislation, outraged Islamists, who declared it "unconstitutional." The king's wisdom in making the decision was questioned: If democratization were truly taking place, then why did the king still maintain sole authority over such important decisions and legislation? The new electoral law immediately cut into any hopes the Islamists had of doing well at the polls. According to the new law, elections would be based on a system of one person, one vote. Under the outgoing slate system (or bloc-vote), electors had been permitted to cast as many votes as there were members in the constituency.

The announcement in early September 1993 of negotiations between the Israelis and the PLO and the subsequent Declaration of Principles signed in Washington on September 13 deflected Jordanian attention from domestic issues. The Islamist movement's reaction to the "peace" agreement was contrary to that of King Hussein, who had been pushing for a formal peace treaty with Israel. This opposition, combined with Islamist rejection of the IMF plan for economic recovery that the king supported, increased tension over the forthcoming election. The monarch was determined not to let an Islamic-dominated parliament scupper any peace deal with Israel, however, and it was quickly rumored that the king would postpone the election. By delaying, he would be able to push through a peace deal with the Israelis without having to consult parliament. The hostility generated within the Islamist camp, and concentration on the issue during election campaigning, however, did not win them support at the polls.

By early October, a month before the election, uncertainty over the poll itself and electoral issues were weakening the stand of the Islamists and the IAF itself. The IAF was still dogged by internal divisions and factionalism as well, which were also weakening its electoral chances.

Shattering the Myth

In contrast to the 1989 poll, the campaign for the first multiparty elections in the kingdom since the 1950s was lackluster and disappointing. The new political parties, most of which had been registered for a year or less, were unable to marshal popular support. The fears that the king might postpone the election dampened election spirits and cast an air of uncertainty over the proceedings. The IAF decided to field thirty-six candidates, a large number of whom ended up competing for votes against each other in the same district.[27]

Nevertheless, the poll did take place as originally scheduled and the results were announced on November 9, 1993. The poll was disappointing for a number of reasons. At a general level, despite three years of democratization and promotion of the concept of political pluralism to the kingdom's citizens, voter turnout was very poor, at only 820,000 (39.5 percent) of the electorate, compared to 60 percent in 1989. The policies of democratization were only serving to marginalize voters rather than encouraging them to interact with their political system. The poor turnout sent a very clear message to the kingdom's political elites in both the parliament and the palace.

The biggest disappointment was for the Islamists, who lost over a third of the seats they had previously held in the 80-member House of Representatives in parliament. Although in 1989 the Muslim Brotherhood and other Islamists had been able to garner a total of 36 seats, this number was cut to a total of 18 (16 to the IAF and 2 to independents) in the 1993 poll. As one journalist noted, King Hussein had succeeded where others had failed. He had "cut fundamentalism down to size by playing the democratic game."[28] However, if the democratic game was played, had it been played fairly? How many players had been removed in elimination bouts, and how many were shackled from the starting line? It was true that the king had played the democratic game, but it was also true that he had drawn up the rules of the game despite the protests of the players. The opposition over his one-person, one-vote legislation provides a telling example of this. Observers noted that the new legislation had "succeeded in diminishing the Muslim Brotherhood's strength in parliament."

The poor polling had been hampered by the internal rifts between the pragmatists and the radicals within the movement. These disagreements became public and affected voter confidence in the bloc. The tensions within the IAF had led to defections by Islamist independents. The small pool of Islamist independent candidates, and poor polling by those candidates to win seats in parliament, also reflected the political games played before the election. The independents had been virtually eradicated from the scene as a result of the show-trial farce conducted against independent Islamists in the previous year.

The only comfort that the Muslim Brotherhood could draw from the election defeat was that it was still able to attract a strong popular base of support from the voters. The votes were there, but the new electoral system and the strategy of fielding too many Islamist candidates had prevented those votes from being translated into seats in parliament. Protest against the new electoral system was soon forthcoming from the ranks of the IAF. In December 1993, the IAF staged a walk-out from the Jordanian parliament to protest the legislature's reluctance to form a committee to examine the November election. In addition, IAF members were among the fifty signatories to a petition issued in late November protesting the new electoral system and the alleged bias against their movement. Although Islamists were able to garner a popular vote and win seats in elections outside the parliamentary system, in both local council and professional association polls they had to realize that they could not count on the political system to work in their favor in parliament. The Muslim Brotherhood could no longer dominate parliament; other blocs had emerged, including independent Muslim Brothers and other Islamists, destroying the fallacy of parliamentary unity in Islamist ranks.

Peace with the Enemy

If the forces of political Islam in Jordan were unaware of their increasing marginalization and lack of political influence over the monarch and institutions of government, the signing of the Jordan-Israel Peace Treaty on October 26, 1994, between Jordan and Israel was irrefutable testimony to the nature of the new political climate in the Hashemite Kingdom. Unlike past regional pacts with Jordan's Arab neighbors, this change in external relations did not augur well for the Islamists. In signing the treaty, King Hussein brought to public fruition years of secret negotiations; in contrast, the Islamist movement committed itself to an intransigent political stand on the issue. Bound by a history of hostility to the Jewish state, the Islamist movement remains a vociferous opponent to the existence of a Jewish state on Muslim soil. In addition, the Jordanian Islamist movement has strong ties with the Palestinian Islamist movement and has always been sympathetic to its goals and methods. Thus, the Islamists of Jordan have been alarmed at the pace with which King Hussein has ended a forty-six-year state of war. The Islamists have been unable to influence the king in his decision to break Arab ranks and become the second country in the region to sign a peace treaty with Israel.

The prospects for the Islamist movement, radical and moderate alike, in the era of the "warm peace" with Israel are not encouraging. The forces against "fundamentalism" both inside and outside the country have declared an open war on radical Islam and its anti-Israel ideology. Even U.S. President Bill Clinton entered the fray, using the opportunity of his presence at the signing of the Jordan-Israel treaty to send a strongly worded message to the Islamists. Clinton declared that Islamic fundamentalism must not be allowed to succeed, adding that the United States would not allow the "extremist forces" of Islam to torpedo the peace process. The Israeli government, already waging its own campaign against the Palestinian Islamic militants in Hamas and Islamic Jihad, would certainly not tolerate the continuance of assistance and support offered by the Jordanian Islamists to their Palestinian brethren. In the light of the new peace the Israelis would look to King Hussein to take action in his own kingdom to restrict or even eliminate this important Islamist lifeline to the Palestinian movement. Within the kingdom, there is now no doubt within Islamist circles that the peace with Israel will further limit their scope and activities.

The Jordanian Islamist movement, however, remains steadfast in its rejection of a peace treaty with Israel. While the king and members of the Jordanian government may resolutely oppose such views, there are many who support them. In a way, the Islamists' opposition to the treaty reflects popular rather than minority support. There can be no doubt that there remains a broad coalition of opinion among the Jordanian populace that is guided and influenced by the Islamist and Palestinian perspective. With a combination of both factors, Islamist leaders in Jordan have found a receptive audience in the mosques. Their Friday sermons, during which the idea of peace with Israel has been denounced, were greeted with a warm response from faithful congregations. An ability to tap into popular sentiment, shaped by years of hostility and domination of the Israeli/Jewish entity, however, has not been translated into an ability to bring political power to bear in the Jordanian legislature or, perhaps more important, on decisionmaking circles in the palace. The treaty is very much the personal product of King Hussein and his brother Crown Prince Hasan, and it is obvious that the pleas of the Islamists have fallen on deaf ears in this quarter. By calling the peace process a "national endeavor," the monarch has made opposition increasingly difficult to organize. Even in the legislature, where the Islamists have had lobbying influence, they were unable to prevent both the House of Representatives and the Senate from ratifying the peace treaty in early November 1994.

In many respects then, the treaty with Israel symbolizes the emasculation of the political power of Jordan's Islamist movement. As the peace with Israel grows warmer and warmer, the king's relations with the Islamists in his kingdom grow colder. Although King Hussein remains a figurehead of Islam (supposedly the descendant of the Prophet, keeper of the Islamic shrines of Jerusalem, and indeed a devout Muslim himself), he has turned his back on radical-political Islam and its ideology. Thus, in an era of a monarch-inspired moderation, the Islamist opposition in the kingdom has been rendered ineffectual and inhibited by the institutions, laws, and security apparatus of Jordan's burgeoning democracy.

Reassessing Future Prospects

The climate of change that has assailed Jordan's Islamist movement since the late 1980s has resulted in a period of trauma for the movement as a whole. The Islamic resurgence in Jordan has been battered by the process of democratization, and the movement has been forced to reassess its future role in the kingdom. For decades the Muslim Brotherhood enjoyed a natural political advantage over other groupings in the kingdom, but their policies in the 1990s have often proved at odds with the strategies drawn up by the monarch and his supporters. Despite a period of close alliance between the two during the Gulf crisis, the king has steadily eroded the power of the Muslim Brotherhood both inside and outside of parliament. The rest of the Islamist movement has suffered a considerable setback in its goals. The campaign against the "radicals" proved successful and has weakened the Islamists' clout in the country. The future for the movement is beset with new problems and obstacles that will have to be overcome.

The most pressing problem is the split within the movement, which has remained unhealed. Within the Muslim Brotherhood, serious rifts over policy issues have continued. Critics have argued that Islamic principles are increasingly sacrificed to the pragmatic stance of a movement determined to survive a campaign against it by the regime. The more moderate stand of the Muslim Brotherhood was reflected in elections to the IAF *majlis al-shura* (consultative council) in January 1994, when the moderates prevailed and the radicals were ousted. In essence, political survival through pragmatism will be the order of the day if the Islamist movement is to remain a powerful force on the Jordanian political scene in the rest of the 1990s.

Notes

1. The Muslim Brotherhood gained 22 of 80 seats in the lower house of the Jordanian Parliament and Islamic independents gained another 12.

2. See B. Milton-Edwards, "Facade Democracy and Jordan," *British Journal of Middle East Studies* 20, no. 2 (February 1994), pp. 191–203.

3. Yusuf al-Athm, interview with author, June 20, 1989.

4. See B. Milton-Edwards, "A Temporary Alliance with the Crown: The Islamic Response in Jordan," in J. Piscatori (ed.), *Islamic Fundamentalisms and the Gulf Crisis* (Chicago: The American Academy of Arts and Sciences, 1991), pp. 88–109.

5. Islamic parliamentarian Laith Shubailat announced that the Islamic movement was not the solution.

6. In this call for struggle there is a strong connection to the perception of a need for jihad, and the prerequisites and "types" of jihad are linked to the "struggle."

7. G. Jansen, "The Afghans—an Islamic Time Bomb," *Middle East International,* November 20, 1992, p. 16.

8. E. Ya'ari, "The Afghans Are Coming," *The Jerusalem Report,* July 2, 1992, p. 30.

9. Abdel Aziz Shabaneh, interview with the author, Amman, Jordan, April 11, 1992.

10. "Deputy Shubailat: Government Excessive," *Al-Ribat,* September 17, 1991, p. 6.

11. "Mohammad's Army: Eight Receive Death Sentence," *Jordan Times,* November 26, 1991, pp. 1–2.

12. Sheikh Ya'aub Qarrash, interview with author, Amman, Jordan, December 30, 1992.

13. For more on the Shadhaliyya and Yashrouti *tariqas,* which were founded in Jordan after originating in Palestine, see F. ed Jong, "The Sufi Orders in Nineteenth and Twentieth Century Palestine," *Studica Islamica* 58, pp. 149–183.

14. Interview with editor of *a-Dastur,* May 8, 1993.

15. Qarrash, interview with author.

16. In 1989 candidates had to run individually due to the continued prohibition of political parties in the kingdom.

17. Qarrash, interview with author.

18. FBIS-NES-92-220, "King Issues Amnesty for Prisoners, Detainees," p. 37.

19. Qarrash, interview with author.

20. FBIS-NES-92-236, "Interview with Jordanian Deputy Laith Shubailat," by Wafa 'Umar, December 3, 1992, p. 4.

21. N. Murad, "The Muslim Brotherhood Reviewed," *Jordan Times,* December 4, 1992, p. 4.

22. *Jordan Times,* December 4, 1992.

23. N. Murad, "Independents Quit Islamic Front," *Jordan Times,* December 28, 1992, pp. 1, 5.

24. Ibid.

25. Amnesty International, "Jordan State Security Court Trial Ends with Death Sentence," January 17, 1994, p. 1.

26. On January 16, 1994, the ten men on trial were all found guilty of the charges against them. Three death sentences, three life sentences, and sentences for fifteen years' hard labor were also levied.

27. In Zarqa, votes for the Islamic movement were split between three IWP candidates out of a total field of six. Al-Urdun al-Jadid, *Jordan's 1993 Election* (Amman, 1994).

28. G. Hawatmeh, "King Trumps Polls," *Middle East International,* November 19, 1993, p. 10.

8

Islamic Governance in Post-Khomeini Iran

ANOUSHIRAVAN EHTESHAMI

The Islamic Republic of Iran has done much to popularize the label "fundamentalist" to denote those Islamist-oriented, politically active individuals and groups who have illustrated a desire to establish "God's government" on earth and to institutionalize *shari'a* law as well as those forces that have organized and agitated toward this end in the Muslim states of the Middle East.

Political Islam in Iran emerged from a revolutionary process culminating in the establishment of an Islamic republic in the region's only Shi'a state. After more than 2,000 years of monarchical rule, the *velayat-e faqih* system (spiritual and political guidance by a jurisconsult), as enshrined in the 1979 constitution of the republic, was to become the cornerstone of the new form of governance in Iran. In order to shed more light on the Iranian revolutionary experience and the debate about "Islamic fundamentalism," I have chosen to explore four key aspects of the region's first revolutionary Islamic regime: the evolution of Iranian power structures since the late 1980s, foreign policy, macroeconomic policy (including Iran's foreign trade regime), and the relationship between politics and religion in the republic. My main purpose here is to question whether the Iranian Islamic revolutionary experience can be emulated and, more to the point, whether Iran has been able to produce a comprehensive socioeconomic and political system that is uniquely Islamic and, as such, is quite distinct from capitalist and centrally planned systems.[1]

I shall argue that the transformations in the republic and policy changes since 1988 are in a sense the secularization of the policies of a regime that itself continues to function as an Islamic state, in the sense that although the place of religion in the state may have been undergoing changes since 1989, the clerical elite continue to dominate the state, *shari'a* law continues to be implemented, the *faqih* system remains operational, and Islamic principles continue to inform much of the regime's public policies (particularly over matters pertaining to gender, dress, Western cultural influences, and public morals).[2]

The debate about the viability of an alternative Islamic socioeconomic system is all the more interesting because of the emphatic failures of Marxist-inspired and Communist-led regimes in both the Second and Third Worlds to offer revolutionary or reformist alternatives to Western-style capitalism. But, although initially the Iranian revolution was welcomed by many as the appropriate avenue for establishing an Islamic state, reviews of the Iranian experience have raised question marks elsewhere in the Middle East over the long-term desirability of an overtly Islamic state and over the practice of gaining power through force and by the violent overthrow of existing orders. It is worth noting in this regard that even prominent Islamist leaders such as Hasan al-Turabi, Sheikh Mohammed Hussein Fadlallah,[3] and Rashid al-Ghannushi have decidedly opted for reformist strategies of creating an Islamic state and not for violent overthrow.[4] In the midst of the raging debate about future orders in the Middle East, where do we put the revolutionary alternative, and how unique and successful can we regard the Iranian experience?

The problem in analyzing the Iranian experience, however, arises in any attempt to ascribe the appropriate tradition to the revolution of 1979. What seems to distinguish Iran from the Third World socialist revolutionary regimes is precisely its anti-Marxism and anti-socialism. Indeed, its leaders have gone to great lengths to portray themselves and their political system as morally superior to both Cold War power blocs. As one Iranian ideologue has stated,

> The school of capitalism . . . has revealed its detestable face and its filthy core in scandals, in crimes, in unreliability, in corruption, in that dangerous illness AIDS, and such illnesses which have created such tragedies in the world and which have truly horrified the West. Marxism and Communism too . . . has itself declared its own bankruptcy. . . . The school which can really run the world is the school of Islam. We must support Islam; we must support it in the world. Now that those two structures are moving towards destruction . . . we must pay attention to the structure which has been designed by the Prophet of God.[5]

In the economic realm, too, the Iranian leadership insists on having created an "Islamic" system.[6]

Although clearly not a Communist-type state, Iran does not easily fit the bill of Western-oriented capitalist Third World states either. Yet, the Iranian case does put on the agenda a new (revolutionary) alternative to Third World socialism(s), evidently capably transmitting its Islamic revo-

lutionary message to many Muslim societies in the Middle East and beyond. This was the first revolution not indebted to European ideologies
and to have survived without a Major Power protector. It was religion-
based and clergy-led, and it allowed a greater degree of expression within
the revolutionary current than other revolutions. Also, there existed no
vanguard or ruling party to lead and direct the masses during the revolutionary phase. Finally, this revolution entrusted sovereignty with deity:
Article 56 of the 1979 Islamic constitution states that absolute sovereignty
over the world and man belongs to God and that it is he who has placed
man in charge of his social destiny.[7] The Iranian revolution was regarded
as a manifestation of divine law and justice, whereas all other modern
revolutions have been products of man's this-worldly aspirations.

It is of course of some significance to establish that the February 1979
uprising in Iran was a "revolution," because it did lead to fundamental
changes in political organization, social structure, and economic property
control.[8] But such transformations occurred in Iran only to a degree, and
many features of the Shah's system in political organization, social structure, economic property control, and economic planning machinery and
techniques were preserved by the new elite.

As already mentioned, the clergy-dominated Islamic Republic has consistently portrayed its model as the only viable, "progressive" alternative
to both (Western-style) capitalism and socialism. High on the agenda of
Iranian revolutionary leaders have been such issues as social justice, economic self-sufficiency, political integrity, an independent foreign policy,
and strict nonalignment. Iran's success in reaching the more modest aims
of this experiment, in terms of creating a prosperous, equitable, and di-
versified economy at home, and its success in universalizing the Islamic
Republic's alternative model, provides for much of the discussion that
follows.

Evolution of the Republic's Power Structures

Ayatollah Khomeini's death and the constitutional reforms of 1989 led to
a gradual "secularization" of the most important offices of the land and
thus diluted the overtly religious basis of authority in the republic. The
reforms abolished the post of prime minister and entrusted executive
powers to the president as the head of the executive branch of government. In itself this change—a main feature of the reforms—was a major
departure from the established tradition of the 1980s and the founding
principles of the republic. But more significantly still, in preparing the
ground for Khomeini's clerical successors, the same reforms redefined the
role of the central institution (the *velayat-e faqih*) in the system. The *faqih*'s

position was more politicized at the expense of its religious authority. With Khomeini's passing, the office that he created and himself occupied for ten years was no longer the leading source of religious authority in Iran.[9]

The two reforms combined were the processes through which the "secularization of Islam" in Iran would be accomplished, to borrow Mehdi Mozaffari's phrase.[10] Iranianism and pragmatism (both institutionally and culturally) had returned to center stage and a process of secularization of power had been initiated. The reduction of the *faqih*'s position to a "political office" has had serious implications for a regime, and state-form, that relies almost exclusively on religious authority for control and distribution of power.[11] But how did this happen and why is the Iranian republican system moving away from, rather than closer to, a puritanical Islam, ironically just as Islamists elsewhere in the Middle East are emerging as a major political force to challenge the status quo in the Arab world?[12]

Although the transfer of spiritual power from Khomeini to Khamenei was speedy and peaceful and did not threaten the political structures of the state, Shaul Bakhash suggests that "under Khomeini's successor, as might have been predicted, the standing of the office has already been much diminished" and that a process of decline could continue.[13] According to him, legitimacy under the current system "derives from the authority of the *faqih*, as heir to the mantle of the Prophet. The principle of government under the supreme authority of the *faqih* assumes that in each age, the most learned, most respected, most pious, most able Islamic jurist of his generation will assume the supreme leadership and that his pronouncements on matters of Islamic law, government, matters of peace and war, social justice and the like will carry weight by virtue of his great learning and grace."[14] The process of succession (and choice of successor in 1989), however, has not only forced the Islamic political elite to change the rules of the game and to compromise the above principles but, more fundamentally still, has caused a serious rupture in the religious and political authority (and symbolism) of the spiritual leader of the Islamic state. Ultimately, as we have seen with Khomeini's successor, emphasizing the political at the expense of the religious has necessarily de-"Islamicized" the most religiously authoritative of offices in Ayatollah Khomeini's doctrine. In the last analysis, with regard to the nature of rule and governance, the republic since 1989 has come to resemble less a purely Islamic state and more a functional one in which a natural division of labor has emerged between the "spiritual leader" of the state and its executive leadership.

In addition, despite the changes to the power pyramid of the country, because the clerical elite did not tinker heavily with the Iranian administrative and government systems, the nature of governance has remained inherently and fundamentally secular. The play of power and politics, therefore, may have acquired an "Islamic" odor about it, but Islam does not actually affect the administration of the state. Even in the Majlis (the legislative body of the Islamic Republic) the number of clerics has been declining steadily, with just 49 clerics elected to the fourth Majlis (1992–1996).

Iranian Foreign Policy

Constitutionally, the republic rejects "all forms of domination; both the exertion of it and submission to it," and supports "the preservation of the rights of Muslims" and "nonalignment with respect to the hegemonist superpowers." The state's foreign policy principle has been "neither the East nor the West,"[15] which since the end of the Cold War can be said to have been transformed into "both East and West."[16]

Taken in its totality, Iranian foreign policy gave priority to the Islamic countries as the republic's natural constituency. By and large the emphasis consistently was on Islam (and Islamic ethics) as the main component of Tehran's foreign policy. The Islamic Republic fragmented the Third World into two camps: Islamic countries and movements and non-Islamic ones. But although it was able in the 1980s to maintain good relations with both the noncapitalist, socialist-oriented Third World states and the myriad of capitalist, pro-Western Third World states, during the Cold War era it proved singularly unsuccessful in bringing about a united "Islamic front" in international terms. This failure may have been partly due to the fact that by attempting to isolate some Muslim states (like Saudi Arabia) as advocates of "American Islam," while maintaining reasonable relations with some other secular or pro-U.S. regimes in the Muslim world (like Malaysia, Pakistan, and Turkey), the republic managed to erode the universalism of its own message.

Furthermore, at the same time that it was propagating Islam internationally and threatening the legitimacy of the traditional Muslim states of the region, Iran seemed anxious to maintain close ties with the secular and "radical" states of the Middle East, particularly Syria, South Yemen, Algeria, and to a lesser extent, Libya. The justification for this dualistic behavior may lie in the fact that Tehran's new rulers had recognized that the country's geopolitical imperatives would not allow the regime to isolate itself from the existing web of regional relations.[17] What Shireen Hunter refers to as "creeping realism" implied recognition by Tehran of the reality that the republic could not exist outside of the given international system, nor indeed function effectively outside of the global interstate system.[18] This creeping realism has become a defining feature of the republic's foreign policy since the late 1980s, and more emphatically since the imposition of the "dual containment" strategy by the Clinton administration in 1992, as illustrated by Tehran's high-level efforts to find new political and economic partners in the Islamic world beyond the Middle East, especially in Central Asia, sub-Sahara Africa, southeast Asia, and (non-Muslim) Europe.

The republic's attitude toward national liberation movements was part and parcel of this process of change in Iran's international relations. Compared with other revolutionary regimes, however, and despite its declared support for a number of liberation movements, the Islamic regime's policies on this matter remained ambivalent. For example, although the secular Palestinian national movement was sidelined in the 1980s by Iranian leaders in order to pave the way for a religion-based campaign against Israel, Tehran has continued to honor the PLO's right to run the "Palestine embassy" in Iran.

All in all, Tehran supported more than a dozen "liberation" movements before Ayatollah Khomeini's death, largely concentrating on both creating and consolidating the position of the Islamic fronts and movements in the Middle East,[19] with the MORO Liberation Front of Filipino Muslims being the main recipient of Iranian support in the Far East. Tehran's support for such sub-state and Islamist liberation movements, however, did not come at the expense of Iran's membership in the many diplomatic, social, and economic regional and international organizations it had joined under the Pahlavi regime. The country's membership in a host of Western-created and -dominated international institutions, including the U.S.-dominated International Monetary Fund and the Western-based World Bank, continued.

More concretely, and despite some deviations, Iran's security and foreign policies during and since the Kuwait crisis of 1990/1991 indicate that pragmatism, and not fundamentalist persuasions, continue to inform Tehran's behavior. As Said Arjomand notes, during the Kuwait crisis "national interest rather than revolutionary zeal formed the basis for Iran's foreign policy decisions."[20] During the crisis, much of the Iranian leadership, including the president and the foreign minister, supported Iran's neutrality in the conflict and were actively engaged in international diplomatic efforts to reverse the Iraqi aggression, having already condemned the invasion and accepted the authority and mandate of the United Nations (in particular the Security Council) to deal with the crisis.

Uncharacteristically, in the aftermath of the war Tehran, in conjunction with another interested party (Syria), supported the creation of a broad coalition of anti–Saddam Hussein forces. This coalition, which included socialists and liberals, integrated Iran's own well-groomed Shi'a alternative (the al-Hakim–led Supreme Assembly for the Islamic Revolution in Iraq) to the Ba'thist regime. Most interestingly, despite the many opportunities that Baghdad's adventurism had provided, the establishment of an Islamic republic in Iraq no longer appeared as a high Iranian priority. Iran's reassessment was such that it even refused to supply military hardware and ammunition to the Iraqi fighters during the 1991 uprising, according to highly placed Iraqi Shi'a opposition groups.[21]

Since the Kuwait crisis, Tehran has continued to improve its diplomatic and economic relations with its Arab neighbors, the tense situation with the United Arab Emirates over the three Persian Gulf islands notwithstanding. It has tried very hard to counter Washington's influence with the Gulf Cooperation Council (GCC) states by offering to participate in collective security measures with its southern neighbors and by trying to depoliticize its relations with all of its Arab neighbors. Its lack of success in such efforts, however, may have less to do with ideological differences between the two sides and more with Iran's position that such discussions should not involve the Western powers and that they should include Iraq.

Foreign policy pragmatism is also in evidence in Iran's relations with the Asian republics of the former Soviet Union.[22] From the outset, in 1991, Tehran showed its keenness to downplay Islam in its relations with the Central Asian and Caucasian republics, capitalizing instead on its cultural and historical ties for improved economic and diplomatic relations.[23] It was, for instance, instrumental in broadening the membership of the Economic Cooperation Organization to include the Muslim republics of the former USSR and in establishing the Caspian Sea cooperation group. Fear of instabilities arising out of political, ethnic, and border conflicts in the Caucasus and Central Asia, and the potential impact of such instabilities on Iran itself, have in part helped to explain Tehran's caution toward these republics and its emphasis on economic cooperation and conflict resolution. Tehran's efforts to calm the situation in post-Najibollah Afghanistan (even at the expense of its own Shi'a allies), its high-profile involvement since 1992 in negotiating an end to the Armenian-Azerbaijani dispute, and its role in ending the Tajiki civil war in 1994 are consistent with this pattern of behavior. More remarkably, far from agitating for change, Tehran seems quite content for Moscow to continue to underwrite the security of the former Soviet territory and to maintain its military presence in the newly liberated Muslim territories of Asia. Tehran's own strategy toward the Soviet successor states is to underline, rather than undermine, the status quo.

Even on the Arab-Israeli peace process, Tehran's position remains surprisingly unchallenging, considering its policies of the 1980s in the Levant. Despite the Tehran-sponsored international conference in October

1991 on Palestine by the rejectionist Arab forces, Iran's vociferous condemnation of the Madrid peace process, and Iranian unwillingness to accept Israeli sovereignty, little active Iranian opposition (or at least concrete examples of such opposition) has been in evidence.[24] In view of the importance of the U.S.-sponsored peace initiatives in the region, it is rather remarkable that Tehran has not as yet engaged in active and total mobilization against the process. Unquestionably, Tehran recognizes fully that the process (and its direction and outcome) is of vital importance to all the regional actors (including Iran itself), for it has already shown itself to be the most important development in the region since the 1940s and one that has the potential to change the entire matrix of the Middle East subsystem. And yet, the president continues to preach patience with regard to the Arab-Israeli peace process: "As to the question of how we can regain the right of the Palestinians, the plan is extensive, and it requires the resources of the Islamic world. . . . Unfortunately, there is division in the Islamic world today. There is no need to go to war [with Israel]. But the allegation that we intend to defend justice by resorting to terrorism is a lie. No one can achieve anything that way."[25]

Away from its regional preoccupations, Tehran continues to manifest its pragmatism and its desire fully to reintegrate into the international system by continuously promoting bilateral and multilateral cooperation in economic, political, and cultural fields. Its active participation in UN-sponsored events, such as the international population conference in Cairo in September 1994, where it was one of few Muslim countries to take part, also demonstrates this strategy.

In the last analysis, a survey of Iran's foreign policy behavior illustrates that even if a revolutionary regime coming to power proves to be religion-based and initially nonconformist, its inability to change the system eventually forces it to reach an accommodation with the existing order. It thus learns to expend its energies on either finding a new place for itself in the existing international system or tries to recover lost ground. The Iranian case shows that such imperatives can override all other considerations, even the revolutionary ideals and Islamicizing mission of the regime in charge. In the end, all "living and breathing" revolutionary regimes will of necessity have to find a modus operandi—to compromise—with the complex set of social, cultural, and historical pressures at home as well as with the uncompromising external environment in which they find themselves. Not surprisingly, Tehran has been keen to get involved in the emerging New World Order—and no longer seems interested in either trying to change the rules of the game, subverting the system, or indeed undermining the regional order.[26]

Recognition of such realities forced the leader of the Iranian Islamic regime, Ayatollah Khomeini, to drink from the "poisoned chalice" in 1988 and has compelled his successors to try and minimize the threats to the republic through consolidation of the country's relations with its international partners in trade, religion, politics, and culture. Although this move in itself may be a revolutionary transformation for an avowedly anti-West and anti-East regime, I submit that such policies are a far cry from the original aspirations of the Islamist revolutionaries who overthrew the Pahlavi monarchy in Iran and looked forward to the establishment of an Islamic *internationale.* The Iranian case suggests that there seems to come a point after which a strictly Islamic foreign policy code of behavior becomes inoperable.

Economic Policies of the Republic

As self-sufficiency was one of the main slogans of the revolution, representing the deeply felt desire of a nation to reduce its dependence on the West, the republican leadership embarked on a strategy of internalizing as much as possible the essentials of a successful import-substitution industrialization process. Following on from the same industrialization tradition established by the Shah's pro-Western and capitalist regime, the state came to play a central role in the republic's economic life. Constitutionally, the state was given the responsibility for the control of the "natural monopolies" as well as direct ownership of the strategic sectors and the commanding heights of the economy. In practice, the state also came to dominate the republic's politico-economic system. The revolution did not much alter the previous economic practice whereby the government made the major investment decisions and had them implemented through the state-controlled enterprises. Although the revolutionary elite did not put into motion the implementation of an alternative economic system when they took power, through implementation of the 1979 law of "Protection and Development of Iranian Industries" they did bring under state control the properties of dozens of Iran's richest and most powerful families, giving the state the control of almost all of the country's large and modern factories, banks, insurance companies, and extractive and agribusiness industries.

The nationalizations also passed to the state the decisionmaking process regarding finance and commercial strategies. Although the net result of these measures was a much greater role for the state, this did not mean either the collectivization and "socialist nationalization" of bourgeois property or indeed the demise of private capital and the decline of the bourgeoisie. In practice, the Islamic state did not redress the societal imbalance between labor and capital or institute reforms (in landholdings and industrial organization, for instance) substantial enough to revolutionize Iran's socioeconomic realities.[27] The revolutionary regime's endorsement of capitalist relations of production, moreover, meant that even at the height of its populist phase, and despite some early gains in reducing the gap between the haves and the have-nots, the state did not attempt major amendments of the country's social structure in favor of the deprived classes.[28]

In concrete terms, the Islamic revolutionaries' main achievement in the 1980s was to alter the relations of production to reflect the country's new (post-Pahlavi) political realities, and at the same time to enhance the state's relative autonomy in the uninterrupted process of capitalist accumulation.

The reversal since 1989 of the populistic economic measures of the early 1980s marks the transient nature of the Islamists' revolutionary economics. Just a decade after the revolution, the post-Khomeini government initiated a complete reform of the economy in a laissez-faire direction. Privatization of many of the nationalized and confiscated industries and businesses; large-scale deregulation of economic activity; reduction in subsidies for foodstuffs and other basic necessities of life; establishment of a number of transnational, capital-oriented, free-trade zones; support for export-oriented development; and the rejuvenation of the forgotten Tehran stock market marked a return to a Western style of economic organization and indeed underlined the disappearance of the mirage of an alternative economic system in Iran. The icing on the cake of the new government's many initiatives came in the form of encouraging direct foreign investment in the country. To whet the appetite of investors, the government raised the limit of foreign ownership from 35 percent (established by the Shah's regime) to 49 percent and more, thus giving a virtual controlling interest of a project to the foreign investor,[29] and also allowed foreign (and expatriate Iranian) capital investment in the Tehran stock market. By the mid-1990s, foreign investors were also being encouraged to invest in Iran's capital and infrastructural projects and in the heavy and hydrocarbons-related industries, hitherto regarded as "strategic sectors" and as such closed off to private investors. The usual guarantees to foreign investors of protection from hostile legislation, tax holidays, subsidized infrastructure and energy inputs, cheap labor, and the like were also being extended.[30]

Whether the economic liberalization drive of the early 1990s was a symptom of the republic's policy mistakes in the 1980s or the dawn of a new beginning for the Islamic Republic was by this time rather irrelevant. For observers, however, the issue is an important one, particularly as one attempts to put the Iranian revolutionary experience in the broader context of socioeconomic change in late-industrializing countries. Some analysts argue that the trend of economic policy in Iran is a testimony to the nonviability of any so-called Islamic economic system. In reality, by 1989 Iranian policymakers had reached a crossroad at which all remaining routes were ending in economic reform strategies. In the absence of other workable models, the elite was finding it difficult to guarantee the system's survival, let alone its prosperity. In revolutionary Iran, then, we will be hard pushed to find economic organizations and patterns of economic behavior that do not resemble the practice of capitalism elsewhere in the developing world. They diverge in almost every detail from the ideal-type Islamic models discussed by such commentators as Muhammad Umer Chapra.[31]

An examination of the foreign trade regime of the Islamic Republic as a barometer of its international economic profile is also crucial to understanding the behavior of such Islamist states in the international capitalist system. The Iranian Islamists had vowed to make the country more self-reliant and less dependent on foreign inputs. Part of this process involved taking the political decision to change the country's foreign trade patterns, with a new emphasis on trade ties with other Muslim countries, to turn import patterns away from "luxury" goods, and to alter the composition of the country's imports.[32] Despite the stated objective of changing fundamentally the composition of the country's exports and reducing the country's concentration on the traditional handful of commodities, however, the proportion of non-oil goods in Iran's total exports has been rising rather slowly (though surpassing the $3.5 billion mark by the mid-1990s) and the variety of non-oil export products has not substantially changed since the 1970s. Iran has become the second largest producer of petrochemicals in the Middle East, for example, but remains one of the main exporters of carpets and dried fruits and nuts in the world.

Nor have Tehran's Third World partners changed very dramatically since the revolution, despite the fact that the volume of trade with some of the same countries has increased substantially.[33] In the context of trade with the industrialized countries, however, significant changes are discernible. First, between 1979 and 1989 the republic expanded its ties with a number of Eastern European countries, particularly Romania, East Germany, Czechoslovakia, Hungary, and the Soviet Union. Nevertheless, as Hooshang Amirahmadi notes, until 1983 none of these countries had found a place among Iran's top fifteen trading partners.[34] Second, Western European countries have been particularly important to the republic as sources of technology and know-how in addition to being key trading partners.

In practical terms, Tehran's foreign policy strategy of "neither East nor West" did not preclude commercial contacts with Western or Communist countries. In fact, by aiming to maintain the correct balance between the two blocs and sufficient distance from the United States, the republic did attempt diversification of its trading partners. What it was unable to manage, however, was a severing of the country's trading links with members of the Organization for Economic Cooperation and Development (OECD). As OECD figures indicate, throughout the 1980s Iran remained in the top six OECD markets in the Middle East. Since the mid-1980s, on average about 8.5 percent of the OECD's total Middle East exports have gone to Iran.[35] By 1990, Iran's imports (of more than $10 billion) from the OECD made it the bloc's third largest trading partner in the region (after the pro-Western countries of Saudi Arabia and Turkey). Indeed, the depth of connections was such that, with the economic liberalization policies of the first Rafsanjani administration, Iran's imports from OECD countries grew dramatically in the early 1990s—in 1990 growing faster than OECD imports to other Middle Eastern countries. In that year, 76.2 percent of Iran's imports originated from the industrialized world. This figure was higher than that for Egypt (76.0 percent) and more or less equivalent to that for Saudi Arabia (76.6 percent).[36]

As already mentioned, over the years the composition of Iran's OECD partners has changed, reflecting by and large Iran's political preferences. By the second half of the 1980s, the smaller OECD countries accounted for over one-third of Iran's OECD imports. Still, much of Iran's trade remained with the developed capitalist world. So, for instance, West Germany accounted for 18.3 percent of Iran's total imports in 1986, compared with 19.4 percent in 1977, and Italy and the United Kingdom for 6.5 percent (5.6 percent in 1977) and 6.8 percent (6.9 percent in 1977), respectively.[37]

Interestingly, this pattern has been strengthened by President Rafsanjani's economic reform policies. In 1991, for instance, German exporters accounted for 26.5 percent of Iranian imports and Japan's market share stood at 16.1 percent (compared with 26.8 percent in 1980), followed by Italy (11.9 percent), Britain (5.9 percent), France (5.8 percent), and the United States (3.4 percent).[38] Together these six countries accounted for 70 percent of Iran's total imports. After the revolution the OECD countries continued to maintain their leading economic role in Iran, accounting for approximately 60 percent of Iran's exports and imports in the late 1980s, compared with 86 percent of its exports and 78 percent of its imports in 1977.[39]

Looking through other important features of the Iranian economy, one is struck by how unrevolutionary post-Pahlavi economic policy has been. One important indicator in this regard is the imports-to-GDP ratio (calculated by dividing total nonmilitary imports by the country's gross national product), which shows an economy's import dependence. In Iran the figure has not been substantially reduced since the revolution and has continued to hover around the 12–15 percent figure. Thus it is lower than the 18 percent average for the 1973–1977 period but still very high considering the general lowering of imports for a time after the revolution.

Other data indicate that the level of consumer goods imports has not been reduced substantially either. In fact, the proportion of such goods rose from an annual average of 17 percent of total imports in the mid-1970s to about 26 percent some ten years later.[40] Thus, the desire to move away from consumerism and dependence on consumer goods imports has not been fulfilled.[41]

Equally important are significant increases in Iran's food imports, costing on average between $2.5 billion and $3 billion in annual imports, despite the increases in agricultural output since the late 1980s. In addition, intermediate products have continued to account for over 50 percent of the country's total nonmilitary imports since the revolution, a figure almost identical to that of the 1970s.[42] According to the Economics and Finance Ministry, Iran's intermediate products imports still require substantial foreign currency outlays—some $3 billion per annum in the mid-1990s.[43]

That the war economy of the 1980s imposed severe restrictions on Iran's revolutionary plans, forcing the leadership to make regrettable compromises, is indisputable. On food imports, for instance, it would be perfectly true to state that Iran's situation worsened after the revolution owing to a number of independent factors: high population growth rates (of over 3 percent per annum for much of the 1980s), lack of investment in agriculture, absentee landlordism and neglect of agricultural lands, rapid permanent migration to the cities, and war damage to some of the country's fertile lands. But some of these problems could have been alleviated through proper planning, on the one hand, and the implementation of a comprehensive land reform policy to transfer land to cooperatives and landless peasants, on the other. In view of differences of opinion at the elite level, the reforms were not implemented systematically. The inconsistency caused confusion in the industry and many policy changes.

On the broader economic front, consumption patterns did not change sufficiently to usher in an era of revolutionary transformation. Luxury goods were harder to come by, but largely as a consequence of import restrictions imposed by the populist government. The shortages of foreign currency, the diversification of resources away from the civilian sector in order to meet the war effort, and the need to proceed with the old strategy of import-substitution industrialization were principal reasons for the relative decline in such imports. But on the whole, all that can be said of the regime's economic policies is that the Islamic Republic's leaders may have indisputably changed the country's position in the world economy, but evidently not its orientation. As we have seen, like its foreign policy, the republic's economic strategy since the late 1980s has been "restructured," marking the Islamic regime's final departure from revolutionary economics and its determined move toward "economic realism."

Rights and Religion in the Islamic Republic

The need for democratic government, freedom (of action and expression), and mass participation in the politics of the country were the key political demands of the masses during the revolution. Two important limitations imposed on the meaning of the word "freedom," however, caused tension among the revolutionary forces. Freedom had two legitimate realms in the Islamic Republic, denoting both the right to organize within the republic's permissible structures and a religious concept.[44] Thus, to function and propose ideas outside of the Islamic legal framework were increasingly being considered illegal.

The uniqueness of the Iranian case lies perhaps in the country's profound ideological opposition to Western democratic principles and its establishment of Shi'a-based Islamic laws as the foundation of the new governing regime. The point is illustrated by the Islamist position on the question of sovereignty: If the people have no sovereignty and sovereignty is said to belong only to God, then it stands to reason that his representatives on earth—the clerics—should have control over the state and in directing social change. This view is precisely the basis of Ayatollah Khomeini's interpretation of Islamic governance and the principle of *velayat-e faqih*.

The commensurate increase in the political power of the clergy, in tandem with the demise of the country's other revolutionary and democratic forces, therefore, should not come as a surprise. The coercive power of the state was utilized to increase the power of the clerical elite within the system. In a more structural way, it was also used to consolidate the new government's control over the country. The clerics' eventual near-monopolization of power brought with it the use of similar control mechanisms developed by the Shah's rule, and the utilization of the machinery of the old regime in turn meant that the clerics did not need to develop a political structure of their own to consolidate their power.

The revolution also provided the clerics with the golden opportunity of reversing the historical trend by putting an end to the nationalization of Islam and enabled them to proceed with the Islamization of the nation. Even the country's frequent and uninterrupted elections came to serve the purpose of this Islamization process. All candidates to the Majlis (and for the presidency), for instance, have to pass through a complex vetting procedure by the religious and political establishment before being permitted to contest in elections. This process has served to ensure that no "undesirables" get elected to high office. It has also helped to define the scope and nature of the debate surrounding national issues by keeping it within the given boundaries of the *nezam* (system).

It was through such mechanisms that the founders of the Islamic Republic maintained full control over the affairs of the country. In post-Khomeini Iran, too, the same emphasis on *yekparchegi* (loosely translated as "uniformity") and *vahdat-e kalameh* (spiritual unity), and skillful manipulation of the restructured power hierarchies of the republic, has brought to the pinnacle of power those clerical figures who have tried to make the system function effectively through the introduction of wide-ranging reforms. But the "new" leaders do not constitute a new political elite, and as such they have shown a reluctance to open up the political system to non-Islamists. Thus, despite the emergence of a more open political atmosphere since the early 1990s, many of the levers of control have remained in place.

In this regard, at least, change has been slow in coming and patterns of continuity with the Khomeini era are much in evidence. In the political realm, the preservation of the *nezam* has taken precedence over all other matters, and here only those political reforms that can strengthen the republic have been considered worthy of examination. Although President Rafsanjani's (probable) establishment of the republic's first elite-generated mass political party[45] since Ayatollah Khomeini's death may help to change the pattern of political interactions in the late 1990s, it is too soon to argue that such a development would automatically or unintentionally lead to more openness in the political arena to non-Islamist platforms. But if it does, and the president's initiative leads to a broadening of the political base and a release of alternative political energies, then the most important of the republic's sacred cows (regarding political power) would have been abandoned, and with it more of the essentially Islamic nature of the regime. Such an elite-initiated development, of course, would be inconsistent with accepted norms about the behavior of Muslim fundamentalists and would contradict the view that Islamists desire only to monopolize all power once in office.

Conclusions

The fact that the Iranian revolution did not use socialist ideals and terminology, and the fact that it was not led by the "oppressed" classes, has enabled me to examine it as a "political" rather than a "social" revolution.[46] Still, it had a very profound impact on the socioeconomic environment of Iran.

The features of the Iranian case chosen for further comment in this chapter have brought to the fore the endemic difficulties, in analytical terms, of dealing with the process of change—whether political, social, or economic—in the modern world. With very few exceptions, until recently such changes in the developing countries were usually socialist-indexed. What the case of Iran illustrates is that the change need not be exclusively socialist. More precisely, Iran's revolutionary alternative, far from being universal, found expression in an exclusivist model stemming from the religious traditions of the country and the religious leadership's concept of an Islamic state. It could be maintained, therefore, that this revolution is by its own admission exclusivist and not universalist. But this has not reduced its relevance, nor indeed its impact, on the Middle East region.

Ian Roxborough notes that the "weakness of any domestic bourgeoisie in [the developing] countries has enabled the elites which have come to occupy state power to transform themselves into new dominant classes."[47] In postrevolutionary Iran, the ulama cannot be said to have become a new "class" (in its Marxian sense) but unquestionably have been the dominant elite in terms of control of political power. By virtue of this dominant position they have been able to extend their influence (and in many instances control as well) to almost all aspects of life in Iranian society, even when not physically present at the decisionmaking level, and to secure a privileged position for themselves and for the merchant bourgeoisie, which traditionally congregates around the bazaar.

Second, the very policies of Iran's post-Khomeini leadership have been designed to strengthen the presence and role of the Iranian bourgeoisie, going as far as inviting back to the Iranian market the exiled comprador classes, which had closely associated themselves with the old, pro-Western, Pahlavi regime. The Iranian political elite thus can be said to be undertaking a "passive revolution" in the 1990s.[48] This passive revolution has necessarily required the return of the expropriated bourgeois property to its original owners, or to the new class of potential entrepreneurs. The strategy of the Iranian government has been motivated not only by the domestic difficulties in dealing with the task of economic regeneration, but also by Iran's inability to recover its former position in the international division of labor. Iranian leaders, never having encouraged departure from the international capitalist system, have found it necessary substantially to again open up to that same global system in order to improve the national economy. In this realm, Islamic economic and political principles cannot inform the policies of the republic. Nor have they. Paradoxically, rejuvenation of the economy, if it happens, in turn could secure the position of the "Islamic" elite and also minimize the threats to it from below.

Perhaps the most lasting impression of the revolution and of Islamic governance in Iran is in the cultural arena. Although much of the realm of practice of government has remained "secular" in form and content, and seems to have been accepted by a great proportion of Iranian Islamists, the desire to Islamicize has found its voice in the social (and within that mainly the cultural) realm. This desire finds expression, across the Islamic ideological spectrum, in rejection of and confrontation with Western cultural influences and values. At the end of the day, the desire to blunt the cultural impact of the westernization process in the Middle East might signify the sum agenda and thirst for power of political Islam. As we have seen in Iran, the urge to create a new moral order fuels the Islamists' drive for control of the state. As such, once in power, such elites seem to devote considerable resources to combating the "cultural imperialism" of the West, and little to the pursuit of finding a new, clear-cut agenda for socioeconomic transformation of their societies.[49]

In the final analysis, what the case of Iran illustrates is that for Third World countries, socialism clearly is not the only route to political independence and freedom of action in the international arena (a criterion that has traditionally been regarded as providing the precursor to economic sovereignty). Nonsocialist alternatives, however, do not necessarily lead to economic independence from the Western-dominated international system.

Notes

1. As the intention here is to provide a hardnosed survey of the Iranian experience as an alternative model for economic and political development, of necessity I have had to take as given the progress the republican regime has made in a number of fields, including rural development, the provision of basic education, and achievements in capital and infrastructural projects, and in the sphere of formal politics (regular and relatively open elections, respect for formal divisions of power as enshrined in the constitution, an independent and powerful judiciary, an independent foreign policy, and so on).

2. Interestingly, though, in some areas of public policy the reach of religion and *shari'a* is quite limited, particularly over matters having to do with population and birth control measures, such as free distribution of contraceptives, and aspects of family law.

3. See Judith Miller, "Faces of Fundamentalism: Hasan al-Turabi and Muhammed Fadlallah," *Foreign Affairs* 73, No. 6, November/December 1994: 123–142.

4. John L. Esposito, *The Islamic Threat: Myth or Reality?* (Oxford: Oxford University Press, 1992).

5. Ayatollah Imami Kashani's Friday prayer sermon, SWB, ME/0600, October 3, 1989.

6. President Rafsanjani has argued, for example, that in theory Islam has a mixed economy that has been struggling against both the communist and capitalist modes of production: "We were in any case in practice confronting the two schools of Marxism and capitalism. . . . The 'mixed economy' of Islam is not the same as the formal socialism that existed in the world or the capitalism that exists today. It is not comparable to either of them. [Islam] has an economy which is free in many ways and indeed respects private ownership. . . . But, on the other hand, it respects the rights of the state as well." *Ettela'at International,* January 3, 1995.

7. Ayatollah Khomeini himself, in a detailed interview after the revolution's victory, stated, "The sole determining principle in a government based on towhid is divine law, but that is the expression of divine will, not the product of the human mind." See *Islam and Revolution: Writings and Declarations of Imam Khomeini,* translated by Hamid Algar (Berkeley, Calif.: Mizan Press, 1981), p. 330.

8. These criteria have been adapted from S. Neuman, "The International Civil War," *World Politics,* No. 1, 1948–1949, p. 333.

9. See Mohsen M. Milani, "The Transformation of the *Velayat-e Faqih* Institution: From Khomeini to Khamenei," *The Muslim World* 82, Nos. 3–4, July–October 1992, pp. 175–190.

10. Mehdi Mozaffari, "Changes in the Iranian Political System After Khomeini's Death," *Political Studies* 41, No. 4, December 1993, pp. 611–617.

11. One aspect of the problem has become apparent over the issue of *Marja'aiyat* (source of emulation) in the Shi'a world, itself arising out of the death of a number of senior Ayatollahs (Ayatollah Ozmas) in recent years. Araki, the latest Grand Ayatollah to die, died in late 1994, a year after Golpaygani's death had precipitated the Marja'aiyat crisis. The problem for the republic's post-Khomeini elite has been how to continue to legitimize the role of the *faqih* as a politico-spiritual authority, and indeed the entire *velayat-e faqih* system, if the position of *Marja'aiyat* (the highest Shi'a authority) was not held by the recognized (Iranian) *faqih* but entrusted to other senior Ayatollahs (some of whom, of course, were not Iranian and resided in the Arab world).

12. They have been doing this despite their narrow vision and other shortcomings. See Olivier Roy, *The Failure of Political Islam* (Cambridge: Harvard University Press, 1994), for an analysis of the Islamists' intellectual and political shortcomings.

13. Shaul Bakhash, "Iranian Politics Since the Gulf War," in Robert B. Satloff (ed.), *The Politics of Change in the Middle East* (Boulder: Westview Press, 1993), p. 82.

14. Ibid., p. 81.

15. This policy has been shown by Tehran's withdrawal from the U.S.-sponsored politico-military CENTO structure in March 1979, its dismantling of U.S. monitoring stations along its northern border, and its cancellation of some $10 billion worth of weapons orders from the United States and Britain.

16. Rouhollah K. Ramazani, "Iran's Foreign Policy: Both North and South," *The Middle East Journal* 46, No. 3, Summer 1992, pp. 393–412.

17. Anoushiravan Ehteshami, *After Khomeini: The Iranian Second Republic* (London: Routledge, 1995).

18. Shireen T. Hunter, *Iran After Khomeini* (New York: Praeger, 1992).

19. Ali Rahnema and Farhad Nomani, *The Secular Miracle: Religion, Politics and Economic Policy in Iran* (London: Zed Press, 1990).

20. Said Amir Arjomand, "A Victory for the Pragmatists: The Islamic Fundamentalist Reaction in Iran," in James P. Piscatori (ed.), *Islamic Fundamentalisms and the Gulf Crisis* (Chicago: The American Academy of Arts and Sciences, 1991), p. 65.

21. *Gulf States Newsletter* 20, No. 503, January 30, 1995.

22. For interpretations of Tehran's behavior toward the Soviet successor states and the implications of the demise of the Soviet Union for Iran, see Anoushiravan Ehteshami (ed.), *From the Gulf to Central Asia: Players in the New Great Game* (Exeter: University of Exeter Press, 1994), and M. Mesbahi (ed.), *Central Asia and the Caucasus After the Soviet Union: Domestic and International Dynamics* (Gainesville: University of Florida Press, 1994).

23. See summary of Deputy Foreign Minister Mahmoud Vaezi's comments in this regard in the Iranian journal *Central Asia and Caucasia Review* 2, No. 4, Spring 1994.

24. This said, Iran has never disguised its support for some Islamist movements in the Levant. These include the Lebanese Hezbollah and, less emphatically, some Palestinian Islamists, such as Hamas. None of the Islamist movements in the Levant, however, owe their existence to Iran, and they continue to survive and prosper thanks to their ability to exploit existing regional tensions and the support they receive from local populations and other Arab patrons. It is fair to say that although Tehran provides funds and helps to supply these groups, its ability to direct, let alone control, the Levant-based Islamists is quite limited.

25. Quoted in *U.S.-Iran Review* 3, No. 1, January 1995, p. 11.

26. I would like to argue that Iran's involvement in low-intensity conflicts (such as in south Lebanon), and its resort to political violence as a method of eliminating and intimidating its opponents, is not inconsistent with Tehran's desire to find a place at the New World Order dinner table.

27. Rahnema and Nomani, *The Secular Miracle*.

28. Vahid F. Nowshirvani and Patrick Clawson, "The State and Social Equality in Post-Revolutionary Iran," in Myron Weiner and Ali Bauazizi (eds.), *The Politics of Social Transformation in Afghanistan, Iran and Pakistan* (Syracuse: Syracuse University Press, 1994).

29. Since the early 1990s the government has been allowing 100 percent ownership of assets by foreign investors as well. For economic reform details, see Ehteshami, *After Khomeini.*

30. *Kayhan Havai,* February 8, 1995.

31. Muhammad Umer Chapra, *Islam and the Economic Challenge* (Leicester: The Islamic Foundation, 1992).

32. Jahangir Amuzegar, *Iran's Economy Under the Islamic Republic* (London: I. B. Tauris, 1993).

33. International Monetary Fund, *Direction of Trade Statistics* (Washington, D.C.: IMF, 1989 and 1992). Trade with the following countries did improve after the revolution: Turkey, Pakistan, Argentina, South Korea, Brazil, Singapore, Thailand, Malaysia, and China. Little expansion in Iran's trade with other Third World countries, even the Muslim ones, has been registered, however.

34. Hooshang Amirahmadi, *Revolution and Economic Transition: The Iranian Experience* (New York: State University of New York Press, 1990).

35. Organisation for Economic Co-operation and Development, *Statistics of Foreign Trade, Series A* (Paris: OECD Secretariat, 1986); *Statistics of Foreign Trade, Series A* (Paris: OECD Secretariat, 1987); *Statistics of Foreign Trade, Series A* (Paris: OECD Secretariat, 1988); *Statistics of Foreign Trade, Series A* (Paris: OECD Secretariat, 1991).

36. Committee for Middle East Trade, "Middle East Trade with the World, 1990," *COMET Bulletin*, No. 35, January 1992. Between 1989 and 1991 the OECD countries doubled their exports to Iran, matching the peak 1978 levels in real terms. See Committee for Middle East Trade, "OECD Exports to the Middle East, 1991," *COMET Bulletin*, No. 37, September 1992.

37. Amirahmadi, *Revolution and Economic Transition*, p. 231.

38. Committee for Middle East Trade, "OECD Exports to the Middle East, 1991," *COMET Bulletin*, No. 37, September 1992.

39. International Monetary Fund, *Direction of Trade Statistics* (Washington, D.C.: IMF, 1986), and *Direction of Trade Statistics* (Washington, D.C.: IMF, 1989).

40. Kamran Mofid, *Development Planning in Iran: From Monarchy to Islamic Republic* (Wisbech, Cambridgeshire: Menas Press, 1987).

41. Amuzegar, *Iran's Economy Under the Islamic Republic*.

42. Central Bank of Iran, *Annual Report and Balance Sheet* (Tehran: Central Bank of Iran, various years).

43. *Kayhan Havai*, February 1, 1995.

44. For an excellent discussion of these issues see Mohsen M. Milani, "Shi'ism and the State in the Constitution of the Islamic Republic of Iran," in Samih M. Farsoun and Mehrdad Mashayekhi (eds.), *Iran: Political Culture in the Islamic Republic* (London: Routledge, 1993), pp. 133–159.

45. Rumors began circulating in Tehran in late 1994 that the political arena was to experience significant developments before too long, as Hojjatoleslam Rafsanjani had indicated his support for allowing the emergence of political parties. To encourage this trend, highly placed individuals argued, he had already put plans into motion to found his own Western-style political party by the end of his second term of office as president.

46. I have used Guido Dorso's definition of a political revolution, who sees it "as entry into the ruling class of new recruits who expel a corrupt and restrictive political class, and social revolution as the wholesale replacement of the ruling class." Quoted by Mark N. Hagopian, *The Phenomenon of Revolution* (New York: Dodd, Mead, 1974), p. 105.

47. Ian Roxborough, *Theories of Underdevelopment* (London: Macmillan, 1986), p. 142.

48. The concept of passive revolution has been defined by I. Roxborough as "any attempt by an elite other than the bourgeoisie to use its control of the state to oversee an attempt at rapid economic development [in the case of Iran economic reconstruction] in which, by and large, bourgeois property is not totally expropriated." Ibid., p. 143.

49. Afsaneh Najmabadi, "Iran's Turn to Islam: From Modernism to a Moral Order," *The Middle East Journal* 41, No. 2, Spring 1987, pp. 202–217.

9

Islamist Movements in Historical Palestine

IYAD BARGHOUTI

Like other parts of the Middle East, historical Palestine has witnessed the dramatic growth of various Islamist movements. In the Occupied Territories, the Islamization of social, economic, and political institutions is accelerating. Previously existing Islamist movements, such as the Muslim Brotherhood, are becoming more active, and new movements, such as Hamas and the Islamic Jihad, have emerged. Though these movements are not isolated from similar movements elsewhere in the Muslim world, their development is a clear indication of the effects of the unique Palestinian experience under the ongoing Israeli occupation.

Inside Israel, the conditions of the Islamist movement are completely different than in the Occupied Territories. Working amidst a Muslim minority inside a Jewish state, the movement has been forced to select aims and methodology far different from those of Islamic movements elsewhere.

Historical Palestine consists of Israel and the Palestinian territories occupied in 1967. Because of its geographical proximity to Egypt, and the Palestinian political reality, Palestine was one of the first areas to be influenced by the contemporary Egyptian Islamist movement. The Egyptian Muslim Brotherhood (established in 1928) was attracted by the political realities and eventual crisis of Palestine in its early years. Consequently, the Brotherhood was the first religo-political movement to emerge in Palestine and had established several branches there before the founding of the State of Israel in 1948.[1]

The establishment of Israel led to crucial changes in Palestinian social and political structures. The majority of Palestinian land fell under Israeli control, Gaza was placed under Egypt, and the West Bank came under Jordanian rule, joining with the East Bank to form the Hashemite Kingdom of Jordan. In areas that came under Israeli control, all branches of the

Muslim Brotherhood were dissolved. In Gaza the movement continued to maintain strong relations with the Egyptian Ikhwan; whereas the branches in the West Bank combined with those in the East Bank to form one organization.

The Islamic Movement in the West Bank and Gaza Before Occupation

Like other political structures and movements, the Islamist movement was greatly affected by the political separation between the West Bank and the Gaza Strip. Thus, under Egyptian administration (1948–1967), the Gaza Strip maintained its Palestinian character, as did the Muslim Brothers' organization in Gaza. The latter's fate, especially in relation to the Egyptian regime, was linked, for better or for worse, with that of the Egyptian Muslim Brotherhood.

The Muslim Brothers in the West Bank integrated with the Muslim Brothers in Jordan to become the Jordanian Ikhwan. Other political factions with supporters in the West Bank demonstrated the same trend in that period. However, contrary to others, the Jordanian Muslim Brothers maintained harmonious relations with the Jordanian regime—particularly the king—even under difficult conditions. Indeed, the regime excluded the Ikhwan from its prohibition of political parties in the mid–1950s.

Because the political situations in Gaza and the West Bank were different, the orientation of the two Ikhwan movements on the Palestinian national issue was equally divergent. The Ikhwan in Gaza placed greater focus on the Palestinian cause than the Ikhwan in the West Bank. The activities of the former, especially in the 1950s, emphasized resistance against projects to settle Palestinian refugees and against internationalization of the Gaza Strip.

Although the membership of the Ikhwan did not differ significantly in size from that of other movements, the group garnered no support from the average citizen. Nationalist feelings and the great popularity of Egyptian President Nasser had an adverse impact on a movement popularly described as an agent of the West. This fact perhaps explains why, even today, the Islamist movement is more popular among the younger than the older generations.

The Islamist movement in the West Bank and Gaza also included the Islamic Liberation Party (ILP, or al-Tahrir). This party was established in 1953 in Jerusalem by Shaykh Taqi al-Din al-Nabhani. Al-Nabhani remained the leader of the party until his death in 1977, when he was succeeded by an old party member, Shaykh Abdul-Qadim Zallum. Although the party considers the Arab and Muslim world as a whole the "sphere of its activity," most of its members are concentrated in Jordan and the Occupied Territories.

The ILP was never legalized in Jordan. At times its members were persecuted by the regime, and many of its leaders and members were arrested along with members of other nationalist and leftist parties. However, this did not prevent the party from participating in parliamentary elections in Jordan in the 1950s. In these elections, one of the "historical" leaders of the ILP, Shaykh Ahmed al-Daur, was elected to the parliament; he served until the regime forced him to resign.

The ideology of the ILP differs from that of the Ikhwan. Essentially, the ILP advocates the revival of the classical Islamic institution of government—the Caliphate—and believes that the head of this institution, the Caliph, should lead Muslims in accordance with the Islamic *shari'a* and endeavor to spread the word of Islam throughout the world. The traditional ideology of the Muslim Brothers, however, seems to have emphasized Islamization of society as a prerequisite to Islamization of the state.

On the organizational level, the ILP is extremely centralized, with membership around the world following one set of orders coming directly from the leadership. With the Ikhwan, in contrast, local leadership has, to a large extent, the freedom to make many decisions. Furthermore, unlike the Muslim Brothers, who sought to establish social services institutions, the ILP placed the lot of society's reform on the shoulders of the Caliph. Consequently, whereas the Muslim Brothers were able to maintain close links with their grass roots through their social services institutions, the ILP seemed to have lost touch with most of its followers.

Politically, the ILP emphasized its fundamental ideology and principles rather than pragmatic considerations and objective material conditions.[2] Accordingly, the party explains most political conflicts as either a conspiracy of non-Muslims against Muslims or as a reflection of the competition between Britain and the United States after World War II.

The Islamist Movement in the Occupied Territories After 1967

The 1967 reunification of the land of historic Palestine under a single political power was one of the most significant outcomes of the third Arab-Israeli War. The political movements in the West Bank and Gaza, including the Islamist movement, were also united. At the same time, the Islamists who remained in Israel reestablished their movement, which had been dissolved in 1948. This movement remained independent despite the strong influences by its counterparts in the Occupied Territories.

The Islamist movement in the Occupied Territories confronted a changing situation after the 1967 Israeli occupation of the West Bank and Gaza. First, the occupation itself constituted a new reality to which all political movements had to adapt in one way or another. Second, Palestinian nationalism became the major power, holding authority similar to that of a state. Third, in the first phase, the Islamist movements lost ties with their outside leadership, after losing the direct presence of the Jordanian regime, with which they had aligned themselves.

When the occupation began, the Muslim Brothers and the ILP were the only existing Islamist movements. Two other movements were established after 1967: the Islamic Jihad movement in Palestine and the Islamic Resistance Movement (Harakat al-Moqawmah al-Islamiyya, or Hamas). These movements had very different ways of dealing with the occupation.

The Islamic Liberation Party

Although the ILP insisted on its view that the Palestinian problem was the responsibility of all Muslims around the world, its program was based on a belief that only through the creation of an Islamic state anywhere in the world could Palestine subsequently be liberated. Thus, the Islamic state remained the ILP's first goal. After freezing its activities in the Occupied Territories for many years, however, the ILP reactivated itself through ideological dialogues with other movements and began distribution of pamphlets and publication of the party magazine, *Al-Wa'i al-Islami* (The Islamic Conscience).

Yet, the ILP's position toward the PLO has not changed since the PLO's establishment in 1964. The party considers the PLO to have surrendered Palestine instead of liberating it, insisting that PLO supporters "disobeyed Allah and his messenger" and that it was forbidden (*haram*) for any Muslim to join, work with, or provide financial support to the PLO.[3] The ILP rejects all political attempts to resolve the Palestinian problem, including the Madrid conference, which it considers a clear case of treason, and automatically rejects any proposal that does not state that Palestine is an Islamic land.[4]

Muslim Brothers: "The Ikhwan"

Only after ten years of Israeli occupation did the Ikhwan reinitiate its activity, primarily through the establishment of Islamist institutions and through Islamic blocs that emerged in universities and institutes. In 1987, with the advent of the Intifada, the Ikhwan created Hamas as a means of national resistance against the occupation. Hamas gained popular acceptance and became the main competitor to the PLO in the occupied territories.

Hamas shares the Ikhwan's position on Palestine: It is an occupied Islamic land and must be returned to the Muslims through holy *jihad*.[5] It has not raised the slogan "Islamic state first," however, nor has it initiated military resistance against the occupation.

Shaykh Ahmed Yassin, a physically handicapped former schoolteacher from Gaza and founder and spiritual leader of Hamas, was sentenced to life imprisonment in Israeli prison in 1991.. Two years ago, the military wing of Hamas attempted to kidnap Israeli soldiers several times in order to demand his release. (The PLO also made this demand, during negotiations, to convince the public that it continued to represent all Palestinians, regardless of political orientation. Israel, of course, refused the PLO's demand.) One soldier was killed in one of these attempted kidnappings, and in response, Israel deported more than 400 supporters of Hamas and the Islamic Jihad to South Lebanon for more than a year. Among the deportees were tens of professors, doctors, engineers, and other intellectuals, indicating that the support for Islamists had spread to these sectors of society. The mass deportation of Islamists during the same period that the PLO was negotiating with the Israelis greatly enhanced public support for Islamist movements.

Hamas and the PLO

Hamas has made repeated affirmations of good intention toward the PLO[6] and declared its readiness to join its ranks if the latter would agree to Hamas's conditions.[7] Despite temporary improvements in relations between the two sides, however, Hamas's political positions since its inception indicate a continuance of competition rather than cooperation with the PLO. This competition manifests itself especially during periodic elections of the professional and mass bodies in the Occupied Territories, which are sometimes accompanied by violent clashes between the two groups.

Historically, the relationship between the PLO and Islamists has passed through a complex process. In the late 1970s, a period of leftist "threat," Fatah "gambled" on the Islamists and attempted to build good relations with them. Relations improved further between the two sides when the PLO left Beirut in 1982. As Palestinians began to fight amongst themselves and relations between the PLO and Syria deteriorated, the Ikhwan stood against the Abu Musa split from Fatah, not for ideological reasons but because Abu Musa was closer to Syria.[8] Currently, Hamas, Abu Musa, and other leftists are forming a united front to oppose the Palestinian-Israeli agreement.

Furthermore, Ikhwan–PLO relations are affected by PLO-Jordan relations. When the PLO and the Jordanian regime have good relations, PLO-Ikhwan relations improve, and vice versa. Ikhwan has always defended the need to maintain strong ties between Jordan and the West Bank for ideological and political reasons. That is why it opposed King Hussein's decision to disengage Jordan from the West Bank in 1988 and asked him to reconsider his position.[9]

Nonetheless, competition between the PLO and Ikhwan has been the dominant factor in their relationship, especially after the Islamists began their violent resistance to the occupation. For years, the nationalists had blamed the Islamists for their lack of resistance to the occupation. When the Islamists started their own military activity, however, the competition with the nationalists became more intense. After the signing of the Declaration of Principles between the PLO and Israel, the PLO stopped its armed struggle but the Islamists' use of armed resistance rose dramatically. This situation posed the nationalists with a very complex problem, particularly with regard to their new position as administrators of Gaza and Jericho.

In the 1992 Student Council elections at An-Najah University, the symbol used by Fatah candidates was the weapon, while the symbol used by Islamist candidates was the Qur'an. Ironically, in 1993 elections, the parties' positions were reversed.

In the Occupied Territories, elections in the various institutions have always been political in nature. Moreover, the results of the elections are used by political factions in the Occupied Territories as indicators of their strength and support among Palestinians. In the 1992-1993 elections, a systematic increase in Hamas's popularity was demonstrated, even in liberal institutions such as Bir Zeit University, with the group typically obtaining between 35 and 40 percent of the vote.

After the signing of the Declaration Of Principles, the Islamists and other opposition factions continued to gain popularity and a new political alliance emerged between the Islamists and the leftists (the Popular Front for the Liberation of Palestine, or PFLP [al-Jabha al-Sha'biyya Li Tahrir Falstin] and the Democratic Front for the Liberation of Palestine, or DFLP [al-Jabha al-Dimogratiyya Li Tahrir Falstin]). The supporters of this new alliance obtained the majority of the vote (52 percent) in Bir Zeit University student council elections. Hamas has proven that it is a pragmatic political movement ready to bypass ideology in order to obtain tangible results.

Islamic Jihad

Many organizations bear the name "Islamic Jihad." The one discussed here is the largest and most influential, the Islamic Jihad movement in

Palestine headed by Dr. Fathi Shaqaqi and Abdul-Aziz Odeh (both of whom were deported from the Gaza Strip to Lebanon by Israel in 1988). The Islamic Jihad aims to reunite religion and patriotism in Palestinian political life. The Jihad condemns the Ikhwan, the "traditional" Islamists, for their "artificial" separation of religion and nationalism.[10]

Many factors encouraged the establishment of the Islamic Jihad. First among these was the Muslim Brotherhood's emphasis on Islamization instead of resistance, until the late 1980s. Second was the effect of the Egyptian Jihad and the ideas of the famous Egyptian Islamist Sayed Qutb, which constituted a turning point in contemporary Islamist thought (many of Jihad's leaders, including Shaqaqi and Odeh, were students in Egypt when the Islamic Jihad became active there). Third was the impact of the Islamic revolution in Iran. It hardly seems coincidental that the Jihad was established in Palestine in 1979, the year that the revolution succeeded in Iran. Thenceforth, the Jihadists have always considered Iran a strategic base for Islamists in the world, and they supported Iran in its war against Iraq.

The Islamic Jihad believes that resistance against the occupation should have begun the moment the land was occupied. It disagrees with the ILP's position that establishment of an Islamic state is a prerequisite to the liberation of Palestine. Likewise, it opposes Ikhwan's view that the Islamization of society is a prerequisite to struggle against occupation.

The Islamic Jihad is known for its emphasis on military resistance over political activity, and the Jihad is generally respected for being more serious than other movements. It differs from Hamas in many respects, including its opinion of Arab regimes, which it regards as part of the "imperialist project" in the region.[11] The Jihad makes a firm distinction between the liberation of Palestine and the PLO's "secular" project, and it has never considered joining the PLO.

The Jihad typically criticizes other Islamists for neglecting the importance of the Palestinian cause. For Islamic Jihad, the Palestinian cause is the central cause for the Islamic nation. There are three reasons for this focus: first, on religious grounds, as Palestine is a holy land; second, for historical reasons, as Palestine was the West's entry point to the region; and third, for strategic considerations, as Israel poses a serious threat to the Palestinian people.

The Islamist Movement and the PLO After the Oslo Agreement

On September 13, 1993, in Washington, the Israeli government and the PLO signed an agreement to establish peace between the two sides. This agreement, known as the Oslo, or Gaza-Jericho First, agreement, changed relations between the PLO and Israel from complete antagonism to a kind of cooperation. At the same time, it changed relations between the PLO, which became the Palestinian Authority, and the other Islamist and leftist organizations, which became the Palestinian opposition.

The Islamist movements, including Hamas, the Islamic Jihad, and the Liberation Party, opposed the Oslo agreement and its consequences, but this opposition, for the most part, remained political and peaceful. Violence against the new Authority and its police, who moved from Tunis to Gaza and Jericho, was limited.

The situation did not prevent contact between the two sides completely, however. In spite of the fact that, according to the agreement, the Palestinian Authority was committed to full protection of the Israeli settlements in the territories of the Palestinian Autonomy, the opposition organizations carried out many military operations against the Israelis. Accordingly, the Authority arrested many supporters of Hamas, Islamic Jihad, and other groups. These arrests were limited and did not intensify the situation to a state of war between the two sides.

Actually, no one can guarantee the continuity of the state of balance in the relations between the Palestinian Authority and the opposition. The Authority faces huge daily pressures from Israel to restrain the opposition. At the same time, it seems that the opposition is not always willing to take into consideration the Authority's critical position under the terms of the agreement with the Israelis. Thus, the possibility of violent conflict between the two sides strongly exists.

The Islamist Movement Inside Israel

The few Islamist organizations established in Palestine prior to the formation of the State of Israel in 1948 were basically branches of the Muslim Brotherhood that emerged in various Palestinian cities and towns under different nominations from the early 1930s. One of these appeared between 1936 and 1939 in northern Palestine under the leadership of Shaykh Izz al-Din al-Qassam. The militant movement was created to oppose both the British Mandate and the Zionist movement.

The occupation of most of Palestine in 1948, and the subsequent mass immigration, was very destructive to Palestinian society and created a deep political vacuum for those Palestinians remaining inside the new Israeli state. All Arab political parties and movements ceased to function, with the exception of the Israeli Communist Party, which included both Arabs and Jews. For a period of time, this was the only movement in which Arabs were active and which worked for their national rights.

The initiation of the Islamic Da'wa organization (an Islamic missionary society) in Israel is credited to Abdullah Nimr Darwish from Kufr Qassem village (in the Triangle area in central Israel). Darwish continues to be regarded as the leader of the Islamist movement in Israel. He initiated Islamic activity in his village in the early 1970s after completing his education in the Islamic School in Nablus (West Bank). His efforts gradually succeeded, especially in the Triangle, and in the late 1980s, his following developed into a broad Arabic political movement in Israel.

In 1979, impressed by the success of the Islamic revolution in Iran, the Islamist Farid Abu Mukh established Usrat al-Jihad (al-Jihad cell), a radical Islamist group that initiated armed struggle against Israel. Darwish was sentenced to three years imprisonment for his contacts with this movement, and when released in 1984, had become a reformist Muslim. He subsequently formed al-Shabab al-Muslim (Muslim youth), a new reformist organization.

Al-Shabab al-Muslim did not discuss armed struggle against Israel but focused on creating an Islamic society and worked in accordance with Israeli law. Its ideology is quite similar to that of the Muslim Brotherhood, calling for the peaceful and gradual development of individuals and society toward Islam. This organization, which has branches in most Arab cities and villages in Israel, is the most important Islamist movement in Israel.

The emergence and growth of Islamist movements in the early 1970s may only be partly attributed to charismatic leaders such as Darwish and Shaykh Raed Salah, the mayor of Um al-Fahim. Their success was also due to the same factors that led to a general resurgence of Islam around the world (such as the Iranian revolution) and other international changes. But two local factors played a heavy role: first, contacts, after 1967, between Palestinians from the Occupied Territories and Arabs living inside Israel, in a period when the Occupied Territories were undergoing a period of intense Islamization; and second, the growth of Jewish fundamentalism in Israel.

The Movement's Concerns

Unlike Hamas, the Islamist movement in Israel did not issue a detailed program or charter specifying its aims and methodology, making it extremely difficult to analyze its positions and strategy. Indeed, these may only be searched in the declarations of the movement's leaders or its publications, such as *'Sawt al-Haq wal-Hurriya* (The Voice of Justice and Freedom, the movement's weekly newspaper) and *'al-Sirat* (The Way, its monthly periodical, which has ceased publication). The movement focuses its efforts in three major areas—cultural, social, and political activities—and targets Muslims in Israel. Culturally, the movement's work in Israel does not differ greatly from that of the Ikhwan elsewhere. Furthermore, both believe "Islam is the Solution" and do their utmost to encourage Muslims to increase their commitment to prayer in mosques and religious ceremonies; thus we note the establishment of institutes of religious instruction in the cities Um al-Fahim and Baqa al-Gharbiya.

In their effort to spread their Islamic ideology, Islamists forcefully condemn all other nationalist, secular, and socialist ideologies as well as the Israeli Communist Party (ICP). In fact, the Islamists exert great efforts to marginalize the ICP, which is perceived as their main competitor in their struggle to be recognized as the main representative power amongst the Arabs.[12]

The Islamists provide numerous social services to the Arab population, especially in those cities and towns where they rule the municipal councils. In the first term of Shaykh Raed Salah, the Islamist mayor of Um al-Fahim, the municipality built a library, nine preschools, a small hospital, several clinics, a drug abuse center, a sports center, and a five-story building housing a mosque. It also established computer training courses and voluntary work groups and provided assistance to the poor locally and to Palestinians in the Occupied Territories, especially during the Intifada.[13]

In Israel, the Islamist movement communicates with the Muslim population mainly through social activity. However, as the main political competitor for other factions, especially the ICP, the movement's political role remains the cornerstone in its evaluation by other factions. At present, the ICP remains the most influential power among the Arabs in Israel. The Islamist movement in Israel emphasizes three major areas of identification: international, regional, and local, in that order. The international sphere corresponds to the Islamic identity, the regional to the Arabic one, and the local to the Palestinian (denoting, in particular, the Palestinians residing in Israel). These emphases and their order of preference undoubtedly affect the political and ideological activity of the Islamist movement in Israel.[14] Thus, on the Islamic level, the movement reciprocates the solidarity of Islamists throughout the world. A case in point was its solidarity with Bosnia. The movement sent a large delegation to that country in 1992 and Islamist activists helped form a committee for the relief of Bosnians.[15] As the focus of Islamist activity comes closer to home, it becomes increasingly pragmatic and politically sensitive.

It should be noted that the Israeli government considers the Islamist movement's involvement in Bosnia quite low on the scale of political sensitivity, whereas positions toward the Intifada or the Gulf crisis and Iraq would be at the top of this scale. The Bosnian issue shares only the Islamic dimension; it is for positions in the national dimension that Israel may interpret any opposition as disloyalty. Thus one notes the quite "moderate" position of the Islamist movement during the Gulf crisis.

However, the movement's position on internal Israeli and Palestinian issues remain the substance of the movement. This is a touchstone that determines how committed the movement is to its Islamic ideology, on the one hand, and to the obligatory laws in their country of residence, on the other.

The Public Islamist Stance and the Israelis

In 1979 several Islamist leaders underwent extreme hardship for their rejection of, and military action (*jihad*) against, the state in which they lived. However, they subsequently moved toward the viewpoint that their organization must stay within the boundaries of legality in order to survive and develop.

In view of this shift, the Islamist leaders seemed to exploit every possible opportunity to confirm their willingness to abide by Israeli law. Darwish once said, "There is no discussion of the Islamic State in Israel, where Muslims are the minority. In Israel, Islam means Muslims living according to their religion and *shari'a* without opposition to Israeli law. . . . I acknowledge that we are a minority in Israel, but I am convinced that as a minority we have a real interest in preserving the law since it is the law itself, which protects the minority."[16]

This viewpoint led Islamist leaders to condemn any act of resistance implemented by Arabs against the Israeli army or institutions inside Israel. When three Islamists killed several soldiers during an attack on an Israeli base inside Israel, the Islamists were strongly criticized by Israeli media. In response, Islamist leaders exaggerated their reaction against the operation, emphasizing that they had no links to it. In another event, when Israeli Arab students in an Islamic college inside an Israeli Arab village were arrested, Darwish stated that the college must be closed if it was going to be a source of troubles for the movement. When students from the Occupied Territories who were studying in Um al-Fahim and Baqa were accused of recruiting their Israeli Arab colleagues, Darwish voiced his opposition to such moves, adding that conditions under occupation resulted in reactions that were inappropriate inside Israel. Darwish further stated that the fact that Islamist activity remained legal allowed the movement to strengthen and continue its struggle for the community's rights.[17] This opinion was typical of leaders of mainstream movements. Other leaders tried to prevent increased integration into the country's political life and adopted ideologies reflecting this view. These different viewpoints led to different positions on participation in local and Knesset elections.

It was much easier to ideologically justify participation in local elections than in national ones, where the legislative dimension and the required oath of national loyalty, such as the one required by the Knesset, complicated matters. Moderate Islamists often saw local elections as opportunities to serve the Arabs living in Israel. This explanation was not sufficient for the Islamic Jihad, however, which considered such a position a support for the government and "in contradiction with the Islamist movement's strategy which states that Palestine is an Islamic country" and accused the movement of "accepting Israeli law and co-operating with Israelis in order to pave a road!"[18]

The results of the local elections demonstrated the increasing influence of the Islamist movement among Muslims in Israel. In 1984 in the Triangle (where the movement was traditionally stronger and more liberal), Islamist leaders won the mayor's seat in one village and members' seats in two other councils. In 1989, out of forty-eight constituencies in Arab areas inside Israel, Islamists won the mayor's seat in five councils, one of them in Um al-Fahim—the largest city in the Triangle—after a bitter competition with leftist Knesset member Hashem Mahamid. In the most 1993 elections, the movement maintained its support, contradicting the position that it had gained influence only because it was in the opposition and that after holding power its popularity would wane. In addition, local Islamist authorities were reelected to their positions, and the movement proved its capacity to succeed and maintain its achievements.

Knesset elections stimulated far more debate than local elections, particularly because there was no consensus among leaders. The movement struggled for a path between participating in elections (developing its own slate of candidates to represent them) and calling upon members to boycott them. Because pragmatic leaders, headed by Shaykh Darwish, conflicted with the fundamentalists who sought ideological legality, the movement never took a conclusive position on Knesset elections. Shaykh Salah offered a compromise when he declared that the movement had decided not to participate in elections but called on supporters to vote according to their conscience.[19]

Shaykh Kamal al-Khatib, a radical leader in the movement, opposed participation in Knesset elections, arguing that there were far better ways to serve the Arabs in Israel and that the Knesset was founded to serve only Jewish Israelis.[20] Some believed it was better to remain in the opposition, as experience suggested that support for Arab political streams declined when they reached the Knesset and could not achieve anything or keep their promises to the people. Remaining a movement (instead of a political party bloc), they added, allowed more room to act in support of Palestinians in Israel and to minimize the effects of discriminatory policies in the country.[21]

Following the elections, there were rumors that some supporters of the movement had voted for the Arab Democratic Party, the Jewish religious movement *Shas*, and the Labour Party; the only candidates who received none of their votes were the leftists. Participation in Knesset elections was interpreted by many Islamists as recognition of the state, its sovereign rule, and non-Islamic law. Moreover, such participation forced the Islamist movement to deal with issues of the totality of a state, which was in contradiction with their very interests and beliefs and was bound to affect their influence among Muslims in Israel.

The Public Islamist Stance and the Palestinians

The Islamist movement in Israel has struggled with two problems. As an Arabic organization, the existence of Israel is in contradiction with its national ambitions, and as Islamists its ideology is in contradiction with the nature of the Israeli state. Hence, the movement faces a twofold dilemma when dealing with the Palestinian problem as a political issue. Islamists throughout the world believe the Palestinian problem is "an Islamic cause" and that historical Palestine is Islamic land. Ironically, this situation does not seem realistic for the Islamist movement inside Israel.

For Islamists inside Israel, the Palestinian-Israeli conflict is a struggle between the state in which they live and the people of which they are part, the Islamic ideology in which they believe, and the Zionist ideology which they at least refrain from publicly opposing. It is difficult for them to take a clear stance toward this conflict. Thus, leaders sometimes take contradictory positions or compromise between the radical fundamentalist stream and the pragmatic one.

Writings in *Sawt al-Haq wal-Hurriya*, the publication of the Islamist movement, have rejected all political resolutions of the Palestinian cause, insisting that Palestine should be for Muslims. The leadership of the movement, however, most often represented by Shaykh Darwish, has expressed a pragmatic position ("Two Peoples, Two States") closer to the position taken by the PLO and other political groups with the support of Arabs in Israel.

Hamas denounced Shaykh Darwish's declaration that a portion of Palestinian land might be conceded to achieve peace.[22] Its leaders stated that their position was not against Judaism but against the two-state solution and against recognition of and coexistence with Israel, as this path stands at odds with the Islamic opinion. Hamas also denied that Darwish represented the Islamist movement inside Israel.[23] This response by Hamas resulted in a crisis in relations between Darwish and the Islamists in the Occupied Territories, despite the fact that the Islamist movement in Israel supported the Islamists in the Occupied Territories, especially during the Intifada and the deportation of activists from Hamas and Islamic Jihad to South Lebanon.

Conclusion

There are two Islamist movements with Palestinian membership, one inside Israel and the other in the Occupied Territories. Although their members share the same nationality and ideology, the different political conditions have imposed divergent stances upon the two movements.

The Islamist movement in Israel must be much more pragmatic in order to survive and take part in the country's political atmosphere. Hence, the movement inside Israel does not take positions that contradict the Zionist "axioms" of the State of Israel. This explains why its position on the Bosnian question, for example, was clearer than its position on other issues such as Jewish immigration to Israel.

Although the basic slogan of the Islamist movement in Israel is "Islam is the Solution," the movement recognizes that Islam cannot solve the problems of a state that is for Jews throughout the world, but not for its own population. Thus the movement tends to limit its rhetoric to the Arab minority in Israel.

The Islamist movement in the Occupied Territories also has pragmatic tendencies. It is not shaped by the will of its occupying authority, Israel, however, but by the will of the Palestinian people, with their great desire to be free of occupation. Therefore, this movement has found itself obliged to act, either to accept or oppose, to ally or not to ally, not on an ideological basis but on a realistic, pragmatic basis to ensure, above all else, its own existence.

Notes

1. For more about the history of the Islamic movement in Palestine before 1948, see Iyad Barghouti, *Islamization and Politics in the Palestinian Occupied Territories* (Jerusalem: Al-Zahra Centre, 1990) (in Arabic).

2. Ahmed Fadil, "The Islamic Political Movements: Between Realism and Principles," *Al-Wa'y*, No. 45, January 1991, p. 23 (in Arabic).

3. ILP, "A Pamphlet Concerning the Aims of the Establishment of PLO," April 19, 1964 (in Arabic).

4. About the Palestinian Islamist position on the peace process, see Iyad Barghouti, "Palestinian Islamists and the Middle East Peace Conference," *The International Spectator*, No.1, January–March 1993, IAI, Rome.

5. *Hamas: The Charter*, August 14, 1988, p. 11 (in Arabic).

6. Ibid., p. 40.

7. Hamas, letter to the president of the Palestinian National Council (PNC), April 6, 1990 (in Arabic).

8. The Islamists at An-Najah University, *Communiqué: December 16, 1983* (in Arabic).

9. *Al-Nahar,* September 3, 1988 (in Arabic).

10. The Islamic Jihad, *The Main Principles of the Movement,* n.d., p. 4 (in Arabic).

11. "The Unity of the Islamic Movement: Toward a Better Way," *Al-Bayan,* No. 3, February 12, 1985, p. 2 (in Arabic).

12. Ibrahim Malek, *The Islamic Movement Between Fundamentals and Pragmatism,* Giv'at Habiba, 1990, p. 2 (in Arabic).

13. *Filistine al-Muslimah,* No. 10, 10th year, October 1992, p. 5 (in Arabic).

14. Mahmoud Mi'ari, "The Islamic Movement in Israel," *Shou'wn Filistiniyya,* Nos. 215–216, March 1991, p. 5 (in Arabic).

15. *Sawt al-Haq wa al-Hurriya,* October 9, 1992 (in Arabic).

16. Malek, "The Islamic Movement," p. 5.

17. *Al-Ittihad,* July 19, 1993 (in Arabic).

18. The Islamic Jihad, "Agreement on the Annexation and Canceling of the Conflict," pamphlet, n.d. (in Arabic).

19. Abdallah Ibrahim, "The Islamists in the Occupied Territories in 1948: What's the Position on the Knesset Elections?" *Filisine al-Muslimah,* No. 6, 10th year, June 1992, p. 16 (in Arabic).

20. Ibid.

21. Ibid.

22. *Davar,* November 10, 1992 (in Hebrew).

23. Hamas, communiqué dated March 9, 1992 (in Arabic).

10 ⚭

Sudan: Ideology and Pragmatism

ABDEL SALAM SIDAHMED

On June 30, 1989, the Sudanese parliamentary system collapsed for the third time in the country's independent history as a result of a successful military coup d'état. The coup, which toppled the civilian government of Prime Minister al-Sadiq al-Mahdi, was led by Brigadier Omar al-Bashir (since promoted to lieutenant general and appointed president of the republic).

After some initial hesitation and speculation, the Sudanese gradually realized that the new regime was either perpetrated or at least supported by the National Islamic Front (NIF, al-Jabha al-Qawmiyya al-Islamiyya)—the Islamist party that grew out of the Sudanese Muslim Brotherhood. Over the course of time, however, the question of whether the NIF had actually planned the takeover or engulfed the new regime after the success of the coup has become largely immaterial. For all practical purposes, the Sudanese state is now controlled by the NIF, administered by its inner circle of leaders and technocrats, and supported by its rank and file.

The fact that a contemporary Islamist movement has been able to seize power, even if through a military coup, is significant in a number of ways. In the first place, it represents a radical transformation of the Sudanese state and politics and is bound to have important implications for Sudanese society. Furthermore, it points to the ability of the NIF to accumulate political, social, and material resources and deploy them at the right moment to achieve power and sustain it against all odds.

Outside Sudan, the success of the NIF represents a breakthrough for the contemporary Islamist movements in the Sunni world of Islam and as such has great potential and implications for these movements. The Sudanese experience is viewed with great interest and enthusiasm by several Islamist movements in the region, as it provided them with a realistic model of an Islamist political order and not just a blueprint.

Yet, to what extent should we regard the present Sudanese regime as a "model Islamic order"? In this chapter I attempt a partial answer to this question through an investigation into the problematics of ideology and pragmatism of the NIF.

For the purposes of this treatment, ideology is defined as "a programmatic and rhetorical application of some grandiose philosophical system, which arouses men to political action and may provide strategic guidance for that action."[1] Such a definition involves three complementary categories: (1) a grandiose philosophical system; (2) a program derived from that system; and (3) a strategy of action for the realization of that program.

In the case of Islamism, the "grandiose" philosophical system is naturally Islam, which is often defined as "a religion and a way of life," or a "religion and a state." The program for all Islamist movements is the establishment of an Islamic state or order—or at least a state that enforces Islamic *shari'a* as the public law of the land. Finally, *jihad* (broadly defined as exertion of all necessary effort, including the use of force) may be regarded as the most classic Islamist strategy. Differences regarding the definition and pursuit of jihad notwithstanding, political activism has become the most common form of Islamist strategy since the foundation of the first Muslim Brotherhood organization by Hasan al-Banna in 1928.

As for pragmatism, in this chapter I adopt the everyday usage of the term as an attitude that emphasizes practical utility and expediency. With these conceptions in mind, I now turn to the investigation of the ideological discourses and pragmatic considerations of the NIF. To set the scene, however, it is necessary to give a brief historical account of the rise and development of the Sudanese Islamist movement.[2]

Background

The first unit of a Sudanese Muslim Brothers' organization appeared in April 1949, when one of the pioneers was appointed as "director general" by Hasan al-Banna, the founder and leader of the Egyptian Muslim Brotherhood. The Sudanese Muslim Brothers' organization was considered an organic extension of the Egyptian Muslim Brothers' Society.

Simultaneously, a faction of Sudanese students was introduced to the Muslim Brothers' doctrine while studying in Egypt. At another level, a spontaneous Islamic-oriented group appeared among the students of secondary schools and colleges, apparently with no connections to either of the two groups mentioned above. This indigenous group, which started to operate under the name Islamic Liberation Movement (Harakat al-

Tahrir al-Islami), must have been an outright reaction to the Communist monopoly of student activities at the time.

In August 1954 a conference was held and attended by representatives from the three main groups to assess possibilities of unification. The conference voted for the establishment of a unified Sudanese Muslim Brothers' organization (Ikhwan) based on the teachings of Hasan al-Banna, with a religo-political structure and the ultimate goal of an "Islamic state." Some of the leaders of the Islamic Liberation Movement who perhaps did not wholly share these principles broke out and formed their own organization, al-Jamma'a al-Islamiyya, which continued thenceforth under different names but without much influence.

Throughout the 1950s members of the Ikhwan remained ineffectual and divided regarding the group's identity and political strategy. They succeeded during the immediate postindependence era (1956–1958) in forging a temporary Islamist coalition pressing for the enforcement of an "Islamic" constitution. However, they were not able to transform that alliance into a durable political influence at the time. During the early 1960s the movement was able to gain a firm footing within the student movement, which henceforth became its stronghold. By the mid-1960s the movement emerged as a definite political party under an umbrella organization called the Islamic Charter Front (Jabhat al-Mithaq al-Islami), founded in December 1964 with the Ikhwan as its hard core. The same period witnessed the emergence of Hasan al-Turabi, the current leader, as the most influential figure in the movement.

Despite the increased politicization of the Muslim Brothers, as indicated by their participation in two general elections during the 1960s (1965 and 1968), they stayed on the periphery of the political system and their influence remained confined mainly to the student sector. The period, however, was not without achievements as far as Ikhwan strategy was concerned. The group managed to mobilize the public in a highly emotive campaign that resulted in banning the Communist Party of Sudan (CPS, al-Hizb al-Shuyu'i al-Sudani) on charges of atheism (1965). Furthermore, and largely through their agitation, the call for an "Islamic constitution" assumed center stage and the mainstream parties—the Umma Party (Hizb al-Umma) and the Democratic Unionist Party (DUP, al-Hizb al-Itihadi al-Dimografi)—were converted to it.[3]

Internally, however, the movement was still ridden with factionalism and uncertainty. Toward the end of the 1960s, differences crystallized around two tendencies: the "political" school, led by Hasan al-Turabi, which advocated that the movement throw its lot in the political sphere with the purpose of influencing public affairs and eventually achieving power as a prerequisite of Islamist transformation, and the "educationalist" tendency, led by a number of the movement's pioneers, which emphasized indoctrination and society's reform as a priority and said that the movement should preserve its puritanical image and refrain from overindulgence in politics. An extraordinary congress was held in April 1969 to resolve the differences, and Turabi's tendency prevailed.

A military coup on May 25, 1969 (led by Colonel Ja'far Nimeiri), forced the Ikhwan underground and froze its effective split into two groups for a while. During the lengthy period of Nimeiri's rule (1969–1985), the Ikhwan was subjected to varying situations and experiences and its fortunes underwent a radical transformation. It was converted from the tiny elitist group of the 1960s into a mass political movement by the mid-1980s.

At the outset, the coup of May 1969 represented a victory for the forces of radical secularism, which were increasingly marginalized by both the hegemony of the traditionalist parties (the Umma Party and the DUP) and their insistence on enforcing a permanent constitution based on "the teachings of Islam." Accordingly, during the first years of Nimeiri's regime the Ikhwan was opposed to it, as it represented a "Communist" takeover aimed at the Ikhwan's very extinction. This hostility continued even after the violent collision between the regime and the CPS in July 1971, which resulted in the oppression of the latter. The Ikhwan was actively involved in all attempts to overthrow the regime (1970, 1973, 1976) staged by the opposition coalition, the National Front, that grouped the traditionalist parties and the Ikhwan.

The National Front, which provided the "right-wing" opposition with a unified platform, was built on the basis of the common enmity to Nimeiri's regime and a common, though vague, identification with Islam. The understanding, at least of the Ikhwan, was that following the ousting of Nimeiri's regime, the parties of the National Front would share power on the basis of an Islamist program. The Ikhwan, however, soon realized that once Nimeiri was out of the way, they would most likely be reduced to a negligible minority in any emergent power arrangement or even excluded altogether. Furthermore, with the failure of the numerous attempts to overthrow the regime by force, the Ikhwan became doubtful about the utility of the National Front as its main platform of political activity.

For all these considerations, the leadership of the Ikhwan resolved to adopt a strategy for the movement to grow as an independent and influential political force competing for power in its own right. However, the leadership realized that such a policy could only be pursued under uninhibited conditions where the movement could operate normally. It needed peace with Nimeiri's regime.

A chance presented itself when Nimeiri made an offer of "national reconciliation" to the National Front opposition. The offer had been negotiated with and accepted by Sadiq al-Mahdi, the Umma Party leader and the National Front's chairman. Accordingly, the leadership of the Ikhwan reconciled itself with the regime after discussing and approving its own deal with Nimeiri. The most significant aspect of this separate deal was that no restrictions would be imposed on the propagatory (*da'wa*) activities of the Ikhwan. This concession was interpreted by the leadership of the Ikhwan as full license for political activity and was fully utilized in their strategy of growth into a mass movement.

By the end of the Nimeiri era in 1985, the Islamist movement had actually grown into a formidable force with substantial influence and resources. This success was achieved through a complex and multiform process. First, at the purely political level, the movement benefited from its freedom of action and participation in power in at least two directions. (1) It was able to expand its ranks through systematic recruitment facilitated by unhampered propagation and discreet political activity; and (2) participation of Ikhwan leaders and cadres in the political system as ministers, members of parliament (MPs), and members of the leading structures of the ruling political organization (Sudan Socialist Union [SSU, al-Itihad al-Ishtirabi al-Sudani]) gave the movement a statesmanship experience and enabled it to penetrate even the most sensitive structures of the state, such as the army and security bodies.

Second, the movement was able to hijack an experiment in "Islamic banking" and investment and deploy it in the service of its own strategy of growth into a mass movement. The growth and proliferation of "Islamic" financial institutions gave the Ikhwan access to substantial financial and economic resources and gave birth to an Islamist business class. The process furthermore strengthened the movement by cementing the ties between the organization and its individual members (graduates could now find employment in Islamist institutions or private enterprises, and other members gained access to credit and other banking facilities).

Third, the Ikhwan's freedom of action and participation in power, combined with its enhanced financial resources, enabled the movement to penetrate other sectors of society outside its traditional constituencies on the student campuses and in some suburban pockets. This goal was achieved, on the one hand, through the appropriation or creation of Islamic missionary and relief organizations to influence the multiplying groups of the rural population dislocated by migration to towns and, on the other hand, through the Ikhwan's virtual control of the student unions, which it used to advance its influence in the rural areas via student tours and other forms of extra-campus activities. In a society that views its educated members with great deference, the Ikhwan saw students as an important medium through which it could take its message to the rural areas. Finally, the Ikhwan's rapprochement with Nimeiri's regime coincided and was partially precipitated by the latter's gradual reliance on Islam as a source of ideology and inspiration. Such a tendency gave the Ikhwan enough grounds to campaign and mobilize for "mandatory" Islamicization of state and society and enhanced its chances of recruitment, expansion, and alliances. The peak moment in this process came in September 1983 when President Nimeiri suddenly decreed the enactment of new laws that included the canonical penalties of Islamic *shari'a* (the *hudud*).[4] Nimeiri's *shari'a* experiment was partially designed to out-maneuver the Ikhwan and take the wind out of its sails. The Ikhwan, however, regarded such a move as a "reward" and sought to make the best of the experiment by throwing its weight behind it. In the process, the Ikhwan managed to forge a "*shari'a* coalition" transcending its own movement that was made up of individuals and groups (particularly the smaller *sufi* sects) who supported the experiment on religious or political grounds.[5]

Sensing that the Ikhwan had become too powerful for a subordinate ally, Nimeiri decided to crush it after pinning it with a draconian and heavy-handed application of the *shari'a* laws. Thus, in early March 1985, most of the Ikhwan leaders and influential cadres were imprisoned amid accusations of plotting to overthrow the regime. As the Ikhwan was the only force that remained behind Nimeiri's regime, the latter's demise followed shortly and swiftly in the face of a popular uprising, or *intifada*.

The *intifada* triggered a coup led by Nimeiri's chief of staff and minister of defense, Lieutenant General Suwar al-Dhahab, who deposed Nimeiri and dissolved the main structures of his regime. The *intifada* restored freedom of association and expression and returned the country to a parliamentary democracy after a one-year transitional period.[6]

After the *intifada,* in May 1985, the Ikhwan founded the National Islamic Front (NIF). The NIF was not just a new name for the Ikhwan. Rather, it represented the movement that grew in breadth and strength during the Nimeiri years. The core of this movement was composed of Ikhwan members. Other factions included the "*shari'a* coalition," referred to above; some businessmen who were attracted to or seduced by the Islamists' financial resources and credit facilities; and some groups and individuals who found themselves in a vulnerable position as a result of their close association with the Nimeiri regime (such as former security and army officers, SSU officials, ministers, and the like).

Because of their collision with Nimeiri on the eve of his departure, the Ikhwan, which supplied the leadership of the NIF, was able to diffuse the criticism leveled against it on account of its association with a corrupt and authoritarian regime. At the same time, because of this very association and the advantages it incurred, the NIF did very well in the general elections of April 1986, coming in next only to the mainstream parties, the Umma Party and the DUP.[7] These two parties joined together in a coalition government headed by al-Sadiq al-Mahdi, the head of the Umma Party, as prime minister, and the NIF formed the official parliamentary opposition.

The main concern of NIF leaders during the parliamentary period was how to secure the gains achieved during Nimeiri's years and expand the movement further. The endeavor proved easier than all expectations. By its emergence as a legitimate party in the post-Nimeiri era and its good performance in the 1986 elections, the NIF had both sustained and cultivated the results of its steady growth under the shadow of Nimeiri. The second step was to lead an assault on the Umma-DUP government with the aim of either inheriting its largely Muslim constituencies or forcing it into giving the NIF a share of power.

Toward this end the NIF launched a fierce and ruthless campaign against al-Mahdi's government utilizing the latter's internal differences and its ineptness in the face of the country's immense problems. In its offensive, the NIF, among other things, emphasized preservation of Nimeiri's *shari'a* laws, or their replacement with yet another "Islamic alternative," and advocated a tough militarist stand toward the civil war in the south. On both stands, the NIF aimed at discrediting the two mainstream parties, presenting itself as the only authentic custodian of Arabo-Islamic culture in Sudan.

The offensive paid off. In early 1988, after barely two years in opposition, the NIF was called to join the Umma Party and the DUP in the government's coalition. One immediate result of the NIF's inclusion was the production of a Criminal Law Bill based on the *shari'a* to replace Nimeiri's September 1983 laws.[8] The bill, which was debated in parliament and virtually supported by the three parties of the coalition, led only to the intensification of the civil war, which was being partially fought for a "secular Sudan."

The impasse, however, was broken by a partner in the coalition, the DUP, which signed a Peace Initiative with the rebel movement in the south, the Sudan Peoples' Liberation Army (SPLA, al-Jaysh al-Sha'bi Li Tahrir al-Sudani), in November 1988.[9] The Peace Initiative was rejected by both the Umma Party and the NIF, each for its own considerations, a position that eventually led to the DUP's withdrawal from government in protest.[10] Consequently, the coalition became one between the Umma Party and the NIF only.

The Umma-NIF coalition, however, proved to be a short-lived one. Popular unrest and pressure from the army led to its collapse by February 1989. The next government was composed, after lengthy negotiations, of all parliamentary parties, except the NIF. The new government also included trade union representatives and was known to have the blessing of the army leadership. The NIF, however, declined representation in the new government on grounds that its program was not committed to the shari'a.

Indeed, the new government had reintroduced peace to the political agenda of the country by endorsing the DUP-SPLA Peace Initiative. The latter called for the shari'a laws to be frozen until the whole matter of religion and politics was discussed and resolved in a "national constitutional conference." Such a position set the peace process in motion, and for the first time since the fall of Nimeiri there were direct negotiations between the Sudanese government and the rebel movement.

Back in opposition, the NIF resumed its assault on the government, accusing it of succumbing to the rebel movement. Once again, the issue of shari'a figured high on the NIF's antigovernment campaign, which took a more emotive form this time (such as raising copies of the Qur'an during demonstrations). The NIF was effectively declaring war on the only government that had taken the issue of peace seriously since the outbreak of the civil war in 1983.

When the June coup took place, few members of the politicized public had any doubt about its true identity.

Ideological Adjustment

The development of the Sudanese Islamist movement throughout its various stages was followed closely by important ideological adjustments necessitated by the changing circumstances in which the movement operated or the changing emphases and priorities of the movement itself. In view of the movement's history, one can discern three major phases of ideological adjustments. The first took place in the 1960s, when the movement converted itself from a religious group into a political party with a religious agenda. The second phase facilitated the transition of the movement from a tiny political group into a mass movement during the 1970s and 1980s. Finally, the third adjustment came on the eve of the movement's taking control of political power in 1989.

When the movement emerged as a political party in the 1960s, significant ideological innovations and adjustments were unnecessary. The transformation was rather of a political and organizational character. As for ideology, the Sudanese Ikhwan remained loyal to the basic ideas and teachings of Hasan al-Banna (but not Qutb or al-Maududi), and as such it remained ideologically dependent on the Egyptian Muslim Brotherhood despite its organizational independence from that group.[11] Yet, the definite politicization of the movement brought with it some necessary adjustments. As a puritanical movement, the Muslim Brotherhood was essentially anti-*sufist* and anti-sectarian. However, with its involvement in politics, the Sudanese Ikhwan found it necessary to reconcile itself to a Sudanese society dominated by traditions of popular Islam and *sufism* in order to get a foothold there. By the same token, it watered down its anti-sectarianist rhetoric and allied itself with the mainstream parties (the Umma Party and the DUP), first to combat communism and then to build a coalition for the enforcement of an "Islamic constitution."

The most important consequences of this process had been first the development of an embryonic sense of *pragmatism* in the movement's discourse. From then onward the movement would pursue what it saw as best for its political priorities at a given period rather than what was considered *right* from the viewpoint of its religious ideology. Second, by focusing its attention on Sudanese political realities, the Sudanese Ikhwan enhanced its political and organizational independence from the Egyptian parent organization (which was being severely suppressed at the time) and even sowed the seeds of ideological independence in due course. This came in the second phase in the wake of the Ikhwan's transformation into a mass movement.

Up to 1976 the movement was governed by a "pressure group mentality," reminding leaders, other politicians, and the public of the necessity of an Islamic constitution or legislation. When the movement reconciled itself with the Nimeiri government in 1977, however, it did so with a clearly defined strategy (known as the central or grand strategy) that emphasized building the movement in such a way that it would be capable of taking power in its own right.[12] Yet this strategy did not involve posing and settling essential questions, such as those regarding the substance and form of the Islamic order, or the means of transition to it. Rather, the "grand strategy" opened the door widely to pragmatism, which became the dominant feature of the movement's activism.

The first manifestation of pragmatism was the reconciliation deal itself, which involved the trading of ideology for the possibility of freedom of action and the opportunity to gain practical experience in the running of the state. [13]Second, rather than agitating for some lofty ideals, all the efforts of the Islamists were now geared toward the objective of strengthening their movement and expanding its ranks by all means. In its turn, this objective involved reducing the level of ideological indoctrination required in the new members to facilitate the rapid growth of the movement in the shortest possible time.

Although the dominance of pragmatism has essentially asserted itself in the sphere of practical politics, it may be argued that there are some theoretical foundations for this attitude in the discourse of the movement's leader, Hasan al-Turabi. As mentioned earlier, Turabi's name emerged in association with the first ideological adjustment of the movement in the mid-1960s, when it was turned into a definite political party. Turabi's authority was confirmed throughout the first half of the 1970s, first through the victory of his line over that of the "conservatives" during the extraordinary congress of April 1969, and second by his leadership of the younger generation of membership, who became the dominant force in a movement primarily based on and active in the student population.[14] With the reconciliation of 1977, the split, which was subdued by the Nimeiri coup, resurfaced once again and became an actuality. The departure of the conservatives, or the "educationalist" school, has left Turabi as the only influential leader of the movement and its sole ideologue.

Of the several pamphlets and books produced by Turabi in the past twenty years or so, two perhaps summarize his main philosophy and approach. The first is entitled *Religious Belief: Its Effect on the Life of Man*; the second, *Renovation of the Fundamentals of Islamic Jurisprudence*.[15] The *Religious Belief*, or *Iman* for short, deals with the concept of religion, its place in this life, its impact on the believer, and the most suitable approach toward religion. The central theme in Islamic religion, according to Turabi, is *tawhid*. Apart from its classical meaning as the unity of God, Turabi employed the concept in a broader manner to indicate the meeting point between religion, the word of God, and this world, the domain of man: "*Tawhid* is the union of the eternal divine command with the changing conditions of human life." Additionally, Turabi believes, "*Tawhid* enriches life, giving every material worldly experience a spiritual otherworldly dimension. It is a dynamic principle which unites the material and the spiritual, the real and the ideal, and subsumes the ever changing reality under the eternally valid principles."[16]

To achieve the concept of *tawhid* as a dynamic and novel principle, Turabi suggested the necessity of *tajdid*, that is, renewal of the faith in order to achieve the required harmony between "the eternal revelation" and changing reality. At another level, renewal is necessitated by the dominance of Western civilization and the challenges it poses to Muslims' lives and societies.

To achieve the required *tajdid* Turabi argued that there is a dire necessity not only to consider new answers to new problems but also to reconsider how to revitalize the fundamentals (*usul*) of Islamic jurisprudence (*fiqh*). Because the fundamentals on which traditional *fiqh* was established were the work of the first generations of ulama, who were guided by the sciences and methodology of their time, *fiqh* has in the course of time stagnated. It is no longer capable of providing answers to current problems. In particular, traditional Islamic *fiqh* was deficient in its treatment of public affairs such as politics, administration, and the economy. The reason for this deficiency, in Turabi's eyes, is that throughout most of their history Muslims did not rule their societies in accordance with the spirit and principles of Islam. Therefore the *fiqh* was not inspired to develop in these fields and concentrated instead on issues related to personal and individual matters.

Turabi emphasized the point that Islam is essentially a progressive religion that welcomes any change (such as material progress) that Muslims can utilize for the worship of God. Yet, for Muslims to be able to do this, it is important to swing the door of *ijtihad* (independent formulation of deduction of laws and theology) wide open for all Muslims who are willing and competent and then to rationalize and coordinate their findings through regular consultations under the auspices and guidance of "Islamic" authorities who could then enforce the *consensus* of the ulama.[17]

On the methodology of *ijtihad* and renewal, Turabi proposed an approach that distinguishes between what is eternal and what is temporal in Islam, as well as between the spirit of legislation and its letter. His emphasized the eternal over the temporal, and the spirit of *shari'a* over its letter. His most significant assessment in this regard was perhaps his statement: "It is not true, as is widely believed, that the community of the Prophet is the most perfect paradigm that could never be improved upon. It is indeed possible with the help of constant regeneration, to improve tremendously on the performance of that first generation." He went on to cite the example of the *shura* (consultation) as practiced by the first generation of Muslims as something that could be perfected further today by using the present "advances in communications."[18]

The implication of this rationale on the movement's ideology and practice cannot be overestimated. On the ideological level, Turabi's treatment of his two cardinal concepts of *tawhid* and *tajdid* placed him at odds with the literalist interpretation of Islam common among a great number of modern and contemporary Islamists. The result was a discourse garbed in an aura of liberalism, innovation, and flexibility. A testimony to this conclusion is that when Turabi attempted to put his idea of *tajdid* into practice, he produced some unorthodox pronouncements that generated much controversy, such as his argument that "the death sentence on the apostate was not mandatory but conditional on his engaging in a war against the Muslim community."[19]

At the practical level, particularly the level of politics, Turabi's ideological discourse rationalized the movement's pragmatism and expediency. By emphasizing unity between the religious and the temporal, he implied to his followers that any worldly object may be utilized or pursued as a worship of God. Accordingly, any political approach to be adopted by the Ikhwan was perfectly legitimate, since its ultimate goal was the establishment of an Islamic order.

The second way in which Turabi's discourse cultivated pragmatism was its preaching of realism. Being overtly disdainful of the rejectionist school of Qutb and al-Maududi, Turabi argued, "The failure of the modern Islamist movement to become an effective force was due to its setting for itself lofty ideals lying well beyond the present reality, without proposing a programme bridging the gap between the ideals and the reality. When their programme failed they blamed society and withdrew from it."[20]

Turabi's realism appeared when he first reconciled his movement to the Sudanese society by tacitly endorsing popular Islam and sectarianism. Then he reconciled the movement to the state without any elaborate ideological conditions attached. Both steps were considered transitory aimed at improving the movement's chances of growth and influence. Both, however, opened the door widely for pragmatism.

Pragmatism, on its part, generated further ideological concessions. As one biographer put it, "In many instances, [the movement] moves first to implement policies which it deems expedient and starts the search for justification later. As a result, theory did not blossom in practice but actually grew out of it."[21] This attitude was first dictated by the postreconciliation era, which witnessed the expansion of the movement among new and diverse sectors and groups. It became almost the norm when the movement penetrated new fields, such as the economy and finances, and became deeply involved in questions of government and opposition during the post-Nimeiri era.

It was these mutually interactive arenas of ideology and pragmatism that gave rise to the National Islamic Front in 1985. Unlike the Ikhwan movement of the 1950s and even the 1960s, which was essentially a religious group with a political agenda, the NIF emerged as a political party with a rather fluid religious agenda.

The Nature of an Islamic State

As stated earlier, the third phase of ideological adjustment came on the eve of the NIF's ascendancy to power in 1989. For an Islamist movement with an emotive agenda of establishing a divinely guided political order, an Islamic state, power raises the all-important question of how this mammoth objective can be approached in reality. In its turn, this question may be broken down into two related ones: (1) What method of transition should be used to reach the required Islamic order or state? and (2) What should be the nature and form of this Islamic state?

The first question may seem irrelevant in the case of the NIF, which had already assumed power through a military coup. Yet it is important to raise such a question because it is at the center of the controversy engulf-ing Islamist movements today. Indeed, the Sudanese Islamists headed by Turabi have repeatedly addressed this question. Yet, as we shall see presently, Turabi's answers have varied in accordance with the changing fortunes of his movement.

At first, the NIF leader championed democracy and freedom as the most essential prerequisites for the transition to an Islamist order. This view was apparently dictated by the pressure group strategy of the move-ment during its early history—a position necessitating freedom of associ-ation and action. Accordingly, the 1965 charter of the ICF (the umbrella organization of the Ikhwan movement at the time) "stressed democracy and individual liberty as basic values." It was with this understanding that the movement contributed to the popular resistance of two military dictatorships (the regime of General Ibrahim 'Abboud in the early 1960s, and that of Nimeiri up to 1977).[22]

With the adoption of the "grand strategy" in 1977, which called for the movement to work for the assumption of power on its own, Turabi's dis-course shifted emphasis from democracy to Islamist control of the state. Nonetheless, he maintained the line that the will of society should as-sume primacy over the state: "You cannot have an Islamic state except in-sofar that you have an Islamic society. Any attempt of establishing a polit-ical order for the establishment of a genuine Islamic society would be a superimposition of laws over a reluctant society. This is not in the nature of religion; religion is based on sincere conviction and voluntary compli-ance."[23]

Turabi also stressed that the state "is only the political dimension of the collective endeavour of Muslims."[24] What is to be understood from this line of reasoning is that an Islamic order can only materialize as a result of the free will of Muslims and as a manifestation of their "collective en-deavor."

This line continued to characterize Turabi's discourse throughout the early 1980s, when his movement was in alliance with Nimeiri's regime—a factor that deterred him, perhaps, from confronting the issue of transi-tion to power directly. Hence, as long as the discourse operates on an ab-stract level, questions of freedom and liberty may be cherished on either religious or political grounds.

With Nimeiri's downfall and the emergence of the NIF, the transition to a projected Islamic order had to be faced headlong. Ironically, despite the climate of freedom and democracy that characterized post-Nimeiri poli-tics, such themes faded almost completely from Turabi's discourse and that of his movement.

In an article published in May 1985 (the same month that the NIF was founded), Turabi drew a comparative assessment of Western democracy and Islamic *shura* systems.[25] After laboring on the respective merits and characteristics of each, he concluded by asserting the superiority of the *shura* system, which had existed from the early days of Islam to the present day. If democracy is not an ideal system for the Islamists, then by what means are they going to attain power? Turabi chose to leave this question unanswered.

Thenceforth, the question of transition to power has become increasingly ambiguous in the discourse of the Sudanese Islamists. For example, in a pamphlet entitled *Features of the Islamic Order* (1987), Turabi emphasized that what matters in fact is who controls the state, and for which purpose, rather than by what means. So if the Islamists are able to lay their hands on the state, then its power will be deployed for the service of the Islamicization process. He maintained that the way to convert individual Muslims, and eventually the state, was through peaceful *da'wa* (propagation), as a pious Muslim would lead to a pious society, which in its turn would produce a pious state.

He then argued that whenever a number of Muslims become inspired enough by the Islamic *da'wa*, they form a group or party that endeavors to become a microcosm of a possible pious and righteous Muslim society. Yet, for such a pioneer group to become successful, it must observe certain conditions. Of paramount importance among these are an established system of leadership and consultation and a strong popular base. As a matter of approach, members of the vanguard group should receive an intensive "Islamic" education, whereas the larger popular base (of the movement) may be mobilized on the basis of generally formulated ideological discourses (such as the call for the application of Islamic *shari'a*, the observation of an Islamic code of ethics, or the denouncement of non-Islamist approaches from the state or adversary parties).

As for the method of change (i.e., the Islamicization process), it involves peaceful propagation, education, and revolutionary means (by which he means use of force). In this process, "if the Islamic movement attains power whether peacefully or by force then it adds the force of the state to its means of changing reality."[26]

Therefore, Turabi first shifted emphasis from the Muslim society to the group of Islamists who had become "inspired enough" to lead the rest on the Islamicization track. Second, instead of being a manifestation of the political will of the community, the state became a mere object by which the Islamists could intensify their Islamicization program. Once again, Turabi left the question of the method of the transition to power unresolved.

The ambiguity appears to be deliberate, though. As stated by the Islamist biographer referred to earlier, "Turabi believes that no option should remain closed in the fight to establish an Islamic order. Being the consummate pragmatist he is, Turabi does not want to be committed . . . to observance of legality and peaceful transition to an Islamic order."[27]

One may conclude that the Sudanese Islamists, led by Turabi, had finally come to emphasize the necessity of establishing an Islamic order as a value in itself, by whatever means. This brings us to the thorny question regarding the substance and form of this Islamic order. It is a thorny question because Islamist leaders generally refrain from specifying a particular model for an Islamic state or government. In the present case, however, Turabi did produce such a model outlining the universal principles that should rule the conduct of an Islamic government, historical and societal specificities notwithstanding.

The scheme was outlined in an article entitled "The Islamic State" that was published in 1983.[28] In the remainder of this chapter I shall review the main themes addressed in this article and then compare them to the realities of the current Islamist regime in Sudan.

Turabi started by describing what the Islamic state is not. First, he asserted that the Islamic state "is not secular," as all public life in Islam is religious. Second, an Islamic state "is not nationalistic because ultimate allegiance is owed to God, and thereby to the community of believers—the *Ummah*." Third, an Islamic state is not an "absolute or sovereign entity," as it is "subject to the higher norms of the *shariah* that represent the will of God." Finally, the Islamic state is not "a primodia, because the primary institution in Islam is the *Ummah*."

He then elaborated the major characteristics of an Islamic state model. In the first place, he established that the form of an Islamic government is determined by the central principles of *tawhid* (again defined as the unity between God and human life), which entail the "freedom, equality and unity of believers." Accordingly, "one can call an Islamic state a republic since the *shariah* rules out usurpation and succession as grounds of political legitimacy." Turabi then posed the question of whether the proper Islamic form of government—elective and consultative—amounts to a liberal representative democracy. To this he answered by stating first that in a large Islamic state, consultation (the central principle in Islamic polity) would have to be indirect. Such a method was recognized by the classical jurists in their reference to *ahl al-hal wa'l-aqd* or *ahl al-shura* (i.e., those who resolve public matters). Likewise, *ijma* (consensus), which is the conclusion of the process of consultation, came to mean the consensus of ulama. The ulama therefore may be regarded as the representatives of the people at large or the articulators of public opinion.

On these grounds, Turabi concluded, "An Islamic order of government is essentially a form of representative democracy." This principle, however, is qualified by the supremacy of the *shari'a*, which rules over both people and government. Yet, he maintained that an Islamic state is a popular government, since "*shariah* represents the convictions of the people and therefore their direct will."

Turabi then argued that an Islamic polity should be a stable system of government "because the people consider it an expression of their religion and therefore contribute positively to the political process. In their mutual consultation, they work toward a consensus that unites them." This issue led him to raise the question of whether an Islamic government may have a multiparty or single-party system. He argued, "There is no legal bar to development of different parties or to freedom of opinion and debate." Again, a measure of qualification was necessary: "While there may be a multiparty system, an Islamic government should function more as a consensus oriented rather than a minority/majority system with political parties rigidly confronting each other over decisions."

In laying down the possible functions of an Islamic state, Turabi first sought to identify the areas where government jurisdiction is limited. He stated that essentially, "not every aspect of Islam is entrusted to the government to enforce." This element, argued Turabi, "is in the nature of a Unitarian religious order of society [which implies] that the individual should enjoy a wide degree of autonomy." Second, "where society could manage, government has no business interfering." In this respect, Turabi expressed his belief that an Islamic polity is "similar to a liberal minimal theory of government." This very "liberal" feature produces the third area of Islamic government's limitation, namely, its power to tax. On the positive side of the government's duties toward society, Turabi ascertained that an Islamic government is duty bound to exercise all powers necessary for providing a minimum of the basic conditions of Muslim life. Again, consistent with the liberalist conception, Turabi argued that where "society on its own manages to realize social justice, then the government does not need to interfere." Should the society fail to do so, however, "the government is bound and entitled to promote education, health services and what have you."

Finally, an Islamic state should respect and uphold the rights and freedoms of its citizens: "The individual has the right to his physical existence, general social well-being, reputation, peace, privacy, to education and a decent life." A significant addition to this impressive "bill of rights" is an affirmation of "freedom of religion and expression" as cardinal principles. "Thus," Turabi maintained, "while a Muslim would not oppose *shariah* because he believes in it, if he does not agree to a particular interpretation of the law, he is entitled to his view."

Turabi's model of the Islamic state may be regarded as the perfect government *par excellence.* It is a representative and democratic republic with due regard to the will of the community and its common interest. Its polity is consensus-oriented rather than guided by divisive principles of majority/minority. It is based on a system that rules out absolutism, because its leaders are guided by the divine law and accountable to the will of the community. The system also ensures maximum autonomy of the individual versus the state, but with due regard to provision and promotion of social justice. Similarly, the scheme guarantees and upholds basic rights and freedoms of individuals.[29]

How does this "ideal type" of an Islamic state compare to the present Sudanese regime, which is controlled and administered by Turabi's Islamist party, the NIF? One is immediately struck by the huge gap that separates Turabi's model from the actual form and conduct of the government controlled by his own party. Indeed, the present Sudanese regime actually violates almost every principle outlined by Turabi in his article.

In the first place, the present Sudanese regime is a usurpation, as it came through a military coup d'état. Second, it is a highly authoritarian regime that has ruled since its inception without a constitution or any representative institution. Third, its policy toward the Sudanese citizenry has been characterized by systematic violations of basic rights and freedoms (of Muslims and non-Muslims alike). Fourth, throughout its years in power the regime has pursued a policy of ruthless prosecution of the civil war in the south, a factor that brought havoc to the region, increased the sufferings of innocent civilians, and complicated any possible prospects of peace in the country. Finally, the present government burdened the Sudanese population, the majority of whom are living under the poverty line, with heavy and unprecedented taxation. Yet, instead of promoting social security and justice, these revenues are being deployed in the civil war and the state apparatus.[30]

It may be argued that Turabi's model is too neat and abstract to be realized in practice. After all, as the author himself has stated, the scheme is merely about outlining "the universal characteristics of an Islamic state." Naturally, one does not expect the literal realization of any model in practice, especially in forms, structures, and policies. Yet some regard for the fundamental principles and guidelines is to be expected. As we have seen, Turabi's state in reality does not even approximate his state model in theory, except maybe in the common reference to the *shari'a* as the source of guidance and legislation.

There are two possible explanations for this curious state of affairs. The first is that Turabi's theoretical model belongs to the realm of ideological discourse, which operates more often than not on the pure abstract or theoretical level. His actual state (the present Sudanese regime), in contrast, belongs to the pragmatist discourse that dominated the practical conduct of the movement during the past decades.

The second explanation is that Turabi's article was written at a time when the movement was in a stage of expansion and mobilization, a context that led him to adopt a discourse characterized by strong hints of liberalism and flexibility. As the movement grew stronger, however, it started, gradually but systematically, to shed its liberal and concessionary attitude. Once power was achieved, regardless of the controversial means, such an attitude was completely discarded and replaced by authoritarianism.

On both accounts the question of the Islamic state-model has become as ambiguous as the strategy of transition to it. The emphasis shifted from the Muslim society at large to the Islamist movement, and the concept of the state changed from an expression of the collective will of the community into a tool to serve the movement's Islamicization program. Hence, with its strong "self-righteous" conviction and attitude, the Islamist movement has appropriated for itself the role of the representative of society per se, and consequently, has become the only legitimate contender for political power. Within such a context, questions of models, ideologies, and strategies are to be left to the discretion of the movement. The answer to the question regarding the Islamic state-model, therefore, becomes simple. An Islamic state is one governed by Islamists!

Notes

1. M. Hagopian, *Regimes, Movements, and Ideologies: A Comparative Introduction to Political Science* (2nd ed.) (New York and London: Longman, 1984), p. 295.

2. For a general introduction to Sudanese history, see P. Holt and M. Daly, *The History of Sudan from the Coming of Islam to the Present* (London: Longman, 1988). For a more elaborate account of the history of the Sudanese Muslim Brotherhood, see Hasan Makki, *Tarikh harakat al-ikhwan al-muslimeen fi'l Sudan 1946–1969* (History of the Sudanese Muslim Brothers Movement in the Sudan, 1946–1969) (Khartoum: Institute of African and Asian Studies, 1984); Hasan Makki, *Al-haraka al-Islamiyya fi'l Sudan 1969–1985* (The Islamic Movement in Sudan, 1969–1985) (Khartoum: Bayt al-ma'riffa and Institute of Research and Social Studies, 1990); Abdel Wahab El-Affendi, *Turabi's Revolution: Islam and Power in Sudan* (London, Grey Seal Books, 1991); Hayder I. Ali, *Azimat al-Islam al-Siyassi: al-jabha al-Islamiyya fi'l Sudan namuzagan* (Crisis of Political Islam: NIF in Sudan as an Example), 2nd ed. (Casablanca: Sudan Studies Centre, 1991).

3. For the general history of postindependence Sudan, see Mansour Khalid, *The Government They Deserve: The Role of the Elite in Sudan's Political Evolution* (London and New York: Kegan Paul International, 1990); Peter Woodward, *Sudan, 1898–1989: The Unstable State* (Boulder: Lynne Rienner, 1990); Tim Niblock, *Class and Power in Sudan: The Dynamics of Sudanese Politics, 1898–1985* (London: Macmillan, 1987).

4. *Gazette of the Democratic Republic of the Sudan, 1983/1984.* For a critical assessment, see Mansour Khalid, *Al-fajr al-kazib: Nimeiri wa tahrif al-shari'a* (On the Shari'a Experiment of Nimeiri) (Cairo: Dar al-Hilal, n.d. [1986]); John Esposito, "Sudan's Islamic Experiment," *The Muslim World* 76, nos. 3–4 (1986): pp. 181–202;

Carolyn Fluer-Lobban, "Islamization in Sudan: A Critical Assessment," in John Voll (ed.), *Sudan: A State and Society in Crisis* (Washington, D.C., 1990); Carey Gordon, "The Islamic Legal Revolution: The Case of Sudan," *The International Lawyer* 19, no. 3 (1985): pp. 793–815.

5. Cf. El-Affendi, *Turabi's Revolution,* chapter 6.

6. For more on the *intifada* and the change of government in 1985, see Khalid, *The Government They Deserve*; and Woodward, *The Unstable State.*

7. Report of the Elections Commision, 1986, Khartoum.

8. The Criminal Law Bill was decreed as Sudan's Criminal Code in 1991 by the present regime. For a critical assessment of the bill, see Peter N. Kok, "Conflict over Laws in Sudan: From Pluralism to Monolithism," in C. H. Delmet Bleuchot and D. Hopwood, *Sudan: History, Identity, Ideology* (Reading: Ithaca Press, 1991), pp. 235–252.

9. The SPLA and its political wing, the Sudan Peoples' Liberation Movement (SPLM, al-Harakat al-Sha'biyya Li Tahrir al-Sudan), were founded in 1983 and have been fighting the successive governments in Khartoum since. For more on the rise and development of the movement, see Douglas Johnson and G. Prunier, "The Foundation and Expansion of the Sudan Peoples Liberation Army," in M. Daly and A. Sikainga (ed.), *Civil War in the Sudan* (London and New York: British Academic Press, 1993), pp. 117–141, and Mansour Khalid (ed.), *John Garang Speaks* (London and New York, Kegan Paul, 1987).

10. For the text of the Sudanese Peace Initiative, see Abdel Ghaffar M. Ahmed and G. Sorbo (eds.), *Management of the Crisis in the Sudan* (Bergen: Center of Development Studies, 1989).

11. El-Affendi, *Turabi's Revolution,* pp. 152–153; Hasan al-Turabi, *Al-haraka al-Islamiyya fi'l Sudan: al-kasb, al-tatwur, al-manhaj* (The Islamic Movement in Sudan: Achievement, Development, and Methodology) (Cairo: Dar al-Qari' al-Arabi, 1991).

12. Cf. El-Affendi, *Turabi's Revolution,* pp. 164–165.

13. Ibid., p. 166.

14. Ibid.

15. Hasan al-Turabi, *Al-Iman: atharhu fi hayat al-Insan* (Religious Belief: Its Effect on the Life of Man) (Manshurat al-a'sr al-hadith, 1984); Hasan al-Turabi, *Tajdid usul al-fiqh al-Islami* (Renovation of the Methodology of Islamic Jurisprudence) (Khartoum: Dar al-fikr, 1980).

16. Quoted in El-Affendi, *Turabi's Revolution,* p. 170.

17. Al-Turabi, *Tajdid usul al-fiqh.*

18. Hasan al-Turabi, "The Islamic State," in John Esposito, *Voices of Resurgent Islam* (Oxford: Oxford University Press, 1983), pp. 241–251.

19. El-Affendi, *Turabi's Revolution.* For an "orthodox" assessment of Turabi's views and methodology, see Ahmed Uthman Khalifa, *Al-Turabi wa mawqifahu min al-shari'a al-Islamiyya* (Turabi and His Position from the Islamic *Shari'a*) (Cairo: Dar al-wuhda, 1994).

20. El-Affendi, *Turabi's Revolution,* p. 163.

21. Ibid., p. 180.

22. Ibid., p. 159 ff.

23. Al-Turabi, "The Islamic State."

198 ABDEL SALAM SIDAHMED

24. Ibid., p. 243.

25. Hasan al-Turabi, "Al-shura wal demogratiyya" (Consultation and Democracy), *Al-mustaqbal al-Arabi* 8, no. 75 (May 1985).

26. Hasan al-Turabi and Salim al-Awa, *Ma'alim al-nizam al-Islami* (Khartoum: Dar al-Fikr, 1987).

27. El-Affendi, *Turabi's Revolution*, p. 164.

28. Al-Turabi, "The Islamic State." In the following summary, no further citation of this reference will be made.

29. For a critical assessment of Turabi's model, see Abdalla An-Na'im, "Constitutional Discourse and the Civil War in the Sudan," in Daly and Sikainga, *Civil War in the Sudan*, pp. 97–116.

30. For a more elaborate assessment of the nature and policies of the present Sudanese regime, see Mansour Khalid, *Al-nukhbah al-Sudaniyya wa idman al-Fashal* (The Sudanese Elite and the Addiction of Failure), an enlarged Arabic version of *The Goverment They Deserve*, vol.2 (Cairo: n.p., n.d. [1993]).

11

State and Islamism in Syria

RAYMOND A. HINNEBUSCH

It is generally accepted that there is no such thing as a uniform Islam, only many specific Islams, each shaped by the particular social milieu in which it develops. Less evident, perhaps, is the fact that Islam and the state are often specifically shaped by their relations to each other. In Syria, the Islamist movement has been distinctively shaped by its character as, in good part, a reaction against Ba'thism; this framework has limited its social base and given it a particularly conservative slant on Islamic ideology. Political Islam has been in the forefront of no less than six major urban revolts against the Ba'th regime; it has so far succeeded in neither revolution against nor accommodation with the regime and remains a "counterculture" unintegrated into the state. The Ba'th regime's development has also been affected by its relation to the Islamist movement; the Islamist rebellion nudged it toward "totalitarianism," and current prospects of liberalization depend on an Islamist-Ba'thist détente and, ultimately, incorporation of the Islamists into the political system.

A Framework of Analysis

Three basic factors shape Islamist movements and their relation to the state: ideology, the political context, and social composition. Islamist movements inherit from Muhammad's prototype a populist ideology accepting capitalism while also valuing small property and fair dealing by the petite bourgeoisie of small tradesmen, artisans, and herdsmen against the elitism and monopoly of the tribal-merchant aristocracy. Contemporary Islamist movements are reactions to the threat posed by the imperatives of the Western-dominated capitalist system to the populism and in-

tegrity of the *umma*, particularly to petty commodity production. Their solution is a "Third Way" that accepts capitalism but seeks to contain the inequality it engenders by an all-encompassing moral law and the moral activism of the faithful. The ambiguity in this formula reflects the typically
cross-class character of Islamic movements. It allows Islamic ideology to
swing between petit bourgeois egalitarianism and a conservative legitimation of capitalist inequality. Thus, in the 1950s Syrian Ikhwan (Muslim
Brotherhood) leader Mustafa al-Siba'i advocated a moderate "Islamic socialism" and insisted that those who declared Islam capitalist were igno-
rant (*jahil*) of it, whereas Muhammad Hamdi Al-Juwaijati, imam of Damascus's Rawda mosque, declared, "Socialism is contrary to the laws of
God."[1] Which ideological variation prevails depends on the political context and the precise social composition of the Islamic movement.

   Closely related to ideology is the political context, the second factor
shaping Islamist movements. Islamist movements typically mobilize
against a state suffering from a legitimacy crisis, which can be rooted in
societal troubles or external factors. The more conservative the regime,
the more likely the Islamic resurgence will take a populist form; the more
populist it is, the more conservative the Islamic opposition. Accommodation between the two depends on bridging this ideological gap, which is
most likely to happen by means of some limited political liberalization
giving the Islamist movement enough power to bring about a certain Islamization of the state. The alternative is Islamic revolution against the
state (as in Iran) or costly repression of Islamic movements by the state (as
in Algeria).

   Social composition is the third factor shaping Islamist movements.
There has been a remarkable consistency in the social composition of
these groups. Followers are typically recruited from the traditional petite
bourgeoisie and the ulama from such families, on the one hand, and mar-
ginal elements, such as migrants to the city or students facing poor job
prospects, on the other. Thus, the persistence of the Islamic ideology can
be seen as a reflection of the failures of capitalist and statist development
to displace petty commodity production and expand employment opportunities in the modern sector. However, the attack on bourgeois interests
by statist regimes in the 1960s pushed elements of this formerly liberal
stratum to embrace Islamism.[2]

   Islamist movements attempt to recruit across classes because, without a
broad social base, they lack the power to successfully challenge the state.
Their ability to do so, however, and especially to bridge the urban-rural
gap, varies widely depending on their ideology and the political context.
The precise class balance within any given Islamist movement between
bourgeoisie, petite bourgeoisie, and lower classes shapes the bias of its
ideology along the conservative-egalitarian continuum, and different ide-

ological wings of the movement typically have a somewhat different class composition. Whether the state and Islam can coexist amicably depends in good part on whether there is an overlap in their social bases.

The Islamist Movement in Syria

Political Context

Syria's Islamist opposition to the Ba'th state was rooted in four basic factors, each of which explains the receptivity of a particular segment of the population to its message. First, it was a reaction, particularly marked among the ulama, against westernization and secularization. The secular Ba'th state made few of the concessions to Islamic sentiment of states such as Egypt or Sudan and has therefore always been suspect to those who sought unity between political power and piety. Second, the Islamist opposition expressed the reaction of the urban establishment against a rural-based regime whose socialist reforms damaged its interests. Islam, interpreted to exclude socialism, was a natural vehicle of protest. The cleavage between political Islam and Ba'thism continues to express the split between the city and the village.

Third, political Islam also expressed Sunni resentment at the disproportionate role played by members of the minority communities, particularly Alawis, in the regime elite. Although this resentment was initially concentrated in the Sunni establishment the Ba'th displaced, as the Alawis abused their power and favored their own kind, resentment of "minority" rule spread. Islamic fundamentalism, denying the legitimacy of rule by other than orthodox Muslims, was a congenial vehicle of this resentment. Finally, in the 1970s, as the regime's nationalist-populist legitimacy declined, authoritarian rule gave no legitimate outlet to dissent and no other secular ideology offered a credible alternative for wider alienated sectors of the population.

The four roots correspond to historically successive impetuses to the Islamist movement. As a result, the movement could be said to be organized in concentric circles, with the antisecular ulama at the core, those antagonized by Ba'th reforms adhering next, then those alienated by sectarianism, and finally, those alienated by the regime legitimacy crisis of the late 1970s.

Social Composition

Leadership. The main leadership of the Islamist movement has been provided by the Ikhwan. The leadership of the Ikhwan shows a progression over three decades from populists challenging a privileged establishment to militant but essentially conservative conspirators who want to restore much of the former order.

In the 1950s a populist preacher, Mustafa al-Siba'i, led the movement. From an *alim* family, and a student of Hasan al-Banna, he fought secularizing tendencies in the 1950s. But he had also been jailed by the French for anti-imperialist agitation when he denounced the old feudal oligarchy and called for armed struggle to liberate Palestine. He built a decentralized movement through personal links to ulama in the mosques and Islamic associations. The movement stagnated under al-Siba'i's successor, Isam al-Attar, who disputed Ba'thist power, abandoned populism, and was eventually exiled.

In the 1960s, a charismatic militant, Marwan Hadid, arose in Hama on the fringe of the Ikhwan. From a cotton-growing family, he expressed the city's rage at Ba'thist rural reforms. He lead several uprisings and launched a campaign of assassinations against the ruling elite. But, though a charismatic leader, he overlooked the fact that the organization needed to really threaten the regime.

By the mid-1970s, the Ikhwan leadership had become a collective group of Islamist apparatchiki, largely from middle-class, ulama-linked families. Adnan Saad ad-Din, a middle-class educator, was made leader (supervisor) in 1975. Sa'id Hawwa, a middle-class *shari'a* graduate, became chief ideologue. Ali Sadr ad-Din al-Bayanuni, an Aleppine lawyer from an ulama family, became deputy supervisor and Husni Abu, from an Aleppine business family and son-in-law of a prominent *alim*, headed the military branch. These men replaced the previous decentralized structure with a formal organization—offices, chains of command, representative bodies, and fighting cells. The scale and durability of the rebellion they mounted in the early 1980s indicated a substantial advance in organizational capabilities. But the movement still lacked a strong leader with unquestioned authority who could rally wide support: Syrian Islam had neither an al-Banna nor a Khomeini.

Cadres. The Islamic mobilization of Syria depended on a cadre of activists. The ulama were a main source of such cadres, and they mobilized against the radical Ba'ths' secularism in the 1960s and worked to introduce Islamic provisions into the 1973 constitution. Many, recruited from the urban merchant class and notable families, or combining their religious functions with petty trade, also pressed religion into the defense of private property, denouncing Ba'th socialism as Marxist and hence atheist.

Islamist disturbances often started with antiregime sermons in the mosques then spilled over into protests in nearby streets, and the call to rise has often been proclaimed from the minaret. But the ulama's numbers and density were limited. In 1970 there were 3,000 ulama in Syria, concentrated in urban areas.[3] There were only 1,000 ulama in Syria's 6,000 villages; by contrast, the Ba'th had cells in most villages. The Syrian ulama also lacked the organization of counterparts such as the Iranian mullahs. Generally, they had no comparable capacity to mobilize Islamic opposition.

The numbers of lay militants varied widely. In Aleppo they grew from between 500 and 700 in 1975 to ten times that in 1978 and perhaps 30,000 nationwide.[4] This rapid growth suggests there was a significant pool of passive sympathizers mobilizable in times of confrontation. Historically, · lay militants have been drawn from traditional middle-class and lower-middle-class families, who are frequently recruited in mosque study circles. As young people from these families grew up and attended the universities, a growing proportion of Islamists came to be drawn from university circles. As the Ikhwan came to express opposition to Ba'th reforms, sons of prestigious families, often professionals who would once have joined the old notable parties, began to join the movement. All this meant a more educated, prestigious, and upwardly mobile pool of activists.

Mass Base. The broader receptivity of mass society to political Islam has varied widely. Syria's political awakening, led by westernized notables, including many Christians, took the form of secular Arab nationalism, originally directed against Muslim Turkey. The clientage networks of the notable parties long constrained the spread of political Islam. In the 1950s, the rise of middle-class parties, such as the Ba'th, Syrian Nationalists, and Communists, was also an obstacle. Indicative of the movement's limited appeal to the modern middle class was its weakness among army officers, who became Syrian Nationalists, Ba'thists, and Nasserists, but rarely Muslim Brothers.

The Ikhwan was thus largely limited to the traditional cities, where the ulama and the mosque were concentrated, as opposed to the modern cities or the villages. In the elections of the 1940s and 1950s, it elected a handful of deputies from some popular quarters of Damascus and reached a high of ten seats nationwide in the 1961 elections. Even here, though, Nasserism was a powerful rival for the loyalty of the urban masses.

With the decline of the notable parties under Ba'th rule and of Nasserism after Nasser's death, the Ikhwan outlasted its major rivals for the support of the urban masses. Under the Ba'th, the movement's core support in the traditional urban quarters was strengthened, since this part of society, from large notable to small trader, paid the heaviest costs of Ba'th policies. Land reform and state agrarian credit and marketing networks deprived the propertied classes of influence and wealth in the villages. Nationalization of industries, which in a few cases touched artisan workshops, was seen as an attack on business and property as a whole. The state takeover of foreign trade, restrictions on imports, and a growing state retail network deprived merchants of business. In the later 1960s, the radical Ba'th government waged a war on black marketers in the *suq* (market), arresting merchants and confiscating stock. Its general hostility toward capital brought private economic activity to a standstill. Rich, notable families with clientage ties in the old quarters gravitated to the Islamic coalition, supplied money, and engaged in conspiracies: There is much to the claim, "Behind the mask of religion stands the Khumasiya"—the power of capital.[5] Protests against socialism invariably linked merchant and professional strikes, violent clashes led by the Ikhwan, and denunciations of the regime from the mosques.

After 1970, Syrian president Hafiz al-Asad attempted to conciliate Muslim and bourgeois opinion. He portrayed himself as a pious Muslim, cultivated the ulama, and launched an economic liberalization program to revitalize the private sector. But a minority-dominated government could not readily overcome its image as an illegitimate sectarian regime among parts of the Sunni city. Moreover, business still had to deal with inefficient and unsympathetic officials and pay off corrupt ones and remained insecure in the face of new state interventions in commercial fields.

In the late 1970s, there was a clear geographic differentiation: Whereas the northern cities, notably Hama and Aleppo, were hotbeds of unrest, Damascus remained quiescent. This difference was in good part due to state policies. Asad co-opted into the regime middle- and even upper-class Damascenes. Close to the center of power, personal connection, and corrupt influence, the Damascene bourgeoisie was enriched by the disproportionate share of public moneys expended in the capital. Many were linked to the political elite in mutually beneficial, often corrupt, business partnerships.

In contrast, traditional Hama suffered under Ba'th rule. A historic center of Islamic piety, it took particular offense at Ba'thist secularism and resented the favoritism shown the surrounding villages it used to dominate. The new factories around Hama largely recruited from rurals, whereas small, inner-city textile industries suffered from the competition of large state factories. The great Hamawi families—the Keilanies, Barazis, and Azms—found the presence of Ba'th provincial officials in the heart of their once exclusive preserve galling. Aleppo was a similar case. The main seat of Syria's agrarian bourgeoisie, it especially suffered from agrarian reform. A political bloc the equal of Damascus in the pre-Ba'th era, it was weakened by the regime's centralization of power.

In the late 1970s, support for political Islam broadened beyond this core to the educated urban Sunni middle class. With high aspirations, it faced growing Alawite favoritism and rural competition for scholarships and jobs. The 1976 Lebanon intervention against Palestinians and Muslims in defense of Christian rightists damaged regime legitimacy among Sunnis. Inflation, corruption, inequality, and the enrichment of the power elite alienated many of the regime's own Sunni supporters.

Nevertheless, the Sunni middle class did not go over to the Islamic opposition en masse and remained politically divided. Upper-middle-class professionals entered tactical alliances with the Ikhwan. But, generally liberal-minded, they were unreceptive to Islamic ideology. The university campuses were not swept by Islamism as they were in Egypt: Opposition was as likely to take a leftist form. There was some sympathy for the Ikhwan among teachers and government employees, but their dependence on state employment, the strength of the secular center and Left among them, and the antistatist ideology of the Ikhwan deterred active pro-Ikhwan opposition. Urban high school students played a role in Ikhwan street protests, but the Ba'th also had an organization in the schools that mobilized counterdemonstrations.

The lower strata were also split. Only traditional labor was in the Ikhwan camp. Although the Ikhwan once had a modest following in the trade unions, in the 1960s leftist trade unionists mobilized workers against the Islamist movement because of its opposition to socialism. In other countries, recent migrants to the city, alone in the large, impersonal environment, have been especially receptive to fundamentalist Islam. Yet many migrants in Syria already have urban relatives with connections to the Ba'th-run state, and the Ikhwan, opposed to rural migration as a threat to its own urban constituency, neglected their recruitment.[6] It also failed to penetrate the countryside, except in a few larger villages near the cities. Rural recruitment was of low priority, and village Ba'thists were obstacles to it. In summary, Syrian Islam failed to reach many sectors of the large middle class, to link up with much of the working class, or to bridge the urban-rural gap, an essential key to mass revolution.

Ideology

During the 1950s, when the Ikhwan expressed middle-class opposition to the old oligarchy, its populist ideology actually spoke of "Islamic socialism." By the 1980s, its ideology, reflecting its marginally more elevated social base and its utter disaffection from Ba'thist populism, was, unsurprisingly, a distinctively conservative variant of Islam. The movement's manifesto[7] began with a call to jihad against the regime—characterized as a sectarian military dictatorship led by Alawi unbelievers and a military that, as a tool of foreign interests and internal repression, was incapable of fighting Zionism. An Islamic state would be established once the

Ba'thists were defeated. Government by *shura* would be institutionalized in a strong, elected parliament, and an independent judiciary of *shari'a* jurists would nullify anything contrary to Islamic law. Freedom of expression and party competition was "guaranteed," but not for parties against Islam or linked to foreign powers—that is, Communists.

Since the majority of the Syrian population is Muslim, the state had to be Islamic, with the rights of religious minorities protected. Nevertheless, an austere republic of virtue seemed indicated: Islamic law would rule every branch of social life; the vices that infect society, such as gambling, extravagance, alcohol, prostitution, and nightclubs, eradicated; and the citizenry morally regenerated by a return to the way of the Prophet. Some more radical Islamic leaders, rejecting democracy, even held that men must be ruled by the command of God through a pious Caliph.

If the Islamic state would be repressive of individual license, its economic order was based on a return to free enterprise. The Ba'th system was said to mix the worst of the West—rampant materialism—and of the East—an unproductive state sector that destroys incentives and is corrupted to enrich a small political clique. Private enterprise would be the basis of the economy "as prescribed by the Qur'an." An Islamic economy would encourage private investment and the "natural incentives" of a fair profit, while preventing excessive concentration of wealth.[8]

The state should not encroach on the trade sector, Islamists said, which is properly private and should be allowed to freely import and export. The bloated bureaucracy had to be cut, and people should be encouraged to work in the private sector. Workers had to cease to malinger. As there was plenty of unused land in Syria, land reform was unnecessary as it only reduced agricultural output. State farms and cooperatives had failed and should be abandoned. The only populist plank was the traditional provision that class gaps be narrowed through payment of *zakat* by the rich to support charitable endowments for the poor and through state guarantee of basic needs—food, clothing, and shelter—for all citizens.

Although this program accurately reflected the interests of the movement's core constituency, the private sector, there was very little populism in it and much to threaten important societal sectors such as the military, the bureaucracy, minorities, and peasants.

The Ba'th State and Political Islam

Failed Revolution and Repression

The Syrian Ikhwan made repeated attempts against the government from 1977 to 1982. But seldom has an Islamist movement challenged the state with such sustained violence and yet failed to topple it. The Islamist uprising began with an intensive campaign of sabotage and elite assassinations. As the Islamist challenge mounted, an internal debate raged in the Ba'th between hardliners, headed by the president's brother, Rif'at al-Asad, and relative liberals, such as Mahmoud al-Ayubi, who wished to defuse opposition through limited political liberalization and anticorruption reforms. Reflective of this struggle, until 1980 the regime mixed appeasement and repression. To shore up eroding support among the urban salaried middle class, it increased bureaucratic and military salaries and tightened anti-inflation price controls. It promised more freedoms to the small leftist and nationalist parties, which made up the pro-regime National Progressive Front (al-Jabha al-Wataniyya al-Taqadumiyya), and opened negotiations with other groups, such as Riyad al-Turk's Communist faction and Jamal al-Atasi's Arab Socialist faction. It sought to defuse discontent by allowing "constructive criticism" within the front and promising new anticorruption moves and restrictions on the use of state security courts. The 7th Regional Congress of the Ba'th Party met in an atmosphere of crisis. Delegates blamed corrupt incumbent leaders—always excepting Asad's inner circle—for damaging the party and replaced them with new men. A new government of middle-class technocrats was appointed under a wealthy but reputedly "clean" Damascene Sunni prime minister, Abd al-Rauf al-Kasm. Some of the regime's moderate critics hoped its vulnerability could be used to reform and liberalize it, but radical leftist groups and the professional middle class calculated that the weakened regime could be brought down or transformed by rebellion and so formed tactical alliances with the Islamist opposition.

In the spring of 1980, the Islamist opposition, buoyed by the revolution in Iran and sensing the isolation of the regime, initiated a new phase of resistance. A campaign of attacks on government installations in Aleppo escalated into urban guerrilla warfare, and mass pro-Ikhwan demonstrations flooded the streets. Whole quarters slipped out of government control. Similar disturbances spread to Hama, Homs, Idlib, Latakia, Dayr ez-Zor, Ma'ret-en-Na'man, and Jisr esh-Shagour. In Aleppo, professional associations staged strikes to back Ikhwan demands for political freedoms and an end to arbitrary security practices. These groups were joined by merchants protesting price and supply controls. The ulama called for the release of political prisoners, an end to martial law, and application of Islamic law. Former political leaders who had been marginalized by Asad's consolidation of power began to organize in the hope of offering an alternative, should the regime collapse. Ba'th Party founder Salah al-Din al-Bitar, publishing a journal in Paris, became a rallying point for disaffected Ba'thists. Antiregime leftists demanded political freedoms and the end to repression. This partial adhesion of leftist and liberal middle-class elements to an Islamist-led opposition made the prospects of a generalized, antigovernment movement under an Islamist umbrella, as in Iran, more real than ever before.

The heightening threat to the regime began to shift the internal balance toward the hardliners, who favored repression over concession. The leaders of the lawyers', engineers', and doctors' syndicates were purged and imprisoned. In mid-April 1980, government security forces carried out a massive sweep of northern cities in an effort to smash the Ikhwan network. When the rebellion continued, the hardliners, arguing that reactionaries had exploited limited liberalization, urged a return to "revolutionary vigilance." The regime charged the opposition was part of a "Camp David conspiracy" by the United States, Israel, and Egypt to break Syria's steadfastness against Arab capitulation. The party attempted a countermobilization of the labor, peasant, and youth unions and recruited armed militia units to defend the revolution. Asad, meanwhile, exhorted peasants not to forget the bad old days, when they were treated as the property of the landlords, and warned that reaction had deep roots that still threatened the peasants' stake in the revolution. The murder of a landowning family in Harem by armed peasants, and an atmosphere of intimidation, which kept landowners from their estates in other villages around Aleppo, was a warning to the old families. Without the protection of a government they disliked, their property rights were unenforceable. Asad, supposedly bowing to peasant demands, decreed a third minor land reform. A decree raising wages and favoring workers against their employers had a similar political message.

An assassination attempt against the president in June 1980 gave the hardliners a free hand to hunt down the regime's adversaries: Terrorism was met by state terrorism. Rif'at threatened a bloodbath in defense of the regime, and prisoners were massacred at Tadmur prison. Membership in the Ikhwan—after an amnesty period—was made a capital offense. The regime sent assassination squads abroad, murdering Salah al-Din al-Bitar and the wife of former Ikhwan leader Isam al-Attar. Raids by security forces on Ikhwan hideouts, in which weapons were seized and military field courts delivered summary executions, sometimes degenerated into indiscriminate killings. The forces took little care to distinguish activists from passive supporters, demonstrating the lengths to which the regime would go to preserve itself. An emboldened Rif'at sent his militant "Daughters of the Revolution" into the streets of Damascus to tear veils from the faces of traditional women. Interminable violence without prospect of resolution enabled the regime to play on the fears of the middle class of a breakdown in public order.

Both sides apparently wanted the showdown that came in Hama, the Ikhwan stronghold, in February 1982. In reaction to regime security operations, militants assaulted government centers, executed officials, and declared the city liberated. Members of the old families, such as the Barazis, were joined in opposition to the regime by followers of their old antifeudalist enemy, Akhram al-Hawrani—a symbol of the extent to which the old class struggle was being superseded by a sectarian one. Since government forces could not penetrate the narrow streets, they used helicopter gunships, bulldozers, and artillery bombardment against the city, virtually razing whole quarters and killing many thousands. The Ikhwan's call for a nationwide uprising failed. The regime's reaction to the Hama uprising was more than the people had bargained for: Those who had joined the opposition less out of Islamic zeal than dislike of the regime melted away. The Islamist movement was decimated. The episode seemed to support Machiavelli's view that repression, provided it was done thoroughly, could work.

What explains the ability of the regime to withstand the rebellion? It proved much stronger than anticipated. The security apparatus mounted a repressive campaign of unusual ruthlessness. This repression was backed by the party, army, and bureaucracy, the best-organized institutions in society; they did not, with few exceptions, split or unravel along sectarian lines, even under the pressures of near-sectarian civil war. This solidarity, in turn, is probably best explained by the roots of the institutions, especially the army and party, in the village, whereas the Islamist uprising represented the urban constituency that used to exploit the village.

Had the Islamist movement been able to mobilize the Sunni majority, it would almost certainly have brought down "minority rule." But it suffered from flaws that prevented it from putting together the ingredients of such a mass revolution. Its leadership, fragmented and in exile for long periods, was no credible alternative to Asad. The movement was too urban and regionally based. Its peculiarly conservative version of Islamic ideology lacked wide appeal, and it threatened the large military and bureaucratic middle class. Rejecting everything Ba'thist, it had little of Mustafa Saba'i's populism. The secular Left, organized workers, government employees, and peasants were wary of any return of power to merchants and landlords. The minorities—a fourth of the population—feared an Islamic state. Finally, where political Islam has been most successful, it has fused religious zeal with nationalist revolt against a foreign or foreign-dependent regime, but the Ba'th has enough of a nationalist character to deprive Syrian Islamists of this weapon.

Despite the regime's apparent victory, the outcome merely aggravated the bifurcation between the state and urban society. The Islamist movement lost the battle with the regime but remained deeply rooted in the *suq*, where a merchant ethos mixes with a pervasive religious sensibility nurtured by the ulama. With a partially autonomous economic base and a counterideology, the traditional city remains resistant to state penetration.

The regime itself was rigidified by the conflict. The limited liberalization begun in 1970 was cut short and set back for over a decade. In its mortal conflict with political Islam, the state ratcheted up its control over society. A purge of mosques, religious associations, and professional syndicates eliminated these as bases not just of opposition, but of civil society. The surviving modicum of press freedom and party pluralism was deadened. The regime came, briefly, as close as ever to "totalitarianism."

Islam and the State Today

Ten years after the repression at Hama, the Ba'th regime embarked on a major wave of liberalization that could open the door to reconciliation with political Islam. Economic liberalization is reviving the private sector and rolling back the state. It is bridging much of the gap between the state and the bourgeoisie as political, business, and even marriage alliances are struck between Alawi elites and Sunni business families. Asad has launched a calculated political decompression, downgraded the role of the Ba'th Party, enhanced access by the Sunni bourgeoisie to regime councils, and tried to broaden his base to the business class.

There is, however, little prospect that the regime will be able to stabilize and consolidate its power base or make substantial advances in political liberalization before a compromise becomes possible between the Ba'th state and political Islam. Can the *suq* be integrated into the political system in a way that would advance pluralization, as long as political Islam remains its dominant political expression? Political Islam is an obstacle insofar as it fosters communal conflict in a mosaic society and a counter-culture not readily incorporated into the secular state. The Islamist movement is not necessarily antidemocratic, however: In the pre-Ba'th era, the Syrian Ikhwan participated in electoral politics rather than creating secret organizations like those in Egypt. In an attempt to broaden its appeal in the 1980s, the movement advocated a semi-liberal state. The notion of violent revolution has now been discredited in most Islamic circles. The moderate Islamic tendencies currently dominant in the *suq* are reconcilable with an increasingly de-Ba'thized regime.

To the considerable extent that the Islamist movement expressed the reaction of the *suq* and sections of the bourgeoisie to Ba'thist socialism, economic liberalization could advance a détente with the regime. The Aleppo bourgeoisie, which supported the Islamic rebellion out of resentment at its marginalization under Damascus-centered étatism, has been increasingly appeased by new business opportunities, such as the chance to cash in on export deals to pay off the Soviet debt. Syria's *suq* petite bourgeoisie survived and even prospered in spite of Ba'th rule; in the

1970s and 1980s, merchants actually increased their proportion of the labor force from 9 to 12 percent.[9] They may be well positioned, with accumulated capital and traditional know-how, to move into the economic space being vacated by the state. Thus, the economic roots of cleavage between the regime and the Islamic opposition are melting away. Ideologically, Syria's Islamic movement has always advocated a liberal economic model; as the regime liberalizes, the ideological gap is narrowing.

Asad is following a multipronged strategy meant to avoid substantial political liberalization by co-opting and appeasing the Islamic mainstream while marginalizing the more radical elements. Since the collapse of the USSR and socialism, he has been trying to "play the Islamic card," that is, to add Islam to the regime's legitimacy formula while downplaying secular Ba'thism.[10] The regime is building mosques, patronizing the ulama, and propagating Islam in the mass media. As part of this effort, Asad has tried to re-Islamize the Alawis, building mosques in the mountains in order to bring them into the Islamic mainstream. The media depict them as genuine Muslims—for example, Asad's son Basil was shown making the hajj; when he died, his funeral was presided over by a Sunni cleric, and the Alawi shaykhs in attendance were shown in Sunni-like rituals, as if there was little difference between the sects.

Asad has also tried to foster a conservative (al-Azhar-like) Islamic establishment to channel Islamic currents and legitimate the regime. This establishment is headed by the Mufti Ahmad Kaftaro; the Minister of Waqfs; several professors of *shari'a*, of which Ahmed Rahman al-Buti, a television preacher, is the most prominent; and the government-appointed preachers of the great mosques. They do have some followings, such as in Sufi brotherhoods and old quarters like al-Midan. At the base, the regime has encouraged moderate "Asad Qur'anic schools."

The regime is also seeking political détente with moderate opposition Islamists. A big 1992 release of Islamists from prison aimed to mollify Islamic opinion. Islamists are allowed to publish a magazine, and some have been co-opted as independents into parliament. Ghassan Abazad, for example, an Ikhwan leader from Der'a who brokered the return of Ikhwan exiles from Jordan, won a seat in parliament.

But can Islamists be incorporated without being allowed to organize politically? The most favorable scenario for their incorporation into the system would be parliamentary elections that resulted in power sharing between the regime and moderate Islamists. Asad has even toyed with the idea of encouraging a moderate Islamic party; at the time of Ceauşescu's fall, a nervous regime wanted Ahmad Abd al-Rahman al-Buti to form such a party. It is not a foregone conclusion that the Ba'th could not hold its own in elections. In fact, in the only free elections of the Ba'th era, those of 1972 to provincial councils, traditional and Islamic forces won in the cities and the Ba'th won in rural areas. The regime can mobilize blocs of votes through the popular organizations and the National Progressive Front. It could count on the support of many westernized Sunni families and working women fearful of fundamentalism or an Algerian type of upheaval. The Jordanian precedent, which suggests Islamist movements can be tamed through participation, may encourage the regime to proceed with such an experiment. Nevertheless, the regime's current line is that no party can claim a monopoly over Islam.[11] It evidently fears that an Islamist party could appropriate the potent banner of Islam, cast the ruling party as un-Islamic, and become a channel of real opposition.

A nonpolitical Islamist movement fostering pious personal behavior is nevertheless spreading, and so long as it does not challenge the regime, it will permit this safety valve. Signs of an Islamic resurgence include new mosques and a turn among youth to Islam, with the daughters of westernized mothers assuming Islamic dress. This resurgence is, however, limited by a large, influential, non-Sunni population (25 percent of the total population) and a consequent tradition of secularism and religious coexistence: Unlike some other Islamic countries, Syria allows church bells to be rung.

An alternative to co-optation is the renewal of political Islam as an opposition movement carried on by the victims of Syria's integration into the world capitalist market under economic liberalization. As the economic winners among the petite bourgeoisie—upwardly mobile into a bourgeoisie co-opted by the regime—adopt a moderate and conservative version of Islam, a wing recruiting from the marginalized and preaching a populist counterversion could split off from the Islamist mainstream and oppose the new alliance of regime and bourgeoisie. The poor are, so far, turning to Islam chiefly as an ideology of escape, but if their condition worsens, Islam is the natural (and only remaining) ideology of protest. There remains an anti-regime Islamic opposition in exile that could exploit this situation: From Iraq, it accuses the Asad family of treating Syria as its private property and of being ready to make peace with Israel to get money and keep power.[12] Capitalist penetration, combined with the less than honorable kind of peace settlement with Israel that seems to be in the cards, could provide oppositionist Islam with fertile ground for proselytization.

Conclusions: A Comparative Perspective

Contrasting the Syrian with the Iranian and Egyptian cases is instructive. In Iran, the state enjoyed little national legitimacy and was associated with indiscriminate westernization. This backdrop generated a powerful and radical egalitarian strain of Islam that mobilized a wide mass base for the movement. The outcome was the revolutionary overthrow and transformation of the old order. ʾ

By contrast, the modern Egyptian state was forged as part of a nationalist revolution and retains a residue of this legitimacy; moreover, being Sunni, it can, with far less risk than the Syrian regime, dilute its secularism to appease Islamic opinion. The state is therefore less vulnerable than in Iran to radical Islam and more able to reach an accommodation with its moderate wings than Syria. The Islamic movement in Egypt is cross-class, embracing rich bankers and the poor of the *baladi* (rural, unsophisticated) neighborhood. Egalitarian and conservative tendencies coexist, but moderates are dominant and have seemed ready to reach an accommodation with the state. If the regime were to return to a strategy of co-optation, begun in the 1980s but later abandoned, the result could be a limited sharing of power between state and opposition, producing both a partial Islamization of the regime and a parallel conservatization of the Islamist movement.

In the Syrian case, opposition to a regime with an initially populist character threw together all those damaged by the regime's secularizing, populist reforms. An alliance formed between the ulama, prominent figures, and *suq* that, as regime legitimacy declined, attracted broader urban support. This composition shaped a particularly conservative variant of political Islam almost devoid of populism. Its adherents pursued not revolution but reaction, attempting to turn back the political clock to the pre-Ba'th era of urban bourgeois dominance. Its social base therefore remained limited, unable to win over the working class or bridge the urban-rural gap, the keys to mass revolution. The regime retained enough nationalist legitimacy and had incorporated enough of the populist interests spurned by the Islamists to survive Islamic counterrevolution. And yet the ideological gap between a secular, minority-dominated regime and a conservative Sunni movement was too wide to admit of an Egyptian-like accommodation. The outcome was defeat for the movement and a drift toward totalitarianism in the regime. However, as the regime alters its social base—incorporating the bourgeoisie and the *suq* through economic liberalization—an Egyptian-like co-optation of moderate Islamists may become a viable strategy. The risk is that, to the extent the regime is conservatized, Islamic opposition may reappear in new populist clothes.

Notes

1. Abdullah Hanna, *Stages in the Formation of Religious Ideologies in the Arab East Since the End of the Nineteenth Century* (Tokyo: Institute of Developing Economics, March 1989), pp. 17–18.

2. Ibid., pp. 37–39.

3. Hanna Batatu, "Syria's Muslim Brethren," *MERIP Reports*, No. 110, November–December 1982, pp. 12–20.

4. H. R. Dekmejian, *Islam in Revolution* (Syracuse: Syracuse University Press, 1985), pp. 118–119.

5. *Middle East International*, February 13, 1981.

6. Thus, even the populist Mustafa al-Sabai declared, "I do not see any need to launch an electoral campaign among the peasants because . . . the middle strata . . . elected me." See Hanna, *Stages in the Formation of Religious Ideologies*, p. 20.

7. See Umar F. Abd-Allah, *The Islamic Struggle in Syria* (Berkeley: Mizan Press, 1983), pp. 201–267.

8. Interview with Sa'id al-Hawwa in *Die Welt*, transcribed in Foreign Radio Broadcast Information Service, December 1980.

9. Syrian Arab Republic, *Statistical Abstract* (Damascus: Central Bureau of Statistics, 1976), pp. 151–152; Syrian Arab Republic, *Statistical Abstract* (Damascus: Central Bureau of Statistics, 1991), pp. 76–77.

10. This, at least, is the perception of such diverse observers as Patrick Seale and officials of the Iranian embassy in Damascus. (Interviews, London and Damascus, Summer 1994).

11. Abdullah ad-Dardari, in *al-Hayat*, reproduced in *Middle East Mirror*, March 3, 1992, p. 13.

12. Baghdad Radio, reported in BBC Summary of World Broadcasts, ME, February 24, 1994.

12

Islamism and Tribalism in Yemen

ERIC WATKINS

Much continues to be written about the worldwide growth of political Islam since the early 1980s and in particular the development of an international Islamic fundamentalism hostile to any values but its own.[1] Certainly, events such as the bombing of the World Trade Center by Islamic extremists, or the Iranian government's *fatwa* against Salman Rushdie for publication of his *Satanic Verses,* are hardly reassuring about the intentions of some Islamists. But such intentions do not necessarily represent the whole of Islam; nor do they provide any convincing evidence of a closely coordinated effort toward a global Islamist regime. Doubtless there are numerous individuals and groups who would like to see such a regime and who will bend their efforts in this direction. But, as I will attempt to show in this chapter, such people have not been successful in Yemen, despite international connections and the apparent support of the central government. In particular, I will show that traditional tribal groups and their allies in the government have used Islamists to eradicate political adversaries, to unify the country under a single political structure, and to consolidate their own grip over that structure.

From Imamite Rule to Tribal Republicanism

"Traditional Arabia," writes R. B. Serjeant, "is dominated politically and socially by the arms-bearing tribal class and its chiefs."[2] Written well over a decade ago, Serjeant's words aptly sum up several centuries of Yemeni history as well as the most recent, but unsuccessful, efforts to re-Islamize the country in the 1990s. To understand those efforts, it is perhaps useful to follow Serjeant at least briefly in examining the underlying principles that appear to govern Yemeni tribalism in its relationship to Islam. In Serjeant's view, "Tribal Arabia is normally conceived of as operating in a state of anarchy. A tribesman is secure in his own tribal territory, but without some arrangements for protection outside it his life and property are at the mercy of others."[3] Serjeant further notes that tribes have developed a system of law among themselves that "is concerned with protection, truces, the payment of blood monies, and damages, all of which involve the essential function of an arbiter."[4] Tribes themselves recognize the crucial role of outside mediators in solving their disputes and, as Serjeant notes, "No potential arbiter is more acceptable than the member of a house upon which Allah has conferred some superior and supernatural quality—for who can quarrel with God's authority?"[5] But a crucial point in the selection of any arbiter concerns tribal honor, in particular, the honor of the tribal shaykh: "Tribal honour among the shaykhly houses is so sensitive that no shaykh or tribal lord can brook submission to the authority of another, unless possibly temporarily to a *muqaddam harb*, a war chief."[6]

Imamic rule, which lasted more than 1,000 years in Yemen, is said to have had its origins in the arrival of al-Hadi Yahya, a descendant of the Prophet Muhammad, to the country's northern regions to settle a tribal dispute in the third Islamic century. "Like the Prophet Muhammad," Serjeant writes, "he made his entrance as an arbiter endowed with authority from Allah."[7] Citing al-Hadi's biographer, Serjeant's account of the arbitration is worth quoting at length:

> The Saad and Rabia tribes of Saada of Khawlan b. Amr came out to meet him where he had camped outside the town and greeted him and he greeted them. He made a moving address so that they wept at his words, unable to contain their emotion, like pilgrims to the Bayt Allah. Al-Hadi then ordered a Qur'an to be brought and made them swear to one another to leave off dissension and hostility—which they did. He then made them swear to himself obedience and support, and they paid allegiance to him on the spot.[8]

Succeeding where local arbiters had earlier failed, al-Hadi was then able to establish a power base in Saada and soon dispatched his own agents to collect taxes in outlying villages. Although Serjeant reports that the revenues were small, they enabled al-Hadi at least to consolidate his position in Yemen and to establish the institution of rule by the Imams, who would govern the country more or less continuously until the 1960s.

Despite his success in arbitrating among the tribes, al-Hadi nonetheless had difficulties with them. In fact, he seems to have overstepped his authority by trying too hard to impose Islamic morality on them and had to leave when they disobeyed his orders, "which were in consonance with pure *shari'a*."[9] In particular, Serjeant says, al-Hadi was "extremely strict":

A tribesman "punished for wine-drinking died under eighty lashes awarded by one of his governors."[10] But drinking wine was only one of several tribal practices that ran counter to al-Hadi's strict Islamic code. Citing verses in praise of wine, women, and song recited in a mosque, Serjeant says the poem "becomes understandable as a reaction against Islamic restrictions" on practices that tribal society viewed in a more positive light; indeed, he says, "the remoter tribal areas" still have "a different moral outlook on them."[11] In the millennium that followed al-Hadi's arrival in Yemen, there was thus, to use Serjeant's phrase, a "seesawing tension" between the tribes and the Imamate.[12] This tension was caused partly by the tribal shaykhs' inherent need for the Imamate as an arbiter and partly by their instinctive fear of the Imamate's efforts to undermine their own authority by imposing Islamic law.

In the course of their history, the Imams made a number of key political blunders, two of which bear directly on the present discussion. The first occurred in 1728 when the Imam's governor in Lahej revolted and broke away, creating the original division between North and South Yemen. Indeed, barely 100 years later, the Sultan of Lahej opened negotiations with the British, leading to their 130-year reign over the south.[13] The second blunder also began in the 1700s when, following a clash with tribesmen, the Imam Husayn ordered the assassination of the prominent tribal leader Ali bin Qasim al-Ahmar and had his head impaled on a spear for public display in Sanaa.[14] That blunder continued into the twentieth century when the Imam Yahya seized Hajja, the capital of the Hashed confederation of tribes, and proceeded to break the power of its ruling al-Ahmar family.[15] Persecution of the al-Ahmar family continued into the late 1950s when the Imam Ahmed—repeating the actions of his forebears in the 1700s—ordered the execution and beheading of the tribal leader Sheikh Husayn al-Ahmar and his son Hamid.[16]

For our purposes, the consequences of those two blunders are clear. The revolution of 1962 saw the al-Ahmar family, headed by Shaykh Abdullah bin Hussein, aligning itself with republican forces against the Imamate and, in the postrevolutionary era, forming a vital element in what Fred Halliday has called the rule of "republican tribalism."[17] Referring to supporters of the republican cause, Halliday notes that tribal shaykhs used the revolution primarily to advance their own cause: "A fourth group comprised tribal leaders who supported the Republic for traditional reasons, knowing that patronising the central government could advance their position; prominent among these were Shaykh Abdullah al-Ahmar."[18] Elsewhere, describing the effect of Egyptian intervention in the war, Halliday says, "The main consequence of their intervention was that they strengthened the centrifugal forces, the tribal leaders who came to represent the most powerful force in North Yemen."[19] And, of these tribal shaykhs, it was Abdullah bin Hussein al-Ahmar who "emerged in time as the most powerful republican shaykh of all."[20] Eventually, says Halliday, "the war was concluded by the republican tribalist forces whom the Egyptians had subsidised and who then turned the country into a Saudi satellite"; as Serjeant confirms, "Under the Republic the position of the Zaydi tribes is still strong and they receive subsidies as in the days of the Imams—the Republic has to rely on Hashid and Bakil for its defence."[21]

The Tribalist-Islamist Alliance

In 1990 Shaykh Ahmar, then arguably the most powerful man in the country, joined forces with Shaykh Abdul Mujeed al-Zindani, the leader of the Muslim Brotherhood in Yemen, to form the fundamentalist al-Islah (Reform) Party.[22] A founder of the Yemeni Muslim Brotherhood, Shaykh Zindani, known for his Saudi-influenced view of Islam, was diametrically opposed to liberal thinking, especially to the communism of South Yemen. In the struggle against the Yemen Socialist Party (YSP, al-Hizb al-Ishtiraki al-Yamani), Shaykh Zindani was to play a key role, not least by urging his followers on against "godless communism." Nevertheless, Shaykh Ahmar's decision to work with him seems to have surprised even his own followers. According to Paul Dresch, the move initially weakened his position among the tribes, perhaps because of their traditional mistrust of the centralizing effect of any Islamic rule and of Saudi Islam in particular.[23] But, as we shall later see, Shaykh Ahmar's political union with Shaykh Zindani seems to have had more traditional and longer-term political ends in view.

Consequences of the Imam's loss of Lahej in the 1700s also appeared at this time, most notably through the emergence of Shaykh Tariq al-Fadhli, head of the Yemeni Islamic Jihad Organization (al-Jihad al-Islami). Encouraged by the independent Sultan of Lahej in the 1830s, the British opened formal negotiations for the purchase of Aden and soon found themselves caught in political intrigues between the Sultan of Lahej and the Sultan of Fadhli.[24] The British eventually came to terms with both sultanates and provided them with considerable economic help in return for their assistance in maintaining control of Aden. Indeed, those two sultanates, being the closest to Aden, were the recipients of virtually all of Britain's largesse during the colonial period: Halliday writes, "Throughout the British occupation there were only two development projects of any significance: both produced cotton; one in Abyan, the other in Lahej."[25] Halliday adds that the first of the two projects, in the Fadhli Sultanate, was "run by the local sultan and by the rulers, who controlled the country up-stream from which the flood waters came. In 1949–50 a cotton ginnery was built at Zinjibar, the capital of Abyan province, and by the mid 1960s over 50,000 acres had been irrigated."[26] The value of this project to the Fadhli family must have been immense since, of the two cotton projects in the country, it had a greater share of the export potential. According to Halliday, "By 1962 cotton alone made up 56 per cent of the Protectorate's exports."[27]

Given its privileged position, the Fadhli family was due for a fall with the coming of Marxism to South Yemen, especially when "all lands of sultans, amirs, and shaykhs who had worked with the British were confiscated without compensation."[28] As Halliday notes, "All the leading Federal leaders had fled by the summer of 1967 and some had been tried in absentia and sentenced to death for treason. But they had found support in Saudi Arabia, and the republican regime in the North had also begun to give them shelter after its shift to the right in early 1968."[29] Among the federal leaders, the Fadhli family also took refuge in Saudi Arabia, where Shaykh Tariq al-Fadhli is said to have taken up Islamist causes. Indeed, reportedly funded by the Saudi businessman Osama bin Ladin, Shaykh Fadhli eventually "divided his time between Iran, the northern borders of Pakistan, and Afghanistan."[30] In a word, Shaykh Fadhli fought with the Afghan mujahideen against the Soviet Union. After leaving Afghanistan, he returned to Saudi Arabia and, with the continued patronage of bin Ladin, quietly filtered back into Yemen as head of its Islamic Jihad Organization.

The full history of the relationship between the al-Islah Party and the Islamic Jihad Organization has yet to be written. But, in broad outline, they appear to have been partly overt and partly covert partners joined by the common aim of undermining the former rulers of the Marxist south, the YSP. Forming the overt side of that relationship, al-Islah leaders frequently stated their distaste for working with the socialists. Their opposition lasted from reunification of the two Yemens in May 1990 until the end of the civil war in July 1994. During that period, al-Islah frequently threatened jihad or holy war against the socialists. This threat and its apparent implementation first became evident in connection with parliamentary debate over so-called scientific institutions founded in the 1970s. Funded by the government but operated by fundamentalist organizations, the institutions supposedly provided an Islamic curriculum. In fact, they were generally understood to be fronts for Islamist militants. They provided staging posts and training facilities for a stream of mujahideen passing between Cairo and Kabul, with occasional stop-overs in Khartoum, home of the exiled Saudi businessman Osama bin Ladin and the Sudanese fundamentalist leader Dr. Hasan al-Turabi.[31] Aware of these purposes behind the apparently innocent facade of the "scientific institutions," the YSP in the summer of 1992 introduced parliamentary legislation to end them. Faced with this threat, members of al-Islah initially lobbied President Ali Abdullah Saleh and disrupted parliamentary debates so extensively that the speaker of the house, Dr. Yassin Said Noman, a YSP member, threatened to resign.[32] As the debate continued, Shaykh Ahmar called for jihad should the socialist proposals pass. Shortly after the bill was passed, the home of Dr. Noman was subjected to a rocket attack, apparently a fulfillment of Shaykh Ahmar's threat.

Forming the covert side of the fundamentalist opposition to the YSP, the Islamic Jihad Organization was responsible for the wave of terrorist actions in the country—including assassinations, attempted assassinations, and bombings—directed mostly at the socialists. There initially appeared to be no connection whatsoever between al-Islah and the campaign of terror being waged. But after the bombing of two Aden hotels in December 1992, southern security forces began a roundup of Islamic Jihad supporters in Abyan, which led to a standoff with Shaykh Fadhli himself in a mountain stronghold near Shuqra on the Gulf of Aden.[33] The link between al-Islah and the Islamic Jihad was soon tacitly confirmed when Shaykh Fadhli was allowed safe passage from Abyan to Sanaa under the protection of Shaykh Ahmar. Any remaining doubts about the link between al-Islah and the Islamic Jihad Organization were finally eliminated during the civil war of 1994, when the two groups fought side by side against the south.

Outwardly, the relationship among Shaykhs Ahmar, Zindani, and Fadhli seems relatively straightforward as a political alliance among fellow Islamists. All three had received Saudi support, including refuge, funding, position, and—to varying degrees—ideological orientation in the direction of Saudi Islam. They were, moreover, opponents of the southern leaders, with Zindani and Fadhli, in particular, having suffered at their hands in the early days of the revolution in South Yemen. And, not least, through their Saudi connections the three shaykhs were in communication with Islamist backers in Sudan and elsewhere. But on another level, the relationship between Shaykhs Ahmar and Fadhli seems to have been founded on tribal grounds. This tribal relationship, in turn, was shared by President Saleh, himself a Zaydi tribesman born in the village of Bayt al-Ahmar.[34] It thus appears, especially in the light of subsequent events, that Shaykh Zindani and his followers were duped into providing an Islamist front—and thus popular support—for what was essentially a tribalist opposition to the YSP.

The Yemeni civil war of 1994, fought from April through July, was in fact largely instigated by al-Islah. Shaykhs Ahmar and Zindani, in particular, had actively promoted the idea of jihad against the south in the run-up to battle and during the war itself.[35] The final defeat of the YSP and its allies initially seemed to fit in with Islamist aspirations, not least in Aden, where Islamist supporters smashed cases of alcohol, burnt down the local brewery, and destroyed religious shrines. Islamists later seemed to have been altogether victorious when the Yemeni constitution was changed, according to their long-standing demand, to read that *shari'a* law would be the sole source of legislation in the country. But Islamist aspirations were soon dashed and, indeed, it seems that those aspirations had been deliberately unleashed only to serve the interests of the Saleh regime.[36] Changes in the Yemeni constitution also included an end to the five-man presidential council and, with it, to the prominent political position of Shaykh Zindani, formerly a member of the council. But the death knell of Islamization in Yemen was sounded most clearly, perhaps, by Shaykh Tariq al-Fadhli. When asked to comment on the ravaging of Aden by his presumed supporters, Fadhli denied any connection with them and explained that the Jihad Organization had consisted of men only opposed to the YSP. With the defeat of the YSP, he added, there was no longer a reason to keep the Jihad Organization in existence and its former supporters could join whichever political party they wished or, for that matter, "get jobs in accordance with the legitimate framework."[37]

Conclusion

There can be little doubt that Islamist thinking will continue in Yemen, in the short term by groups such as the salafis and over the longer term by members of the al-Islah Party now in the government.[38] But equally, there can be little doubt that the main thrust of Islamization has already seen its day in Yemen. In retrospect, it can be seen that tribalist forces, in alliance with the central government, encouraged, controlled, and directed the growth of Islamist forces in Yemen, both to secure and to extend their own positions of power throughout the country. This is most evident in the case of Shaykh Tariq al-Fadhli, whose primary motivation was revenge against the YSP and restoration of his family lands in Abyan. Once those ends were achieved, he dropped all pretense of Islamism and reverted to his traditional role of tribal shaykh. Now appointed by President Saleh as paramount shaykh of the region, Tariq al-Fadhli is a member of the ruling order and entrusted with retribalization of the former South Yemen. Shaykh Abdullah bin Hussein al-Ahmar has likewise assured himself of increased power—not least, in the favors he will be owed by President Saleh in helping to defeat the YSP. More important, perhaps, in helping to restore Shaykh Fadhli in the south, Shaykh Ahmar has now extended his own domain of influence, becoming the country's predominant tribal ruler.

As we have seen, the political role of Islamic forces in Yemen has always been relatively precarious and based largely on the intrinsic need of tribes for arbiters. Islam initially filled that mediatory role in the person of al-Hadi and later in the rule of the Imamate. But, ever wary of the Islamic tendency to impose its own law and undermine their authority, tribal shaykhs maintained a pragmatic relationship with the Imamate, using it when necessary, avoiding it when possible, and finally, eliminating it when expedient. Events have shown that, with the increased consolidation of Yemeni tribes over time, Islamist activity is now even more precarious. In a sense, it could be reasonably argued that the tribalists' use of the Islamists was part of that longer historical tension between the tribes and the Imams. Thus, an altogether new tribalist ascendancy may be occurring in the country, one that increasingly can dispense with anything more than the thinnest of facades of Islamist thinking.[39] In a word, the house of al-Ahmar appears after centuries to have reasserted its ancient role as arbiter and thus to have eliminated the need for Islamic mediators altogether. The forces of republican tribalism thus appear to have consolidated their position considerably through the war and to have done so at the expense of both the Islamist and the Socialist opposition. Serjeant's words seem applicable to Yemen today: Traditional Yemen is still dominated politically and socially by the arms-bearing tribal class and its chiefs.

Notes

1. The number of books about the growth of Islam is legion. For a recent comprehensive view, see Farzana Shaikh (ed.), *Islam and Islamic Groups* (Harlow, U.K.: Longman, 1994).

2. R. B. Serjeant, "The Interplay Between Tribal Affinities and Religious (Zaydi) Authority in the Yemen," in *Al-Abhath: Journal of the Centre for Arab and Middle East Studies, Faculty of Arts and Sciences, American University, Beirut* 30, 1982, pp. 11–50. I am indebted to this work and to that of several other academic scholars. The late Robin Bidwell, author of *The Two Yemens* and former secretary of the Centre of Middle Eastern Studies at the University of Cambridge, is to be credited for my decision to reside in Yemen. He advised me in early 1989 that changes were coming to the country and that living there would enable me to document them. Renaud Detalle, currently a doctoral student attached to the French Centre for Yemeni Research and my closest associate during my five-year stay, has given unstintingly of his time, hospitality, and unrivaled understanding of the political scene in Yemen. Paul Dresch, author of *Tribes, Government, and History in Yemen* and a Fellow of St. John's College, Oxford, has likewise been generous with his authoritative observations of tribal life in Yemen and its role in political affairs. Bernard Haykel, a Postgraduate Fellow of St. John's College and a specialist in

Yemeni religious history, has contributed substantially to my understanding of Islamic groups in Yemen and their role in contemporary politics.

3. Serjeant, "The Interplay Between Tribal Affinities and Religious (Zaydi) Authority in the Yemen," p. 12.

4. Ibid.

5. Ibid.

6. Ibid.

7. Ibid., p. 21.

8. Ibid.

9. Ibid., p. 18.

10. Ibid., p. 20.

11. Ibid. The moral outlook that defeated al-Hadi eventually found its way into the very Imamate that he established. Recounting his journey to Sanaa in 1836, a British midshipman describes meeting the Imam at his palace: "Twice we were at the private apartment of the Imam, and each time we left perfectly disgusted. The Imam, with five or six dancing and singing girls, got shockingly drunk, and he seemed surprised at our refusing to join him in drinking raw spirits. The liquor is made in Sanaa and tastes like bad whiskey." The story is cited in Gordon Waterfield, *Sultans of Aden* (London: John Murray, 1968), pp. 35–36.

12. Serjeant, "The Interplay Between Tribal Affinities and Religious (Zaydi) Authority in the Yemen," p. 46.

13. Fred Halliday, *Arabia Without Sultans: A Survey of Political Leadership in the Arab World* (London: Vintage Press, 1975), p. 95.

14. For a fuller discussion of the importance of the al-Ahmar family in Yemeni history, see Serjeant, "The Interplay Between Tribal Affinities and Religious (Zaydi) Authority in the Yemen," pp. 28–31, 37–41. For a detailed treatment of the Imamate's fall in the 1960s, see Halliday, *Arabia Without Sultans*, pp. 93–138.

15. Serjeant, "The Interplay Between Tribal Affinities and Religious (Zaydi) Authority in the Yemen," p. 30.

16. Ibid., p. 29.

17. Halliday, *Arabia Without Sultans*, pp. 126–130.

18. Ibid., p. 117.

19. Ibid., p. 126.

20. Ibid., p. 129.

21. Ibid., p. 127; Serjeant, "The Interplay Between Tribal Affinities and Religious (Zaydi) Authority in the Yemen," p. 42. According to Foreign Office files, Shaykh Ahmar, following the cessation of hostilities in 1970, "became responsible for the distribution of government subsidies to the tribes." Elsewhere the files say that Shaykh Ahmar has been "criticised in tribal circles for not distributing Saudi largesse more widely."

22. Foreign Office files say that Shaykh Zindani was born around 1936 in the central Yemeni province of Ibb and received his early education in Aden under the British. He went on to Ain Shams University in Cairo where he initially studied chemistry and biology. Under the influence of Imam Hassan al-Banna and Sayyid Qutb in Egypt, though, Zindani switched to Islamic studies. In 1966 he returned to Aden, but with the rise of the National Liberation Front, he fled to Saudi

Arabia in 1967. There he followed the teachings of the Saudi Mufti Abdul Aziz bin Baz and became a senior official in the Islamic Call Organization, then headed by Dr. Abdullah Naseef. In 1970 Zindani returned to Yemen where he was appointed an adviser in the Ministry of Education and, in collaboration with Qadhi Yahya al-Fusayil, an ex-royalist minister, formed the Yemeni Muslim Brotherhood.

23. This view was expressed in personal conversation.

24. British negotiations for Aden are documented in Waterfield, *Sultans of Aden.*

25. Halliday, *Arabia Without Sultans,* pp. 176–177.

26. Ibid., p. 177.

27. Ibid.

28. Ibid., p. 259. It is worth noting that confiscation of private land was part of the broader program of the National Liberation Front to detribalize the south. Indeed, with aims similar to those of the Imamate in North Yemen, the NLF struck a radical blow at the tribes "through the enforcement of non-tribal law. Tribal conflicts were centred around real conflicts over issues of economic scarcity—water rights, grazing rights, and caravan tolls. Conflicts between tribes were handled by vengeance and prolonged by feuds. Such law as existed was *urf,* traditional tribal law. The NLF set itself up as a supra-tribal institution which would remove these spurs to tribalism." Ibid., p. 258.

29. Ibid., p. 248.

30. *Al-Wasat,* London, January 11–17, 1993.

31. Yemeni newspapers were full of such reports at the time. *Sawt al-Ummal* reported on May 28, 1992, that the Voice of America had broadcast complaints from Egypt, Algeria, and Tunisia about a training camp established in Yemen by the Sudanese fundamentalist leader Dr. Hasan al-Turabi. Suggesting Saudi complicity, the newspaper claimed that the camp was part of a wider plan to disrupt Yemen's coming elections and install a fundamentalist regime in the country. A similar article appeared in *At-Tas'heeya* on June 2, 1992, adding that Turabi planned to make Yemen a staging point for further fundamentalist activity throughout the region. *Al-Mustaqbal* reported on June 8, 1992, that Yemen was already one of three routes used by mujahideen en route to Afghanistan and was the favored route of "a Saudi-backed fundamentalist group coming from Egypt called the Jihad Organization." The Yemen government did not acknowledge the Jihad's responsibility for terrorism in Yemen until January 1994. On January 10, 1994, the official armed forces newspaper *26th September* ran a story quoting the minister of the interior, Yahya al-Mutawakkil, as saying, "The al-Jihad Organisation is behind all terrorist activities in Yemen including the hotel bombings in Aden and political assassinations."

32. Noman's threat of resignation was reported in *Al-Thawri* on July 9, 1992.

33. It was no coincidence that Shaykh Fadhli was cornered near Shuqra since the area has traditionally been the ancestral home of the Fadhli tribe. Describing British efforts to bring the Fadhlis to heel in the 1800s, Waterfield says that Captain Haines "sent the Company's brig *Euphrates* to blockade Shuqra, which was the main port of supply for the Fadhli tribe, in the hope that this would divert the tribe from maintaining their control of the roads to Aden." Waterfield, *Sultans of Aden,* p. 107.

34. During the lead-up to the 1994 war, southerners made much of the family connections between Ali Abdullah Saleh and Shaykh al-Ahmar. More relevant, perhaps, are notes from Foreign Office files on political and military relations between the two. "He [Saleh] showed ruthless decisiveness in crushing the National Democratic Front's guerrilla campaign in the autumn/winter of 1978, but was caught napping with an undermanned, under-equipped, and poorly-led army when the Peoples' Democratic Republic of Yemen attacked in support of the NDF in February 1979. He was saved by the intervention of the Arab states, particularly Iraq, *and the rallying of Hashid tribesmen to defend their homeland"* (italics added). The same files report that Shaykh Ahmar "and his Hashid tribesmen came to the support of the government in the YAR/PDRY fighting in early 1979 and during the following summer moved closer to the President." Elsewhere the files say that Shaykh Ahmar was "appointed a member of the President's Advisory Counsel at its creation in May 1979, and given special prominence in government circles thereafter. He was regarded as a leading light in the Islamic Front's opposition to the NDF, in the summer (of) 1980." Shaykh Ahmar's role in Saleh's party, the General Peoples' Congress, is also noted: "He was appointed a member of the Permanent Committee of the General Popular [*sic*] Conference in August, 1982."

35. During the fighting Shaykh Ahmar told journalists that the war was "a holy war that must not be stopped, even if it costs millions of lives." In his own name Ahmar repeated the *fatwa* earlier issued by Abdul Wahab al-Daylami, another al-Islah leader, which said that "a cease-fire in the war against the atheists is against the Islamic *shari'a*." The *fatwa* had been broadcast by the official Sanaa Radio.

36. Mr. Abdul Rahman Ali al-Jifri, exiled leader of the moderate Sons of Yemen League and of the post–civil war opposition movement, commented on President Saleh's use of the Islamists in an interview with *Al-Hayat* on September 29, 1994. "Ali Abdullah Saleh," Jifri said, "presents himself to the world, and especially to Egypt, as someone who is capable of resisting extremism, whilst domestically he has been encouraging this very extremism."

37. Reported in *Al-Hayat*, London, September 4, 1994. I am indebted to Bernard Haykel for drawing my attention to this article along with several others and for translating excerpts of them.

38. In its report on the political conditions in Yemen prior to the 1993 elections, the U.S. International Republican Institute described the salafis as a part of al-Islah "directly associated with the Wahabbi sect of Islam based in Saudi Arabia." International Republican Institute, *1993 National Elections in the Republic of Yemen*, p. 11. The salafis were later held responsible for the destruction of shrines in Aden following the end of the civil war. Al-Islah Party members currently hold a deputy premiership as well as ministries in the government including religious guidance, health, justice, local administration, and supply and trade.

39. In "The Interplay Between Tribal Affinities and Religious (Zaydi) Authority in the Yemen," p. 29 ff., Serjeant discusses the traditional mediatory role of the al-Ahmar family.

Part Three

Parallels

13

Islamism in Algeria and Iran

MEHDI MOZAFFARI

Islamic fundamentalists succeeded in seizing power in Iran but failed in Algeria. Unique circumstances in each country and other factors offer plausible explanations for the different outcomes. In this chapter I shall examine these and discuss possible scenarios for Algeria's future following the interruption of the democratic process, looking in particular at the Khomeinists in Iran and the Front Islamique du Salut (FIS) in Algeria. The comparison shows that despite some substantial similarities, these two fundamentalist groups are quite different from each other.

I define *Islamic fundamentalism* or *Islamism* as a militant and antimodernist movement growing out of a belief that Islam is simultaneously a religion (Din), a way of life (Dunya), and a form of government (Dawla). This definition contains three elements. First, the Islamic fundamentalists have a holistic concept of Islam. They believe in the absolute indivisibility of the three famous D's. This characteristic marks the main difference between them and the liberal Muslims, who believe that at least a kind of separation between Islam and politics is possible and thus make an effort to conciliate Islam with modernity. Having a holistic view of Islam is not specific to Islamic fundamentalism, however; the huge majority of Muslims throughout history believed and continue to believe that Islam is holistic.

Thus, what sets the Islamic fundamentalists apart from other Muslims? The main questions are: What are the distinctive characteristics of Islamic fundamentalism? Is it enough in itself to believe in the three D's to be a fundamentalist? Or is it something more than a pure belief in holistic Islam? This "something more" is *militancy*. That is, not every militant Muslim is a fundamentalist (e.g., Mojahidin-e Khalq in Iran), but an Islamic fundamentalist is necessarily a militant. Professor John Voll thinks that the term *activist* is more appropriate than the term *militant*, because in his opinion, militants are "those groups who utilize violence in achieving their goals and this is not the case for all Islamic fundamentalists, like the Muslim Brotherhood in Egypt."[1]

Militancy is not necessarily equivalent to violence, however. In France, for example, ordinary members of political parties are called "militants." The Egyptian Muslim Brotherhood has also used violence to achieve its goals. For example, in December 1948, Egyptian Prime Minister Nuqrashi Pasha was shot and killed by a young member of the brotherhood, and in October 1954 the brotherhood made an unsuccessful attempt on Nasser's life. Finally, no Islamic fundamentalist group has deliberately eliminated the use of violence from its strategy. Violence may come right at the start (e.g., Fadayan-e Islam [Zealots of Islam] in Iran in the 1940s) or on the road to political mobilization (e.g., the Front Islamique du Salut [FIS, Islamic Salvation Front] in Algeria), but it always comes, sooner or later. Therefore, I maintain that militancy, and more than that violence, is a distinctive characteristic of today's Islamic fundamentalist groups. After the holistic outlook, militancy and violence form the second element of Islamic fundamentalism.

The third element is Islamic fundamentalism's clear antimodernist tendency. One has to distinguish *modernity* from *modernization*. While *modernity* is an intellectual position based on liberty of criticism and also *criticism* of criticism, *modernization* or *modernizing* is essentially technical, consisting of the use of modern instruments and facilities. Islamic fundamentalists reject the concept of modernity (or confuse it with modernizing), but they use modern facilities in abundance.

In my discussion of Algerian and Iranian Islamic fundamentalists, I use a broad spectrum of variables: the discourse; organizational dimensions; the leadership; religious and cultural specificities; political and social dimensions; and finally, the geopolitical and international environment.

The Discourse

Iranian and Algerian Islamic fundamentalists share the same ideas and discourse and act in similar ways. They believe in and work toward the same ideal model (the Medina model under Prophet Muhammad). Both believe in the *reversibility of time*, as Lévi-Strauss put forward in another context. The minor differences that exist concern their source of inspiration (the Iranians are Shi'a and the Algerians are Sunni). In Iran, because they are Shi'a, their first reference point (after the Prophet) is the line of twelve Imams. However, they also respect certain Sunni figures, such as Ghazali (1058–1111), Bukhari (810–870), Ahmad Ibn Hanbal (780–855),

Tabari (839–923), Muhammad 'Abduh (1849–1905), and the contemporary figures Maududi (1903–1979) and Sayyid Qutb (1906–1966).

The Algerian fundamentalists, who are Sunni (Maliki rite, derived from the name of Maik Ibn Anas, 708 or 716–796), also have a deep respect for the first Shi'a Imam (Ali Ibn Abi Talib), who is also the fourth and last "righteous" Caliph (Rashidun). Furthermore, they admire the success of Ayatollah Khomeini in establishing an Islamic regime in Iran.

Despite some internal disputes between the so-called radical and moderate fundamentalists, the majority agree on the necessity of a strong and severe Islamic regime with respect to the political, social, and cultural life of Muslim society. Politically, neither Iranian nor Algerian fundamentalism is democratic. Ali Belhadj, one of the prominent leaders of the FIS, has repeatedly declared that "democracy is *Kufr* (atheism)."[2] Khomeini likewise did not believe in democracy. His interpretation of "Islamic" political rule was based on the new concept of *velayat-e faqih* (the governance of Shi'a jurisconsult). This concept was later elaborated and revised by Khomeini himself, taking the form of *velayat-e mutlaqah-e faqih* (absolute governance of the Shi'a juriconsult). Concretely, this means not only that the guide of the republic must always be an ecclesiastic but that all the power of the Prophet must be vested in him. Both assumptions are clearly in opposition to the fundamental principles of democracy.[3] Regarding political tolerance, neither the Algerian nor the Iranian Islamic fundamentalists tolerate any real opposition (Islamic or non-Islamic). Ali Belhadj made it clear that "any party who opposes the Islamic solution is the party of the devil."[4] The Iranian political situation under the Islamist regime is a plain illustration of the fundamentalists' lack of tolerance.

Socially, both desire permanent control and supervision (*amr bi ma'ruf—nahy can al-munkar*) of all private and collective activities of the people. Culturally, the sublimation of traditions is encouraged. With regard to the economy, the main trend in both forms of fundamentalism is a kind of liberal economy focused on the promotion of the private sector, especially the merchants. In the FIS program of March 7, 1989, a long chapter is dedicated to the economy. According to this program: "Commerce . . . constitue le système nerveux de l'économie qui canalise la production des richesses, coordonne les divers intérêts et réalise l'équilibre."

In Khomeini's view, the economy was only a secondary issue of little importance.

Algerian and Iranian fundamentalists also share a particular vision of the West as evil. Whereas Iranian fundamentalists accord the role of the Great Satan (Shaytan-é bozorg) to the United States, France represents the evil of the West to Algerian fundamentalists.

This short overview of fundamentalist discourse indicates a great degree of similarity between the Algerian and Iranian fundamentalists.

There are also some significant differences between them. These differences could partially explain the success of the one and the failure (so far) of the other. The first difference concerns the organizational aspect.

The Organizational Dimension

Algerian fundamentalism has been organized as a recognizable and legal political party; Iranian fundamentalists, in contrast, only function as part of a movement. The Algerian Front Islamique du Salut (FIS, Islamic Salvation Front), which encompasses an agglomeration of different Islamic organizations and movements, was formed on February 18, 1989, in the Ibn Badis mosque (or on March 10 in the Al Sunna mosque, according to another source).[5] On September 16, it was officially recognized by government authorities. The fact that the FIS has taken the recognizable and legal form of a political party marks a qualitative difference to the Iranian case. In Iran, since World War II a group of small organizations, parties, and circles have existed with the main objective of establishing an Islamic government. The most active of them was the Fadayan-e Islam. When the revolutionary process in Iran began in 1977–1978, however, there was no political party (not even a clandestine one) that could fully represent the fundamentalist idea and program,[6] only a huge and diffuse movement with which almost all the anti-Shah opposition groups could identify. The movement as such was disparate, nonstructural, and nonformalized. It was indeed everywhere and nowhere at the same time. This does not necessarily mean that the fundamentalist movement was out of control; the priesthood under the supreme leadership of Ayatollah Khomeini was able to give specific direction to the movement.

The absence of such a party in Iran and its presence in Algeria have led to diametrically opposed consequences. Because it was a *movement*, Iranian fundamentalism could easily survive and escape dismantlement by the police and military authorities, despite being extraordinarily active. Similarly, it was impossible for the Shah's regime and the judicial authorities to dissolve the fundamentalist network. Another benefit of being a movement was that there was not any single recognizable organism behind the riots, the destruction of public and private buildings and properties, and the general chaos and rebellion. Authority for the movement was assumed by Khomeini himself, who remained in his Paris suburb when the real crisis and rebellion started in Iran.

In contrast to the Iranian movement, the Algerian FIS was officially recognized and had founders who were responsible for the party (Abbasi Madani and Ali Belhadj). Furthermore, the party consisted of formal structures (committees, a general assembly, and a consultative assembly). Despite efforts to keep the names of the influential members hidden, it soon became evident that this strategy had not been successful. The arrests of Abbasi Madani and Belhadj on June 30, 1991, followed the arrests of other influential leaders (Hashani and others). Finally, the massive arrests of 2,500 members and sympathizers of the FIS clearly showed that the strategy of forming a party is indeed risky and can be a very costly enterprise. The dissolution of the FIS, which had been stripped of its powers on April 29, 1992, by the Algerian Supreme Court, was yet another clear demonstration of the deep vulnerability of the organizational model that the Algerian fundamentalists had chosen.

The Leadership

The Iranian and Algerian fundamentalists' methods of leadership are quite different. There are two main and perhaps determining differences that deserve attention. The first is the presence of an ulama hierarchy as an autonomous group able to manage the tasks of leadership in critical situations. The second concerns the personality of the leader. In both instances, the Iranian and Algerian models differ from each other.

In Iran, the Shi'a priesthood (ulama) has traditionally been one of the country's strongest political forces. The ulama have, during the nineteenth and twentieth centuries, repeatedly demonstrated their political influence and permanent interest in the struggle for leadership. Thus animated by the idea of being the true leaders of the Iranian people, they have played an active role in a series of extremely important political events, such as the tobacco revolt in 1891–1892, the constitutional revolution in 1906 (*mashrutah*), the movement for the nationalization of Iran's hydrocarbon resources (1951–1953), the agrarian reforms (1961–1963), and the Islamic revolution (1979). The ulama have never been financially dependent on the state but receive financial resources mainly from Shi'a devotees and in particular from the merchants (the *bazaaris*). By the same token, they are not dependent on the state when nominating clerics. At the high and medium ranks of the Shi'a hierarchy, the nomination is carried out on the basis of an autonomous co-optation system. At the bottom, there is no recruiting network. Theoretically, the doors to Islamic scholarship are open to everybody. The Iranian fundamentalists' interpretation of Islam is quite ecclesiastical. As Khomeini has repeatedly emphasized, "Islam is *akhondism* [ecclesiastical]."[7]

The Shi'a ulama hierarchy (despite factionalism and internal conflicts) has the advantage of being highly regarded by the people. In their eyes, it is not only the authentic watchkeeper of the religion and its survival but also the latent alternative to the Pahlavi political regime, which before the Islamic revolution was regarded as a usurper.

Regarding the personality of the leader, there is no doubt that the presence of a charismatic and strong leader in the person of Ayatollah Khomeini had a very important (if not determinant) influence on the course of the revolutionary process that led to the victory of Iranian fundamentalism. By his charisma and authority, Khomeini was able to impose himself not only as the leader of the fundamentalists but also as the uncontested leader of the revolution. During the whole period immediately before the fall of the Shah, he symbolized the movement itself. Because of this role, Khomeini was accepted as the sole alternative to the Shah.

The Algerian opposition's experience of leadership was completely different from that of the Iranian movement. In Algeria, the leadership of the fundamentalist movement has not been assumed by a "priesthood" (apart from a few exceptions, such as Sheikh Ahmed Sahnoun, who is not a member of the FIS) but by the laymen. In other words, Algerian fundamentalism is far from ecclesiastical. For example, neither of the two key figures in the FIS, Abbasi Madani and Ali Belhadj, is a regular 'alim. Madani (born in 1931 in Sidi Okba) received a state education with a Ph.D. in education from London. After his return to Algeria, he became a professor at Algiers University. Belhadj (born in 1956 in Tunis) has an elementary theological education and has been trained in the framework of the courses administered by the Ministry of Religious Affairs.[8] Furthermore, he has functioned as an itinerant preacher in different mosques in Algeria. Before his arrest, he was a teacher at a secondary school. Abdelkader Hachani, another leader who became responsible for the FIS after the arrest of Abbasi Madani and Belhadj, is an engineer. And his case is far from unique in the FIS leadership.

In Algeria, as in other Muslim countries, there has always existed a ulama. However, the ulama in Algeria did not represent an autonomous and distinct social category as in Iran, and thus none from its ranks could emerge to monopolize the religious heritage and logos.[9] Theoretically, this meant that religion was the property of almost every Muslim in Algeria. In the absence of an organized ulama, Islam was submitted to a very particular form of secularization, not in the Western sense of the word (a clear separation of church and state) but as the lack of legitimacy and authority to interpret the Qur'an and the Sunna. The discourse, attitudes, and general opposition of the leaders of the FIS to the Algerian government were perceived first and foremost as political behavior. They acted more as political leaders than religious and spiritual ones. For example, the FIS leadership did not succeed in transforming its activities into religious duties. No one in Algeria had the necessary religious authority to deliver a *fatwa* (authoritative religious decree), condemning, for example, the government or declaring, as Khomeini did in Iran, that the government and the regime were illegitimate and that it was the religious duty of all Iranian Muslims to disobey them. Algerian fundamentalists chose no such course of action, and it is possible that the FIS leadership was not even aware of the importance of distancing itself from the regime. This attitude could possibly be explained by the fact that the FIS intended to exploit public opposition to the government and come to power democratically. Hence, it became a political force, the most powerful one in the country. It failed, however, to be a *religious* authority. Maybe the key to the success of the Iranian fundamentalists is to be found in this crucial difference. Day after day, the Iranian fundamentalists, under the leadership of Khomeini, managed with great success to interpret every political action against the Shah as a pure religious obligation that was imposed on all believers.

Besides not having an organized ulama, the Algerian fundamentalists have not had a charismatic and strong leader like Khomeini. Whereas Khomeini's leadership remained uncontested, Madani's authority was challenged by members of the FIS's central organ (such as Bashir al-Faqih), who accused him of manipulating Islam.[10]

The Religious and Cultural Specificities

One can find more differences between Iran and Algeria with respect to religion and culture. The Algerian fundamentalists are Sunni, as are the majority of Algerian citizens, and belong to the Maliki theological and judicial school. The Iranian fundamentalists, in contrast, are Shi'a Imami, like the majority of the Iranian people, and belong to the Ja'fari theological and judicial school. The major difference here is not really between two different theological and judicial schools but between different political concepts and attitudes.

Followers' attitudes toward the subject of legitimacy are a case in point. The Shi'a Imami position on the issue of the legitimacy of the ruling elite can be summed up in two essential points: First, no regime is fully legitimate during the period of Grand Occultation (Ghaybat al-kubra), where the Twelfth Imam continues to be in hiding. In essence, this means that in the absence of the Mahdi (the Twelfth Imam), all governments are considered temporary. Second, the general tendency among the Shi'a jurisconsult has been to regard rulers as usurpers (*zalama*)—sometimes "good," sometimes "bad," but always usurpers. With the victory of the Islamic revolution in Iran and Khomeini's assumption of power, this view changed because the majority of Shi'a believers considered him a true

Vicar of the Imam (Nayib-e Imam). During the prerevolutionary period, however, the ulama never recognized the Shah's regime as legitimate. The Shi'a literature was full of subtle hints comparing the Shah's regime with that of Yazid (the second Caliph of the Umayyad dynasty), who in the eyes of the Shi'a is the best illustration of a typical usurper. Consequently, to the Shi'a, political usurpation is more than a pure political issue. It is also a *religious* one.

The situation is radically different in Sunni tradition and hence in the Algerian context. Almost unfamiliar with the idea of the Occultation, the Sunni are also unfamiliar with the concept of the *provisional* character of the government. According to the Sunni view, every government is legitimate if it behaves in accordance with general Islamic rules. Furthermore, the rulers are not usurpers, per se. Thus, condemnation of the ruling regime on religious grounds becomes a difficult task. How can one proclaim that a regime or a prince is illegitimate—and convince a large majority of the population of this fact—if the leader pretends to be a true Muslim? It is not impossible to do, but it is difficult. In Egypt after the signature of the Camp David accords, some Islamic fundamentalists proclaimed President Anwar al-Sadat as illegitimate and even non-Muslim and hence licitated his assassination. Despite the assassination, the Egyptian population, including some fundamentalists, was not convinced that the proclamation was justified.

Another problem for the Sunni is their inability to provide a clear picture of a typical usurper. Unanimously, the Sunni have accepted the regularity with which the Prophet's succession has been carried out. Generally, they have also accepted the rule of both the Umayyads and the Abbasids, and so on. Obviously there have been criticism and contestations against these rulers, but these have usually taken a pragmatic form instead of a religious one. Thus, we end up with two distinct concepts of legitimacy: the Sunni, in which the contestation of power takes an almost purely political form, and the Shi'a, in which the religious challenge is of primary importance.[11]

Another important difference between Algerian and Iranian fundamentalists concerns the sphere of rituals. Attaining a successful mobilization of the masses, especially during the relatively long period that generally characterizes the revolutionary process, requires, among other things, a sense of cohesion, a set of symbols, and a discourse that is simultaneously ambivalent and universal. During this process, revolutionaries may either use already existing rituals or create new ones. On this point, the Iranian and the Algerian cases diverge. Among Muslim sects, the Shi'a is undoubtedly the richest with regard to symbols and rituals.[12] The sect shares Islam's genuine symbols and rituals (the anniversary of the Prophet, Ramadan, the Day of Sacrifice [Qurban] and other rituals) but at the same time has its own specific rituals. All Shi'a recognize them, live with them, and indeed identify themselves with them. Two examples, namely the "cult of the martyr" (*shahadat*) and the "death rituals" (*ta'ziah*) will illustrate the point.

Shi'ism is a religion of martyrs. According to its doctrine, all eleven Imams have been killed by usurpers. The sublime figure of martyrdom is al-Hussein (Sayyid ul-shuhada/Lord of martyrs), the third Imam, who was killed with his relatives and disciples in Karbala on October 10, 680. During the revolutionary process in Iran, Khomeini and his entourage exploited the cult of martyrs to such an extent that in the popular imagination, the Shah and his police were almost made responsible for the sufferings of all Shi'a martyrs. The same discourse was used to encourage people to sacrifice their lives, if necessary, for the revolution. The "sublimation of death" was one of the Shi'a leadership's master strategies during the revolution and the Iran-Iraq War.

These different rituals related to death were also used as a very effective weapon against the Shah's regime. The movement commemorated the deaths of people killed in clashes with the army and the police every third day (*sewwum*), every seventh day (*haftum*), every fortieth day (*chehellum*), and for the most fortunate, every year (*sal*). By employing this tactic, Islamic fundamentalists in Iran succeeded in transforming ordinary weekdays into political and religious events. In other words, every day—even the most ordinary days—became a day of commemoration. The regular Shi'a celebrations, such as *muharram* (the most tragic month for the Shi'a) emphasized these mourning celebrations. The effective use of such events made the Shah the first hostage of the Islamic fundamentalists of Iran.

Algeria has not produced anything similar to this Iranian phenomenon. The Algerians lack the cult of martyrdom. Although during the years of the struggle for independence alone, 1 million Algerians were killed, strangely enough, even though they were considered martyrs, no commemorative ceremonies were held except for very official ones. The different attitudes concerning the sublimation of death are also manifested in the different names given to the foundations for those killed in respective countries; in Iran this very powerful foundation was dubbed the Foundation of Martyr/Bonyad-e Shahid, whereas the Algerian counterpart was named the Organization of Combattants (Mujahideen). The commemoration of persons killed during demonstrations in Algeria has been very limited. Again, nothing comparable to what was seen in Iran in 1978. The lack of both the cult of martyrs and the rituals in their honor in Algeria has had a real impact on the process of mass mobilization and especially on the daily efforts to keep the process alive. Precisely because of this, the demonstrations in Algeria were more or less sporadic. The only lasting momentum has been generated by the Friday prayers. But owing to their very nature such set pieces as Friday prayers lack dynamism. There were occasions for the FIS to demonstrate its huge force, but once the prayers ended, the FIS had to wait until the following Friday. Furthermore, since the prayers took place at a specific point of time, Algerian authorities did not have much difficulty monitoring the movement and indirectly controlling it. In Iran, by contrast, every day was like a Friday.

The Political and Social Dimensions

A detailed analysis of political and social factors in Algeria and Iran is outside the scope of this chapter. Instead, I will take a broad look at the political picture during the period in which the real and general crises started in these two societies. The years 1977–1978 for Iran and 1986–1988 for Algeria seem crucial for such a study.

Although the specific causes of the crises in the two countries differed, they both involved the failure of modernization models—in Algeria in the form of a centrally planned economy and in Iran in the form of a liberal economic model. As a result of the failures (whatever the causes), both societies were disintegrating and had come to lose their balance. The huge immigration of young peasants to city suburbs, the housing crisis, rising unemployment, the shortage of basic food-products, and the like were the direct consequences of these modernization projects. Furthermore, as both countries are rentier states,[13] they are deeply dependent on oil revenues and extremely sensitive to fluctuations in international markets; the fall in oil prices may dramatically and suddenly alter the whole picture. In the case of Algeria, the fall in oil prices in 1986 had a real and dramatic impact on the entire fabric of Algerian society.

Both societies had closed political systems. Whereas the Algerian system consisted of three components, the party, the army, and the bureaucracy, the Iranian system had only one, the Shah, despite the fact that he also had a "ruling" party (Rastakhiz) and a very strong army. Thus, the essential difference between Algeria and Iran lay in the fact that the Algerian political model was constructed on the basis of a partnership in which all components were more or less autonomous. The Algerian partnership was rather limited, but compared with the Iranian model, the Algerian model was relatively more flexible. In Iran neither the party nor the army could aspire to even a minimum of autonomy (vis-à-vis the Shah). This difference set the stage for the different outcomes. In Iran, the fundamentalists overthrew the regime precisely because the regime's power structure was dependent on a single pillar: the Shah. Hence, when the Shah fell, the whole structure followed. In Algeria, in contrast, when

Jabhat al-Tahrir al-Watani (Front Liberacion Nationale, FLN) ceased to be the ruling party, in 1989, the regime was able to stay in power, primarily because of the presence of the army. The army immediately dissociated itself from the party, and later from the president of the republic, Chadli Benjedid, despite Chadli's previous affiliation with the army.

Likewise, in both countries general political openness came far too late to prevent opposition, though it came in Iran quite a bit later than in Algeria. When the Shah finally addressed the Iranian people on radio and television in late autumn 1978, promising political openness and the beginning of a new era, the revolution had already reached the point of no return. In Algeria, political openness came in the form of annulment of the FLN's constitutional right to rule the country, the establishment of a multiparty system, and entry permits to exiled opponents like Ahmed Ben Bella and Hocine Aït Ahmed. These developments (in 1989–1990) gave the democratic opposition an opportunity to start organizing itself.[14] Indeed, the presence of nonfundamentalist organized groups indirectly prevented the fundamentalist party (the FIS) from presenting itself as the only opposition force. The antifundamentalist demonstrations by 300,000 Algerians on January 2, 1992, illustrate the existence of other organized opposition groups. The situation was quite different in Iran. Because of the nature of its political system, there were no legally organized opposition groups or parties. (Parties such as Nehzat-e Azadi-e Iran, or Movement of the Liberation of Iran, MLI, led by Mehdi Bazargan,[15] Mojahidin-e Khalq,[16] and the Communist Tudeh party were illegal, and all three accepted the Khomeini's leadership at the beginning of the revolution.) Thus, no one could openly criticize the Shah's regime and resist the fundamentalist pressure. As a result, the final struggle was set between the Shah and Ayatollah Khomeini. The resistance that Shapour Bakhtiar, Dr. Mosaddeq's loyal disciple and the Shah's last prime minister, demonstrated against the Islamic fundamentalists came too late and had no real impact on the course of events.

Despite the importance of the differences between Algerian and Iranian politics, social characteristics played an even more significant role. The main and perhaps determinant difference between Algeria and Iran in this respect is that Algerian fundamentalists had nothing like the support that Iranian fundamentalists received from the Bazaar. Compared with other social groups, the Bazaar remains the most homogeneous group in Iranian society.[17] Furthermore, from the second half of the nineteenth century until the Islamic revolution of February 1979, the Bazaar was constantly in conflict with political elites in power. At the same time, there was always an organic alliance between the Bazaar and the ulama. Their relations were not hierarchical or vertical but defined in terms of interdependence and reciprocity. Through its financial contributions, the Bazaar made itself a guarantor of the ulama's financial independence from the state. In return, the ulama often interpreted Islam so it would conform to the interests of the *bazaaris*. Thus, private property became sacrosanct, the state administration was considered unjust, and the agents of the state were considered agents of oppression (*zalama*).[18]

The ulama institution in Iran did not lead the rebellion and the revolution against the Shah by itself. The ulama and the Bazaar were in reality the two pillars of the Islamic revolution, even though other groups and individuals also took part. The revolution was essentially led and orchestrated by these two forces. Because of their social base, the ulama were able to carry the burden of events and cover costs.

The social base of the FIS seems to have been rather widely dispersed and lacking in homogeneity. Despite the fact that the results of the municipal elections in 1990, and the first round of parliamentary elections in 1991, clearly demonstrated its huge popularity (polling 54.25 and 47.27 percent of votes, respectively), the FIS did not have a social base as solid as that of the Bazaar in Iran. It was mainly a protest movement with a diffuse and unorganized clientele. As an Algerian scholar put it, Algerian Islamism is neither urban nor rural. It is a consequence of the disintegration of the traditional Algerian society: "C'est le lumpen-prolétaire issu de cette destruction qui constitue la force principale de l'islamisme. Ce sont tous ces anciens ruraux, qui à cheval sur deux modes de vie, l'ancien et le citadin, en proie aux difficultés de la vie et à l'injustice sociale, qui forment le gros des troupes du mouvement et qui lui confèrent son indéniable popularité."[19]

That is, in order to organize the movement, Algerian fundamentalist leaders formed the FIS as a new political party. But even as a party, it could not gain support from any clear and distinguishable social group. A very necessary precondition for the success of a social movement is the existence of such a core. The FIS lacked this core. In other words, the movement was socially fragmented and without an epicenter. The social movement was structurally weak, despite the fact that social discontent and deprivation were ripe. The unemployed, young men and women, the discontented, the *trabendists*, regardless of their number, could not—on their own—produce a historical change, a revolution. Following a French maxim: "Les clochards ne font pas de révolution." "Les clochards" here is a metaphor for people who have nothing to fight for and no weapons to attack with.

The lumpenproletariat, the young and unemployed, and the discontented cannot alone produce a fundamental change. A revolution requires the support of a coherent social group. In Algeria, the only socially coherent group is the army, as the Bazaar is in Iran. Although the Bazaar in Iran, as the only socially homogeneous group, supported the Islamic fundamentalists, the army in Algeria opposed it. These differences led to opposite outcomes: in Iran to a successful revolution and in Algeria simply to turmoil.

The Geopolitical and International Environment

Algeria and Iran both occupy important geopolitical positions: The former is situated in North Africa with an extended coastline along the Mediterranean Sea, and the latter has the largest coastline on the Persian · Gulf and an almost 2,500-km-long border with the former USSR. Furthermore, Iran is located between the Middle East and Asia. However, the geopolitical importance of these two countries is mainly due to oil and gas. Both countries (members of OPEC) are major producers and possess very large hydrocarbon reserves. Generally speaking, as numerous events (coups, political and military interventions) have demonstrated, it appears that the international system as a whole has been and still is more sensitive to fluctuations in the Persian Gulf region than to those in North Africa. Two factors explain this: First, the Gulf region is much richer in oil than North Africa is, and thus the Western countries and Japan are more dependent on oil supplies from the Gulf. Second, the proximity of the former USSR to the Gulf region increased the sensitivity of both superpowers to developments there. Furthermore, North Africa is often considered a European and especially a French "zone d'influence." The presence of more than 2 million North African immigrants in Europe obviously makes European countries more sensitive to events in North Africa than the United States and other major international actors. France, which hosts more than 800,000 Algerians (and several hundred thousands of other Maghrebi immigrants), has more interest than any other Western state in what goes on in North Africa.

Despite the importance of their respective geopolitical positions and oil and gas reserves and production, the real and determinant difference is to be found in what Theda Skocpol has dubbed "world time."[20] As a matter of fact, world time for the Iranian Islamic fundamentalists has been very different from that of the Algerian fundamentalists. In the period between the Islamic revolution in Iran in 1979 and the interruption of general elections in Algeria in January 1992, the international system changed substantially. In 1977–1978, when the Shah's throne began to crumble, the international system was still bipolar with the United States and the Soviet Union continuing their antagonism. World time was at this point—just before the fall of the Shah in February 1979—in "Brejnevian time." The Shah ruled as a powerful subhegemonic pro-American in the Persian Gulf and indeed even in the Middle East. For two decades he succeeded in hindering the USSR in extending its influence in the Gulf. Until the 1980s, despite various attempts, the Soviet Union was unable to establish diplomatic relations with any other Gulf country apart from Iran and Iraq. The Shah had also neutralized Marxist-inspired rebellions—for instance in Dhofar in Oman—in the late 1960s and the beginning of the 1970s. The fall of this strong American ally, right at the door of the USSR, could only have pleased the leaders of the Soviet Union. Indeed, they welcomed the Islamic revolution and indirectly supported it. As a matter of fact, the presence of the USSR had a deterrent effect on a possible U.S. military intervention in Iran aimed at overthrowing Khomeini's infant regime.

Contrary to the Iranian case, the Algerian crisis and the turmoil that followed happened at a time when the entire international system was undergoing unprecedented transformations leading to the replacement of the rigid bipolar system with a U.S. hegemonic system. The second Gulf war, in which the United States led the allied forces, demonstrated that in regional matters, *overlay* was the new model for intervention. Even though the international system had not been changed and the USSR remained a superpower, the Soviet Union would probably not have intervened in favor of the Islamic fundamentalists in Algeria since, for the last three decades, Algeria had been an informal ally of Moscow. The USSR would not encourage the fall of one of its friends. In any case, under these new circumstances, the anti-West—especially the anti-U.S.—revolutionary movements have a poor chance (maybe no chance at all) of seizing power.

Almost thirteen years after the Islamic revolution in Iran, when the Islamic fundamentalists in Algeria seriously began their march on the regime, the world, having already witnessed a similar experience, did not demonstrate the same sympathy it had shown earlier. We have to recall that the Iranian revolution was received with sympathy not only by the USSR and China but also by many Western countries. The U.S. ambassador to Iran (William Sullivan) in his cable to President Carter (as late as November 9, 1978) called Khomeini a "Gandhi-like" figure and speculated that under Khomeini "elections would be likely to produce an Islamic republic with a *strong pro-Western* influence" (emphasis added).[21] The actual outcome was very different, but the world learned its lesson, and the Algerian fundamentalists paid the price for the Islamic experience in Iran.

Conclusion

This analysis has demonstrated that, despite their similarities, Algerian and Iranian Islamic fundamentalists are inherently different in some ways and arose from diverse circumstances and environments. The inherent differences include organizational, leadership, religious, and cultural domains, whereas the second factor concerns the sociopolitical, geopolitical, and international dimensions.

These differences provide the key to an understanding of the Islamic fundamentalists' inability to seize power in Algeria in the slipstream of their Iranian brothers' success. In comparative analysis it is always difficult to accurately separate the more important factors from the lesser ones. However, differences in leadership and the Algerian Islamic fundamentalists' lack of a homogeneous social base equivalent to the Iranian Bazaar seem to have been particularly important factors. The Iranian leadership was ecclesiastic, charismatic, and unified in the hands of Ayatollah Khomeini. These characteristics gave clarity and direction to the revolutionary movement. The Algerian leadership, in contrast, was "secular," noncharismatic, and collective. Consequently, Khomeini succeeded in spiritualizing politics and convincing the populace that the Shah and the United States were the embodiment of "Satan," whereas the Algerian FIS politicized religion but was not able to create a "Satan."

Despite the imprisonment of FIS leaders and the banning of their party, however, the Algerian crisis is not over. On the contrary, the assassination of President Boudiaf on June 29, 1992, and the daily clashes between Islamic fundamentalists and government troops indicate that tension remains.

My final remarks concern the future of democracy in Algeria. The main question is how to democratize a society and at the same time prevent nondemocratic or antidemocratic forces from seizing power and putting an end to democratic processes and ideals. It would not be time to say that there exists a universal solution or a predetermined "shining path." The road to democracy is bound to be state-contingent, and consequently as diverse and complex as the societies and situations examined.

Since the interruption of the democratic parliamentary elections in Algeria in January 1992, two different approaches to democratization have emerged: the judicial and the pragmatic approaches.

The *judicial* position holds that formal democratic procedures should have been followed; that is, the Algerian authorities had an obligation to organize the second round of parliamentary elections even though these would undoubtedly have led to a victory for the Islamists. This position advances three points: First, it is impermissible to interrupt a democratic election process except in the case of war or natural catastrophe. Any other excuse, especially if motivated by political objectives (such as the present case, the maintenance of power) is improper and dishonest. Second, interrupting the democratic process will inevitably disappoint a population that is starting to believe in democracy as a political regime.

This disappointment will be more profound and serious if the democratic process is still in its infancy. In the case of Algeria, there is a genuine risk that the population will lose faith in the future of democracy. Third, in the case of Algeria, the interruption was not wise because the only way to establish democracy there is through the gradual deliquescence of Islamic utopia, which can only occur under the rule of the Islamists themselves.[22] In other words, the conquest and exercise of power by the Islamists is a precondition for the establishment of a true democracy.

At least two objections can be put to the judicial or formal thesis. First, the interruption of the elections, even though imposed by force, does not necessarily imply an interruption of the democratic process. On the contrary, if the Algerian government had allowed the second round of the parliamentary elections to proceed, the Islamists would undoubtedly have prevailed, leaving no guarantee against the Islamists' usurping of democracy. An Islamic republic would have been announced and the *shari'a* imposed, and simultaneously the constitution and the multiparty system would have been abolished. As a result there would be no place for democracy and a fortiori for the pursuit of the democratic process. Hence, the interruption was a necessary step in keeping the democratic process afoot. The second objection is related to the Iranian experience. One should recall that during the revolution, Ayatollah Khomeini promised to respect freedom of speech, freedom of the press, and democracy, though within an Islamic framework. Thus, he was more cautious with regard to his public position on democracy than the Algerians were, since he never emphasized the non-Islamic character of democracy, as did Ali Belhadj. Khomeini, however, never fulfilled his promises of basic human rights but instead established an authoritarian regime, neglecting his repeated promises. The Islamists have now been in power for well over a decade, and even though public faith in the Islamic utopia probably is not as strong as it was in the beginning, there is no indication that democracy will soon replace the Islamic regime. The Iranian experience has demonstrated the fallacy of the "wait and see" thesis; once in power, it is very difficult to wrestle the Islamists out of office, despite rising social and economic problems. Handing power over to Islamists is almost equivalent to asking wolves to watch over the sheep.

The *pragmatic* thesis, which obviously represents the position of the Algerian army and its allies, distinguishes between the interruption of elections and interruption of the democratic process. Proponents argue that handing over power to the Islamists is tantamount to putting an end to the democratic process. They claim that the population does not share the Islamist thesis, even though a majority of Algerians voted for them. The population is voting Islamist because they feel socially, culturally, and economically deprived. Their votes are more a protest than a support for Islamism. Consequently, they argue, the solution to the problem involves addressing the country's social and economic problems, which by the way is an important part of the democratization process. Once these problems are solved, people will be much more inclined to reveal their true preferences when they vote. This line of argument sounds fundamentally valid and sound. However, it is less convincing when confronted with reality. The true facts of the matter are that those in power today have held their positions since Algerian independence from France in 1962. If Algeria is in crisis today, it is because of the policies implemented by the party (FLN), the army, and the technocrats. Who, in the face of such evidence, can believe in their sincerity about the introduction of and respect for democracy? The problem essentially concerns the credibility of the regime.

Whatever the path chosen toward true democratization, the preconditions remain the same. If these are not met, there will be a deadlock. The conditions can be expressed by the concept of *intellectual modernity*. A society that is not critical of the social, economic, and political life of the country cannot be democratized. As Edgar Morin has pointed out, democracy is based on dialogue.[23] Exchanging views is the very essence of democracy. Hence, simply introducing *instrumental modernity*, that is, *modernization*, is not enough. Modernization (*Industrie Industrilisante,* in the Algerian case) without intellectual modernity can never lead to democracy. It is not a question of lack of goodwill on behalf of the leaders; good intentions, however, are far from sufficient to establish true democracy.

It is a fact that a huge majority of the Algerian population, among them many "intellectuals," voted for a nondemocratic party (the FIS), just as the Iranians did soon after the Islamic revolution. Thus, the antidemocratic constitution of the Islamic Republic of Iran was adopted by a mandate of over 90 percent of the vote. How can this be explained? The Iranian vote, unlike the Algerian, had nothing to do with a protest. With the Shah no longer in charge, the Iranians voted for change—as it turned out, change from an absolutist regime to an exclusivist one. The reason might precisely have been the lack of intellectual modernity, the absence of criticism, and consequently the absence of dialogue.

In short, democratization of Algeria cannot be effectively implemented without the introduction and practice of critique. The first step would be to allow all the democratic forces to participate in the national debate as well as in the exercise of power. A regime that monopolizes debate cannot introduce democracy. The current Algerian regime would undoubtedly gain credit if it introduced dialogue, even if the price is loss of power. In an ideal world this would be the historical role of real leaders.

Notes

1. John Voll, correspondence with the author.

2. Interview in *Horizons,* February 23, 1989.

3. See Ruhullah Khomeini, *Hukumat-e Eslami* (Islamic Government) (Najaf, 1971), pp. 91–142.

4. Aissa Khelladi, *Les islamists algérians face au pouvoir* (Alger: Editions Alfa, 1992), p. 108.

5. The date of February 18, 1989, is given in Arun Kapill, "Les partis islamists en Algérie: éléments de présentation," *Maghreb-Machrek,* No. 133, July–September 1991; March 10, 1989, is given in Abdelkader Djeghloul, "Le multipartisme à l'algérienne," *Maghreb-Machrek,* No. 127, January–March 1990.

6. On small and fractionalized Islamic groups, see Seyyed Javad Madani, *Tarikh-e siyasiy-e moaser-e Iran* (The Contemporary Political History of Iran) (Tehran: Islamic Publications, 1984).

7. Khomeini's speech is reproduced in the *Keyhan,* Tehran, September 16, 1979.

8. On Abbasi Madani and A. Belhadj, see Aissa Khelladi, *Les islamists algérians face au pouvoir,* pp. 131–135, 147–155.

9. In 1966 the Islamic Supreme Council was established in Algeria. The council was given a monopoly on the interpretation of the *shari'a* and the delivery of the *fatwa.* However, as the council was a governmental institution, it could not but justify the policy of the government.

10. Bachir Figh's interview with *Horizons,* July 25, 1991, and *Maghreb-Machrek,* No. 133, pp. 118–119.

11. See Mehdi Mozaffari, *La conception shi'ite du pouvoir,* thèse de doctorat d'état (science politique), Université de Paris I (Sorbonne-Panthéon), 1971.

12. On Shi'a mourning ceremonies, see Jean Calmard, "Muharram Ceremonies and Diplomacy," in *Qajar Iran* (Edinburgh: Edinburgh University Press, 1983), pp. 213–218.

13. See Hazem Bedawi and Luciani Giacomo (eds.), *The Rentier State* (London: Croom Helm, 1987).

14. Since the establishment of a multiparty system in Algeria, many parties have either obtained legal recognition or were created after the legalization of the multiparty system. In addition to well-known parties like the FLN and the FIS, the most important parties are: (1) Front des Forces Socialistes (FFS) of Hocine Ait Ahmet; (2) Rassemblement pour la Culture et la Démocratie (RCD) of Said Saadi; (3) Mouvement pour la Démocratie en Algérie (MDA) of Ahmed Ben Bella; (4) Parti Social Démocrate (PSD); and (5) Parti de l'Avant-Garde Socialist (PAGS).

15. On MLI, see Mehdi Mozaffari, *Iran* (Paris: LCDJ, 1978), pp. 185–189, and H. E. Chehabi, *Iranian Politics and Religious Modernism* (Ithaca, N.Y.: Cornell University Press, 1990).

16. On Mojahidin-e Khalq, see Ervand Abrahamian, *Radical Islam: The Iranian Mojahedin* (London: I. B. Tauris, 1989).

17. Mehdi Mozaffari, "Why the Bazar Rebels?" *Journal of Peace Research* 28, No. 4, November 1991, pp. 377–391.

18. Ibid., pp. 381–381.

19. Khelladi, *Les islamists algérians face au pouvoir,* p. 102.

20. Theda Skocpol, *States and Social Revolutions* (Cambridge: Cambridge University Press, 1984), p. 23.

21. Zbigniew Brzezinski, *Power and Principal* (New York: Farrar, 1983), pp. 367–368.

22. Lahouari Addi, "Islam politique et démocratisation en Algérie," *Esprit, Revue Internationale,* No. 184, August–September 1992, pp. 8–9.

23. Edgar Morin, *Penser l'Europe* (Paris: Gallimard, 1987).

14 ✐

Women and Islamism: The Case of Rashid al-Ghannushi of Tunisia

MUHAMMAD MAHMOUD

A Movement in the Making

Compared with the Islamist movements in the eastern part of the Arab world, the Tunisian Islamist movement began relatively late.[1] The movement's beginnings go to the late 1960s, and it was during the 1970s that it started to gather momentum and acquire its distinctive features. The immediate dynamics leading to the movement's emergence may be traced to internal and external factors. Internally, the turmoil within the system of the Parti Socialiste Destour (PSD), following the abrupt break in 1963 with its socializing experiments, led to a great deal of disenchantment and disillusionment among young people, who started questioning the entire performance and ideological props of the PSD and the Left. Externally, the military defeat of Nasser's Egypt in the Six-Day War in 1967 effectively meant the collapse of Nasserism as a political project of Arab liberation. This was a time that witnessed the resurgence of Islamism in Egypt and the Sudan and its eventual expansion to engulf North Africa. An important factor for the Tunisian scene was the upheaval of May 1968 in France, which projected, as one leading Tunisian Islamist put it, a crisis-ridden West bereft of satisfactory solutions living through an "intellectual disarray" similar to that gripping the Arab and Islamic worlds.[2]

Though the Islamists were antagonistic to Habib Bourguiba's secularism, the initial phase of their organizational evolution was characterized by the bitter animosity they showed against the Marxist Left. This antipathy may be explained partly in terms of the constituency they tended to target, that of students—a constituency that was under the political and intellectual influence of the Left (in this respect, the Tunisian movement was similar to the Sudanese Islamist movement, which grew up as a student-centered movement). Another characteristic of this phase was the movement's appropriation of the discourse of the Egyptian al-Ikhwan al-Muslimun (Muslim Brothers), whose writings provided the fledgling movement with its intellectual sustenance. Between 1972 and 1979, the Islamists published a review that made an important contribution to the formulation and development of their ideological position.

It was, however, the Iranian revolution of 1979 that gave the Islamist movement in Tunisia, alongside the other movements throughout the Arab and Islamic worlds, a decisive boost. The event was seen as heralding a new phase of a militant and assertive Islamism that regarded itself as the legitimate and rightful alternative to existing regimes. In October 1979, the Tunisian movement convened a constitutive conference in which the Mouvement de la Tendance Islamiste (MTI, Movement of the Islamic Trend) was given its organizational identity. Rashid al-Ghannushi (b. 1941), a schoolteacher who had studied philosophy and social sciences in Damascus and who had forged close links with the Syrian Muslim Brothers, was elected head of the MTI. Being infused by the Iranian event, al-Ghannushi was so elated that he confidently announced in November 1979 that Islam was winning new positions and passing from the defensive to the offensive and that the century was poised to be the century of the Islamic state.[3] Ironically, the same Iranian event was exploited by the regime when it started its repression campaign as early as December 1979.

The MTI's second conference, which took place in April 1981, drew on a double strategy of keeping a clandestine base, on the one hand, and of gaining recognition by joining hands with other opposition forces in forming a united front, on the other.[4] Two months after their conference, the leaders of the MTI held a press conference in which they declared their organization and called for its recognition as a party. This demand was shortly turned down by the government, which escalated its confrontation with the movement.

Following the MTI's involvement in a series of opposition incidents in the early 1980s, the regime engaged in a ruthless campaign of repression against the MTI and detained its leaders. In August 1984, there was a shift of policy and the majority of Islamist detainees were released. This move reflected a tendency within the regime to view repression as counterproductive and expressed a willingness to legalize the Islamists as a party. This rapprochement, however, received a serious blow in 1987, when the MTI was accused of having plotted against the government and scores of its members were put on trial.

With the deposing of Bourguiba in November 1987 and the coming of General Zayn al-Abidin Ben Ali to power, the regime made some symbolic gestures meant to please the Islamists. The new government did, however, move firmly against the Islamists after their powerful showing in the April 1989 elections, in which they won 12 percent of the national vote. In June 1989, the government rejected the Islamists' application to register under the name of Hizb al-Nahda (Party of Renaissance), signaling its return to repressive policies. The movement was identified as an "extremist religious current,"[5] and its legalization was seen as a direct threat to the regime and the institutions of civil society. Since then it has been subjected to systematic repression. Its leader, Rashid al-Ghannushi, left the country, first going to Sudan, which has become a sanctuary and training center for Islamists since the Islamist coup d'état of June 1989, and then to Britain, where he has been granted political asylum.

Like his mentor, Hasan al-Turabi (b. 1932), the leader and chief theoretician of the Sudanese Islamists, al-Ghannushi projects himself as a liberal-minded Islamist who wants to harmonize his concepts of Islam with the realities of the modern world. But unlike his mentor, he has not been in power yet. Islamists who are actually in power (in Iran and Sudan, for example) have set up a pattern of repressive, intolerant, and closed regimes.

Responding to Modern Challenges

After independence Tunisia witnessed a vigorous drive to implement a program of social transformation that would bring about a clear break with traditional structures and values. An important aspect of this plan was the Personal Status Code of 1956, which replaced the given stipulations of the *shari'a* organizing the laws of marriage, divorce, and children's custody. The code outlawed polygamy and the traditional unilateral repudiation that men enjoyed. Another radical section made it possible for Muslim women to marry outside their faith. A minimum age for marriage for girls and boys was established, and both sexes were given rights in choosing their spouses when they attain the legal age.[6]

The change in the traditional status of women was at the time an integral part of the ideological position of the PSD and received the firm and personal commitment and support of Bourguiba. The state resolutely combatted resistance to this program on the part of conservative elements, and the general social context of the late 1950s and 1960s reflected the new policies. These decades were characterized by rising rates of education among both males and females and rapid urbanization. Advances in education were an important factor in reconditioning the Tunisian value-system in favor of women's emancipation. The political changes following the demise of Ahmed Ben Salah and the dismantling of his socialization program, however, led to a significant change in the regime's orientation. After his victory over the Left and the liberals and his confirmation as president for life, Bourguiba became more conservative and his commitment to women's rights started to waver. Surveys of public attitudes toward women conducted in the early and mid-1970s revealed a conservative shift in opinion.[7]

As conservatism has tended to rely on Islam in arguing its positions regarding women's roles, it was natural for the Islamist movements to pay a great deal of attention to the gender issue. I broadly distinguish between two currents within contemporary Islamism on the subject of women. In those countries where women have been on the whole excluded from the domain of public life (such as Saudi Arabia), the Islamists project a thoroughly conservative position. In contrast, in those countries where women have been allowed a degree of participation in public life (such as Tunis or Sudan), the Islamists have produced what may be described as a "mixed discourse"—and hence they express on a surface level a degree of identification with the changes in the status of women while remaining at a deeper level committed to the traditional position of *shari'a*. (Hence, according to this position a woman can be a member of parliament and take part in formulating legislation but still remains a legal minor.) This position, and the discourse of Tunisian Islamists, is clearly demonstrated in Rashid al-Ghannushi's *Al-Mar'atu bayn 'l-Qur'an wa Waqi'i 'l-Muslimina* (Women: Between the Qur'an and the Present Condition of Muslims).

In this work, al-Ghannushi assumes a double role: On one hand he is reform-minded, firmly entrenching himself within the camp of earlier reform pioneers like Muhammad Abdu (1849–1905) and Rashid Rida (1865–1935), and on the other hand he is an activist concerned about promoting an antisecular discourse in the Tunisian and Muslim societies. Hence, he distances himself markedly from some of the recognized positions of traditional authorities on women while at the same time constantly anathematizing what he sees as a systematic denigration of religion on the part of Bourguiba's regime. It should, however, be pointed out that while condemning the general tenor of Bourguiba's religious policy, al-Ghannushi is careful not to renounce the reform provisions promulgated by the Personal Status Code.

In expounding his position, al-Ghannushi's starting point is a reiteration of the traditional conviction that Islam is the final and universal answer to all man's ills and that Western civilization has run out of steam and is drawing to a close. It is quite interesting to note that his depiction of the status of women in present-day Western societies tends to be negative through and through, reflecting a common characteristic in the writings of Islamists. Nevertheless, he makes use of some of the arguments put forward by Western feminism, particularly those highlighting some aspects of female exploitation under the conditions of capitalist production, though he does so with a marked lack of depth. What he lacks in depth, however, is made up in a pronounced tendency to adopt a broad and flexible perspective. Thus, al-Ghannushi is quite willing to express his admiration for Sigmund Freud and Karl Marx (besides two representatives of "Western" science, Galileo Galilei and Isaac Newton), and he is in fact not disinclined to incorporate some of their arguments in developing his own position. This strategy constitutes a clear departure from the traditional position to which the vast majority of Islamists adhere.[8]

Al-Ghannushi's reading of Islamic history assumes a sharp division between the period of the Medina state (from A.D. 622 to 661) and the subsequent Umayyad rule. He identifies the first period with "authentic" Islam and calls the second one "fallacious" Islam. He describes the latter period also as *'asr 'l-inhitat* (the time of decadence) and traces back to it all the ills that befell the Muslims. This division is subscribed to by many an Islamist, but what characterizes al-Ghannushi's treatment is the virulent and resentful·tone of his statements. One suspects that in spelling this out he is not addressing himself primarily to the traditional Sunnite audience but rather to a different audience that is likely to be disillusioned with the status of women under Islam. By this audience I refer to that sector of Muslim societies which has been exposed, in the process of its education and contacts, to Western liberal values and which tends to live in urban centers and to be largely middle class or aspirant to middle-class status.

According to al-Ghannushi, the community of the Prophet and his immediate successors was absorbed by the consuming preoccupations of building up *the* new model society, *the* new civilization. The Muslim *umma* (community) led a life of great seriousness and relentless *jihad* (holy war, combat). With the coming of the Umayyads the pre-Islamic spirit of tribalism was regenerated, reviving a value-system that debased the humanity of women and degraded them to the status of mere sex objects. During the Medina phase, the interaction between men and women was characterized by spontaneity, cooperation, and mutual giving. In contrast, the Umayyad phase consecrated the sharp discrimination against women and gave rise to a society of *harim* (secluded womanhood).[9] The key terms used in identifying the Prophet's time are *jidd* (seriousness), *jihad*, *'fwiyya* (spontaneity), *ta'awun* (cooperation, concord), and *'ata'* and *badhl* (giving); the key terms employed in delineating the Umayyad phase and after are *qabaliyya* (tribalism), *lahw*, *'abath* (lasciviousness), *jins* (sex), *fasl* (segregation), *mata"* (property, object), *harim*, and *inhitat*.

Al-Ghannushi states that the final objective of his movement's program is to set up an industrialized, civilized society guided by the principles of "Islamic humanism."[10] Unfortunately, he does not define his two key concepts, "civilized" and "Islamic humanism." It is in the light of this objective that he sets out to outline his criticism of present-day Tunisian society. This society is described as *munhal* (permissive), and Bourguibism is adduced as the fountainhead of this "permissiveness." He makes his judgment without any qualification as regards the social milieu to which he refers as he also rails against rural values that tend to be conservative and restrictive regarding women—a state of affairs far from being "permissive." This contradiction highlights in fact a tension that is common in some present-day Islamic movements with urban social roots but an outlook based more in traditional rural value systems.

Al-Ghannushi is, however, ready to assimilate his views with a traditional Islamic discourse that tends to be highly sensitive about sexual morality and other issues usually given prominence by the Tunisian Left. So, he states that the Tunisian Islamists should address the problems of "unemployment, housing, economic exploitation, political repression, bad health services, bad transport and the problems of children and women."[11]

In lashing out against the present state of affairs, he does not spare his own camp either. The *fuqaha'* (jurists) of the past are singled out as a group hostile to women and pictured as ministering to the backward-looking tendencies within Muslim societies to restrain women and perpetuate their subjugation. Besides, the *fuqaha'* are depicted as having played during the period of colonialism the role of custodians of traditional culture, a culture al-Ghannushi views as being incompatible with "authentic" Islam.[12] Likewise, he accuses the Islamist movement of his own time of having failed to grasp "authentic" Islam and says that in its overreaction against the challenge of Bourguibism it propagated an outlook that was influenced by the dominant tradition of the age of *inhitat*. In his view, the Islamist movement failed to appreciate Tunisian society's historical specificity, and applying obsolete principles formulated under a different social reality is bound to end in futility. Maintaining that the status of women during some past Islamic periods was but a specific expression of Islam under specific social conditions, he stresses that the potential of Islam is such that when social conditions change, it can regenerate itself and come up with the appropriate expression.

In expounding his own reformist position, al-Ghannushi is keen to affirm certain basic principles that constitute the foundation of his outlook. In arguing his position he offers a highly selective reading of the Qur'an, besides a limited body of Sunna, *fiqh*, and historical material. From the outset, he asserts the human and hence relative nature of *tafsir* (Qur'anic exegesis). Whereas the Qur'an is absolute and not subordinate to history, *tafsir* is subject to the specific historical, social, and epistemological conditions of the exegetes who produce it. In considering the Qur'an, al-Ghannushi has to deal with an old problem that is crucial to his position: To whom is the Qur'an addressed? He cites the story of Um 'Ammar Al-Ansariyya, who protested to Muhammad about the Qur'an's male-centered address, and the Qur'an's quick response in including women in Q33:35, as categorical evidence demonstrating divine impartiality. The point is, however, brought home in Q33:35 by repeatedly juxtaposing women alongside men, and as this is not the rule in Qur'anic composition, al-Ghannushi, like the exegetes before him, opts for a mere assertion that the Qur'anic address is characterized by *'umum al-khitab* (universal address).

In discussing the creation story in the Qur'an, al-Ghannushi sides with the view that stresses a unity of origin for men and women. Citing Sunnite (Muhammad Abdu and Sayyid Qutb) and Shi'ite (Muhammad Husayn Al-Tabataba'i and Ali Shari'ati) authorities, he rejects the biblical story about God creating Eve out of Adam's rib.[13] It is interesting to note that al-Ghannushi uses the term "mythical" in describing those elements of the Bible that do not appeal to him and censures the exegetes for including these elements in their works. But the exegetes relied on traditions attributed to the Prophet that state unequivocally that the woman was created from a "crooked rib." In any case, al-Ghannushi insists that a "literal" reading of these traditions is unwarranted and that the Prophet was using the expression as a "figure of speech" to indicate to men the particular psychology of women. He does not examine the Prophetic "figure of speech" analytically to explain the nature and source of the particular image.

Al-Ghannushi is, however, determined to carry out his liberation program from within Islam and so has to devise procedures to overcome his textual problems. In the face of problematical elements he either plays them down or omits them altogether. As far as the story of creation goes and whether it should be read in terms of a unity of creation or a dependent creation, he is acutely aware of the crucial implications of adopting either position: The traditional reading (which says the woman was created out of Adam's rib) affirms the subordination of women to men and hence justifies women's subjugation, whereas the reading he supports affirms the equality of women and men and hence contributes to women's emancipation. Though he argues from within the Qur'anic text, he is honest enough to admit that it is with this external consideration in mind that he has come to adopt his position. On the basis of God's "universal address," al-Ghannushi maintains that the general tendency of *shari'a* is in favor of equality between men and women as they are united in their origin, their human value, and their obligation to serve God by bringing prosperity to His earth and to live in accordance with his command-ments.[14]

In dealing with the image of women in the Qur'an, al-Ghannushi fo-cuses his attention on three verses: Q3:36, Q12:28, and Q3:14.

In Q3:36 we come across the statement, "The male is not as the fe-male."[15] Al-Ghannushi places this problematic statement firmly within the context of its verse and the larger narrative of the chapter. Q3:35 and Q3:36 run as follows: "When the wife of Imran said, 'Lord, I have vowed to Thee, in dedication, what is within my womb. Receive Thou this from me; Thou hearest and knowest.' And when she gave birth to her she said, 'Lord, I have given birth to her, a female.' (And God knew very well what she had given birth to; the male is not as a female.) 'And I have named her Mary, and command her to Thee with her seed, to protect them from the accursed Satan.'" As the Qur'anic text lacks punctuation, the verse gives rise to two possible readings of the statement "The male is not as a female." Either we read it as an inseparable part of the parenthetical clause, "And God knew very well what she had given birth to," or we read it as a continuation of the statement of the woman of Imran.[16] The first reading assumes that it is God himself who passes the judgment, whereas the second reading attributes it to a human voice. Al-Ghannushi does not only hold that the statement is made by the wife of Imran but goes further to say that it reflects in fact an instance of false conscious-ness. The woman is dismayed and distressed because she feels that a fe-male is less competent to carry out her promise of divine service than a male. What turns out later is contrary to the mother's expectations as her daughter is made instrumental in giving birth to Jesus. Al-Ghannushi's argument is still problematical, however, because he predicates Mary's worth on her motherhood of Jesus and hence her relationship to a "man" rather than on her own independent worth.

The Qur'an narrates in Chapter 12 what passes between Joseph and his master's wife, who tries to seduce him. In refusing her advances, he makes for the exit and she tears his shirt from behind. They encounter the master at the entrance, and the wife is quick to accuse Joseph of having made an attempt to ensnare her. The fact that the shirt is torn from behind substantiates Joseph's denial and hence the master's response as de-scribed by Q12:28: "When he saw his shirt was torn from behind he said, 'This is your women's guile; surely your guile is great.'" Should the mas-ter's statement about female "guile" be taken to mean a general Qur'anic characterization pertaining to female psychology or should it be confined to its face value as an understandable reaction of a rancorous husband?[17] Al-Ghannushi maintains that Q12:28 is not meant to be read as a divine judgment on women and that its significance should be strictly confined to its narrative context. His position on the concept of *kayd* (guile) is, however, ambivalent. *Kayd* is attributed in the Qur'an to God, Satan, and man, and hence in itself is neither good nor bad. The goodness or badness of *kayd* is determined by its ends and means. Al-Ghannushi is, however, willing to give female *kayd* the benefit of the doubt and to see in it a dynamism of character, sharp wits, and unflagging patience.[18] This almost celebrative tone shifts, nevertheless, to one of repugnance when he elaborates on the relationship between *kayd* and women's class background, pointing out that a woman living in affluence is more prone to *kayd* owing to the free time at her hand, whereas a woman living in poverty or engaged in work has other, more pressing concerns.

Q3:14 reads, "Decked out fair to men is the love of lusts—women, children, heaped up heaps of gold and silver, horses of mark, cattle and tillage. That is the enjoyment of the present life; but God—with him is the fairest resort." The problem with which al-Ghannushi grapples in dealing with this verse is the equation of women with lust and their inclusion in a set comprising gold, silver, horses, cattle, and land as its representative elements. Though he quotes Rashid Rida's *Tafsir al-Manar*, which tries to show that the verse is addressed to both men and women, al-Ghannushi's own reading assumes that the verse is addressed to men. He sets out to answer the following questions: (1) Why does the liking of women take precedence over the other desires? (2) Why does the verse mention only the liking of men for women and omit the opposite? (3) What is meant by the *fitna* (lure) that attracts men to women?[19]

In dealing with questions 1 and 2, al-Ghannushi marshals numerous quotations from various sources that tackle the issue of male and female sexuality. Positing complementarity and mutual attraction between the two sexes, he concludes that there is a qualitative difference between the way men and women express themselves sexually. He then proceeds to ground that observation on the gender philosophy to which he subscribes. According to him, men's sexual expression tends to be brief and transient, with the genitals as its focal point, and women's sexual expression, by contrast, is more profound, total, and subtle. A woman is predisposed to lose herself in the sexual act as she tries to be completely united with the man. For a woman, her body is just a stage beyond which lies an eternal hankering of merging into man. As far as man is concerned, woman is only a facet of his character—a facet from the grip of which he can release himself by concentrating on and promoting other facets. But the matter is different for women. Man is the axis around which the woman's life is destined to revolve, and he is the mirror in which she sees herself and her history.[20] In trying to advance what may appear as a "romanticized" celebration of female sexuality, he only sinks into the quagmire of an essentially male-centered position. He overlooks the other ele-

ments in the verse and its overall negative tone and engages instead in a
digression (a tendency frequently encountered in the writings of Islamists).

In dealing with the third question, al-Ghannushi reinterprets the meaning of *fitna* to signify "test," in the sense that God subjects man to unceas-
ing trials. He shifts the emphasis from a woman's *fitna* on man in favor of
a more complex situation where they act mutually on each other. Going
up the sublime path of God or sliding into the downward course of Satan
is thus a mutual responsibility of man and woman.

Toward an Alternative

In his bid to offer an alternative program, al-Ghannushi addresses specific, practical problems. He focuses on five themes: (1) education, (2) the
mixing of the sexes, (3) Islamic female dress, (4) work, and (5) polygamy.

He takes issue with those who want to keep the education of women
within a minimum that qualifies them to be good housewives. He maintains that such a position is incompatible with the precepts and intentions
of Islam, which encourage women to gain as much knowledge as they
want. In his view, education is vital in many respects. Through education,
both women and men can be liberated from the dominant legacy of the
age of *inhitat* and the horizons of women can be significantly expanded
and their bondage to their present world of trivialities broken. Education
can also offer an alternative model of a well-cultivated Islamic female to
counter what he describes as "Bourguibist permissiveness." He adds that
Islam does not confine the education of women to any particular fields
and that the determining factors are individual aptitude and social needs.
Furthermore, an educated Muslim woman is better placed to penetrate
governmental and nongovernmental institutions and hence to communi-
cate the message of Islam in these arenas. Although al-Ghannushi's arguments seem to be directed to Tunisian society in general, their main thrust
may in fact be aimed at his own co-Islamists, whom he repeatedly accuses, either explicitly or implicitly, of having been molded by the legacy
of the age of *inhitat*.

As regards the mixing of the sexes, al-Ghannushi views complete segregation as foreign to Islam. He draws a sharp distinction between two
conditions of gender mixing. The first is a condition conducive to sexual
seduction (such as the presence of a man and a woman in a "suspicious
circumstance," in an atmosphere likely to induce "license," or in a posture of physical contact).[21] The second, by contrast, is a condition under
which sexual temptation is unlikely to arise (such as in a mosque, a ses-
sion of learning, a field of jihad, or a protest march).[22] Inasmuch as he in-

dicts the presence of women under the first condition, he defends their right to be present (and even effectively so) under the second. He dismisses the argument raised by some that a woman's voice is *'awra* (vice). It is interesting to note that in dismissing this point, he steers clear of the *hadith* and *fiqh* material and turns instead to historical material, building up his argument inductively. And so from the historically documented presence of women in certain situations he reaches the conclusion that women are allowed and even encouraged to be present under the second condition. He recasts the concept of jihad to embrace a constant combat on the part of the whole society against "sin" and "corruption." The · Prophet's tradition, "The jihad continues up to Doomsday" (*al-jihadu ma-din ila yaumi 'l-qiyamati*), is subjected to this reading.

In dealing with Q33:33 and its controversial injunction, "Remain in your houses," he adopts an evasive approach. He does not address the verse and instead plunges into an impassioned plea, recommending that society throw away segregation and embrace gender mixing subject to Islamic conditions. This approach reveals a tendency that may be seen in many an Islamist when the activist side of their personality, concerned above all with the movement's survival, gets the better of them and determines the mode of their reasoning.

In discussing the way a Muslim woman should dress, al-Ghannushi does not come up with new suggestions that could upset the traditionalists. He concedes that a woman's dress should be long enough to cover the body and that her head should always be covered. In reflecting on the human body, he posits a simple dichotomy between a lust-ridden existence and an existence that dominates lust and transcends it to attain a sublime bliss similar to that enjoyed by prophets and angels.[23] The key concepts given prominence in this connection are *'iffa* (chastity, virtuousness, probity) and *hishma* (decency, propriety). He also refers to the concept of *al-shakhsiyya al-qaumiyya*, the national character, in opposition to a process of *maskh* (distortion, alienation) that has been taking place over a long period of time. He expresses his admiration for Japanese and Chinese women who opened themselves up to modernization without allowing their national character to be "distorted" by the West. He does not define his terms or give sufficient elaboration, and so the reader may be left, on the evidence of the context within which he raises and places his arguments, with the impression that the determinant factor of a "national character" as far as women are concerned is the way they relate·to their bodies and the way they project it.[24] It is also noticeable that his key concepts of *'iffa*, *hishma*, and "national character" are advanced as if they are constants operating outside the specificity of their socio-historical context.

Al-Ghannushi, however, incorporates his traditional position on the question of dress into a more flexible standpoint regarding the issue of women working in urban centers. He notes that his more conservative coreligionists have never opposed the involvement of women in cottage industry in rural areas and their mixing with men under the conditions of agricultural production. He argues that as long as a woman puts on her Islamic dress and behaves in accordance with the religious teachings, she has earned the right to take an active part in the process of social production.[25] The limits of his position are, however, quite clear as he cannot break out of an essentially patriarchal framework. He is quite categorical about his view that men should take precedence when a situation arises where equally qualified men and women are competing for the same job, and he says that Islam would not consent to female employment while men are unemployed, as women can always take care of home and family. Yet he is willing to accept a new measure of policy reform according to which a woman's work at home is considered a wage-earning job (no Islamic model is offered in this case, but a reference is made to a tendency in the thinking of French policymakers). His position may thus be summed up as follows: A woman's "natural place" is in the home and her main social role is taking care of the family, but if necessity arises she may go out and work as long as her employment is regulated in accordance with the dictates of Islam.[26]

In addressing the question of polygamy, al-Ghannushi puts across the familiar arguments advanced by modern Islamist thinkers. Polygamy is seen as a safety valve when the numbers of female and male populations are upset by exceptional events like wars. The Islamic legislator has, however, given the woman in a marriage the right to lay a condition in her marriage contract obligating the man not to take another wife. In discussing the issue, al-Ghannushi is keen to stress the "precautionary," "remedial," and "exceptional" nature of Islamic polygamy and states that the practice is admissible, with certain restrictions, without being obligatory or recommended.

As an Islamist activist, al-Ghannushi stresses always the importance of offering the Tunisian society, and the world at large, a "model" demonstrating the intrinsic superiority of Islam as a way of life. This issue was apparently high on the agenda of the MTI, and so al-Ghannushi directs his attention to a brief assessment of the movement's experience in realizing "Islamic" marriages. The 1970s witnessed the birth of the MTI in Tunisia, and according to al-Ghannushi, the movement succeeded over ten years in creating a small social milieu that was cohesive and ideologically confident. This situation, however, was to change, and the movement, like any other movement, began to suffer crises and setbacks. The reversals in the MTI's political fortunes (being subjected to harsh repressive measures by Bourguiba between March 1987 and May 1988) affected the family relationships that had sprung up within its encouraging and protective context. Al-Ghannushi attributes the connubial conflicts to a lack of enlightenment on the part of the men, whose social origins were predominantly rural, and the detrimental influence of the Bourguibist liberation brand on the women.[27] To rectify the situation, he comes up with a series of proposals, the most important of which are the following:

1. The relationship between men and women in Islam is one of equality but not similarity. This is bound to affect the social division of work.
2. The absolute priority concerning a woman's obligations falls on marriage and motherhood.
3. The man is the family's guardian.[28] A wife should not meet other men or accept presents from them without his consent. A man has the right to limit his wife's freedom of movement and can prevent her from leaving the house. A woman has no legal right to object to a change of residence or living with her in-laws.
4. The man is the family's maintainer. If he fails completely or partially in that respect, the wife may work after securing his consent. The husband, however, may terminate his wife's work whenever he deems it necessary. What she earns out of work belongs to the family. The wife has the right to cease working at any given time and demand to be maintained by the husband.
5. The primary tasks of marriage and motherhood should not infringe upon a woman's inalienable right to education.

Al-Ghannushi's treatment of women's issues demonstrates the predicament of Muslim reformers who are at the same time political activists. The logic of reform is one of constant questioning and revision; the logic of political involvement, in contrast, must take into account the status quo, make allowances and compromises, and, quite often, qualify radical reformist positions in the process. Though al-Ghannushi is quite vehement in stressing the complete equality of women and men as human beings and as agents carrying out the precepts of *shari'a* who must assume their full individual responsibilities at the Day of Final Judgment, he does not in fact go far when it comes to translating this notion into a specific code of legal rights for women. And though he takes a dim view of Bourguiba's policies as regards the status of women, it is possible to argue that his own relative open-mindedness and his professed disenchantment with the traditional standpoint are to a considerable degree outcomes of the changes that took place under Bourguiba (besides the pioneering work of Tahir Al-Haddad [1899–1935]). In putting his view, al-Ghannushi constantly appeals to what he describes as "authentic Islam"; on closer examination one may realize that his is a hybrid discourse that

strives at a synthesis between a certain reading of Islam and some elements of "Western" feminism that have already made inroads into
Tunisian and Muslim societies—so much so that he avoids any reference
to some problematic and central issues that any serious treatment of the
status of women in Islam should try to resolve. He, for example, drops
completely any reference to *talaq* (repudiation, divorce), *mirath* (inheritance, succession), and the testimony of women in courts.

The participation of women in the production process, particularly in
urban centers, and the spread of education among them released in Muslim countries vigorous dynamics that undermined their suppression. Al-
Ghannushi's theorizing is based on the assumption that social dynamics
can be subordinated to ideology and that Islam is capable of controlling
these processes and channeling them into a "proper" direction to realize
its final objectives. His project expresses a firm commitment to women's
education but wavers on the right of women to work. As his overall treatment of the issues concerning women is informed by an entrenched patriarchal position, such wavering is likely to lead to further concessions to
the conservative-minded Islamists. The changes that have already taken
place within Tunisia and in the Islamic world have produced a feminist
movement that is acutely conscious of the setback the Islamist program
represents. Al-Ghannushi's project goes beyond the traditional Islamic
position, but it does not go far enough to satisfy the legitimate aspirations
of women in Muslim societies to see inequality and gender discrimination redressed.

Notes

1. By "Islamist," I refer to the specific contemporary expressions of Islam that
have sprung up in the form of primarily radical political movements that insist on
predicating political legitimacy on religion and insist on a universalistic approach
to Islam, extending it from the realm of religion to all the realms of social activity,
such as politics, economics, law, culture, and so on. The Islamist movements in
Sunnite countries project the Medina state and the community of the Prophet and
his four immediate successors as the model at the base of their radical program.
This program applies to all the Sunnite Islamist movements except two, as far as I
am aware. The Sudanese Republican Brothers' Movement (Harakat al-Ikhwan al-
Jumhuriyin), founded by Ustadh Mahmud Muhammad Taha (1909–1985), maintains that the Islamic ideal is yet to be realized. The Tunisian Movement of Islamic
Progress (Mouvement du Progrès Islamiste, MPI) does not cherish any past
model and wants change to take place according to a model arising out of present
needs and realized in conjunction with future dynamics. For the views of Taha see
Mahmoud Mohamed Taha, *The Second Message of Islam*, trans. Abdullahi Ahmed
An-Na'im (Syracuse: Syracuse University Press, 1987). For an exposition of MPI
views, see Krichen Zyed, "Pour une nouvelle exegese de l'islam" (Toward a New

Interpretation of Islam), *Peuples Méditerranéens,* No. 21 (1982), 15–21, and Norman Salem, "Tunisia," in Shireen T. Hunter, ed., *The Politics of Islamic Revivalism* (Bloomington and Indianapolis: Indiana University Press, 1988). On the differences within the Islamic movement in Tunisia according to the MPI, see the interview with Shaykh Hamid Al-Nayfar in *Middle East Report* 8, No. 153 (1988), 24–26.

2. This sense of deep intellectual disappointment after the 1968 events was expressed by Ahmida Enneifer, one of the founders of the Tunisian Islamist movement. See François Burgat, *L'islamisme au Maghreb: La voix du Sud* (Paris: Éditions Karthala, 1988), 205.

3. Ibid., 287.

4. Ibid., 213.

5. François Burgat and William Dowell, *The Islamic Movement in North Africa* (Austin: University of Texas, Centre for Middle Eastern Studies, 1993), 239.

6. For general comments on the Personal Status Code, see Jean Magnin, "Autour du code de statue personnel tunisien," in Jacques Berque and Jean-Paul Charnay, eds., *Normes et valeurs dans l'islam contemporains* (Paris: Payot, 1988), 313–324.

7. See Mark A. Tessler with Janet Rogers and Daniel Schneider, "Women's emancipation in Tunisia," in Lois Beck and Nikki Keddie, eds., *Women in the Muslim World* (Cambridge, Mass.: Harvard University Press, 1978), 148–154.

8. This position earns Al-Ghannushi the admiration of a Western scholar who says, "The MTI leader . . . expresses a conciliatory Tunisian idiom equating Islam and reason that seems far removed from the passions of a Khomeini or the Egyptian Sayyid al-Qutb." C. H. Moore, "Tunisia and Bourguibisme: Twenty Years of Crisis," *Third World Quarterly* 10, No. 1 (1988), 189. By contrast, the Tunisian Shukri Latif, in his *Al-Islamiyun wa 'l-Mar'a: Mashru' 'l-Idtihad* (The Islamists and Women: The Project of Suppression) (Tunis: Bairam Publications, 1988), maintains that Al-Ghannushi's position and that of his movement is tactical and that the real program of the Islamist movement is rooted in ideological hostility to women's rights.

9. Rashid al-Ghannushi, *Al-Mar'a bain 'l-Qur'an wa Waqi' 'l-Muslimin* (Tunis: Tunis Press, n.d.), 16.

10. Ibid., 27.

11. Ibid., 10.

12. Ibid., 17.

13. The Book of Genesis in the Old Testament offers two versions for the creation of man. According to one version, God created man of the dust of the ground, and breathed the breath of life into his nostrils, and then when He realized later that he needed a helpmate, He caused him to sleep, took one of his ribs, and made a woman (Genesis 2:7 and 21–22). According to the other version, God decided to create man in his own image and so, "in the image of God created He him; male and female created He them" (Genesis 1:27). The two versions reflect two divergent attitudes, one of separate creation and one of simultaneous creation. Al-Ghannushi's treatment of the biblical material fails to mention the simultaneous creation version and gives the impression that the Old Testament offers only a separate creation version.

14. Ibid., 22.

15. I have used throughout Arthur J. Arberry's translation of the Qur'an entitled *The Koran Interpreted* (London: Oxford University Press, 1964).

16. Arthur J. Arberry's translation adopts the first reading, whereas A.Yusuf
Ali's translation (*An English Interpretation of the Holy Qur-an* (Lahore: Sh. Muhammad Ashraf, 1975), for example, favors the second reading.

17. I am following here al-Ghannushi's assumption on p. 86, *Al-Mar'a bain 'l-
Qur'an wa Waqi' 'l-Muslimin*, that Q12:28 is a statement uttered by the husband,
though the context of Q12:26 and Q12:27 does not make this sufficiently clear and
so one may assume, as had already been suggested, that Q12:28 is a judgment
passed by the character referred to as "the witness of her folk." Al-Ghannushi is
aware of this ambiguity and is less categorical on p. 88.

18. Ibid., 90.

19. Ibid., 54. The term *fitna* is used in Islamic terminology in two contexts: the
context of the politics of the Islamic community, where it denotes disorder or sedi-
tion, and the context of man's relationship to women, where it denotes temptation, enticement. The relationship between the two senses is established by the internal logic of the Islamic perspective, as disorder is seen in the political act of
disobeying the sanctioned authority, which represents the collective will of the
community, and in the sexual act when it takes place outside the lawful institutions of marriage and concubinage.

20. Ibid., 101.

21. Ibid., 28.

22. Ibid.

23. Ibid., 46.

24. On the way Islamist women view their bodies and the Islamic dress, see
Souhayer Belhassen, "Femmes Tunisinnes Islamistes," *Annuaire de l'Afrique du
Nord* 19 (1980), 255–288.

25. Al-Ghannushi, *Al-Mar'a bain 'l-Qur'an wa Waqi' 'l-Muslimin*, 23.

26. Al-Ghannushi's wife mentioned that she had to put an end to her university
career at the birth of their first child when her husband persuaded her that her
place was in the home. Quoted in S. Waltz, "Islamist Appeal in Tunisia," *The Middle East Journal* 40, No. 4 (1986), 662–663.

27. For a wider treatment of family conflicts in Tunisian society, see Lorna Dur-
rani, "Tensions and Role Conflict in the Tunisian Family," in *The Maghreb Review* 2,
No. 3 (1977), 13–17.

28. In an interview, Abdelfattah Mourou, a leading member of the MTI, said,
"We Tunisians are on the Mediterranean, and the Mediterranean tradition is the
patriarchal family, which has been the tradition of all humanity except in a few
parts of the world where there was a matriarchal family guided by women. Even
French law today accepts the father as the head of the family." Nikki R. Keddie,
"The Islamic Movement in Tunis," *The Maghreb Review* 11, No. 1 (1986), 31. It is interesting that Mourou does not trace his patriarchal position as an Islamist back to
Islam but rather prefers to place it at the door of the "Mediterranean tradition."
This position is apparently not universally accepted within the MTI. Responding
to whether men should be the head of the family, Seida Akreni said, "It is up to
the partners to choose if one of them is needed to be the head, and it could be ei-

ther the woman or the man. The woman is often more occupied in the home and often heads the home. As I am a woman it is logical that I want a more feminist statute. Also, women and social relationships have changed with time. . . . I do not think Islam oppresses women, and so a statute drafted in the name of Islam should not be patriarchal." Ibid., 35.

About the Book

The phenomenon of political Islam continues to dominate the political and social map of the Arab world, with the increasingly open struggle between ruling elites and Islamists becoming the main source of political instability in many states. This volume offers an in-depth analysis of the rise of Islamic and fundamentalist movements in the Middle East and North Africa. Through detailed case studies, the contributors examine the various manifestations of political Islam, highlighting differences across movements and evaluating the varying circumstances in which they arise. They also assess the influence of such movements on the emerging post–Cold War order in the region and consider questions of a general nature, such as Islamic state theories and the impact of Islamicism on international relations.

About the Editors and Contributors

Maha Azzam is head of the program on Security and Development in Muslim States at the Royal United Services Institute for Defence Studies, London.

Iyad Barghouti is professor of sociology, Department of Sociology, An-Najah National University, Nablus.

Youssef Choueiri is lecturer in Arabic and Islamic studies, Department of Arabic and Islamic Studies, University of Exeter.

Anoushiravan Ehteshami is reader in international relations, Centre for Middle Eastern and Islamic Studies, University of Durham.

David George is lecturer in politics, Department of Politics, University of Newcastle.

Raymond A. Hinnebusch is professor of political science, College of St. Catherine, Minnesota.

Muhammad Mahmoud is a member of the teaching staff of the Oriental Institute, University of Oxford.

Beverley Milton-Edwards is lecturer in politics, Department of Politics, Queen's University, Belfast.

Mehdi Mozaffari is professor of political science, Department of Political Science, University of Aarhus, Denmark.

Abdel Salam Sidahmed is visiting research associate, Faculty of Social and Political Studies, University of Cambridge.

Claire Spencer is deputy director of the Centre for Defence Studies, King's College, University of London.

Suha Taji-Farouki is lecturer in modern Islam, Centre for Middle Eastern and Islamic Studies, University of Durham.

Charles Tripp is senior lecturer in politics with reference to the Near and Middle East, School of Oriental and African Studies, University of London.

Eric Watkins is director of St. Malo Press and an Honorary Fellow of the Centre for Middle Eastern and Islamic studies, University of Durham.

Index